for
David Page

with
compliments
Subhash

PARTITION

JIHAD & PEACE

In remembrance of

SADAT HASAN MANTO
author of the Partition classic
TOBA TEK SINGH

PARTITION
JIHAD & PEACE

SUBHASH CHOPRA

Lancer • New Delhi • Frankfort, IL
www.lancerpublishers.com

LANCER

Published in the United States by

The Lancer International Inc
19558 S. Harlem Ave., Suite 1,
Frankfort, IL. 60423.

First published in India by

Lancer Publishers & Distributors
2/42 (B) Sarvapriya Vihar,
New Delhi-110016

ISBN-13: 978-1-935501-17-6 • ISBN-10: 1-935501-17-8

Online Military Bookshop
www.lancerpublishers.com

IDR Net Edition
www.indiandefencereview.com

Contents

Preface

It might have been heaven to be alive in that dawn of freedom for most Indians in 1947, but for millions from Punjab and Bengal it was hell in all its different shades. Those uprooted or about to be uprooted from their hearths and homes could see not the multicoloured rainbow but a dark cloudy sky with blood red patches.

Partition memory is remembrance of brutality past. Brutality born of the animus of division of the Indian sub-continent and the speed with which the division was carried out by the departing British imperial power still defies imagination.

Partition, Jihad and Peace is in parts an eye-witness account of the era by this writer whose family, among millions of others, was catapulted across the new Punjab border in 1947. Sixty years on we are still grappling with the aftermath of that partition and the animus it spawned.

Earlier perceptions have certainly changed with time and for me personally a visit to my old hometown, house and school after 57 years was a rewarding experience, reaffirming my faith in the ordinary people and their goodwill beyond borders.

As a journalist covering Indo–Pak dialogue, observer and self-confessed peacenik, I am sanguine in the hope that peace is inevitable between India and Pakistan, and across the South Asian region, historical and ruling differences notwithstanding.

The rise of the South Asian conglomeration of SAARC, however fitful, has lit a flame of hope. Given cool heads, the battle for that elusive peace and cooperation, especially among the quarreling troika of India, Pakistan and Afghanistan, must be won. Any other alternative is simply unthinkable.

Personal experience and memory apart, the writing of this book would not have been possible without the invaluable help of books and documents like those relating to the Punjab and Bengal Boundary Commission Chairman Sir Cyril Radcliffe and Major General TW Rees, Commander of the Punjab Boundary Force, besides magazines and newspapers of the day at the British Library, King's Cross, London, and other associate offices.

Equally valuable were the facilities at the Nehru Memorial Museum and Library, the Central Secretariat Library, the Press Information Bureau, the Defence Ministry, and the *Hindustan Times* photo library, New Delhi. I am grateful to the staff of all these institutions for their kind help. I am also grateful to my cartoonist friend Dhirendra Kumar for his Indo–Pak dialogue sketches.

Subhash Chopra

10 October, 2009

New Delhi

Introduction

The triumph and tragedy of the 1947 partition and independence of the Indian sub-continent remains a terrifying paradox in the annals of modern history. The object of this text is not to examine why and what led to partition but to cast a cold eye on the animus that consumed one million lives in the immediate instance and its gory reminders 60 years on like the December 2001 attack on the Indian Parliament and Mumbai 26/11, 2008. It also looks at the failure of the parties to the partition agreement — the British, Indian Congress and Muslim League leaders — to prevent the carnage that has ensued since then.

The book also looks at the sabotage of samjhota (rapprochement) dialogue between India and Pakistan over the years since 1998 and how that was targeted by the jihadi saboteurs who eventually took on their masters with attacks on targets like Lal Masjid (Red Mosque) in January 2007, Marriott Hotel in September 2008 and Pakistan Army's General Headquarters in October 2009 killing six soldiers including a Brigadier and a LT- Colonel in the heart of the national capital, dealing a body blow to the Pakistani state itself.

The surrender of the paradise Valley of Swat to Taliban forces by Pakistan in a "Sharia" peace deal and the loss of control over Buner and other nearby districts and the belated military action, under US pressure, to recapture the areas led to the displacement of over two million people. Their eventual return to the bombed out ruins of their homes and towns added a dangerous new dimension to Pakistan polity.

The sharpening of the 1947 animus against India has for long been turned into a political necessity by successive regimes in Pakistan. India-bashing in the name of Islam and 'liberation' of Kashmir has become a potent tool in the hands of Pakistani rulers for self-survival and as a ploy to deflect public attention from failure of government and development at home. Economic assistance from Saudi Arabia in the name of Islam and from the USA in the cold war game of containing Soviet influence under treaties like SEATO and CENTO came handy in keeping the anti-India pot boiling. The Saudi–American campaign to drive out Soviet troops from Afghanistan during the 1980s presented a golden opportunity to Pakistan's military regime under General Zia-ul Haq to merge the anti-Indian animus with the Islamist jihad for Afghanistan's liberation from Soviet influence. A good part of the funds and weaponry for the Afghan jihad has for long been diverted by Pakistan to a low-cost mini-jihad in Kashmir too, while America and Saudi Arabia conveniently looked the other way.

There was perfect convergence of American and Pakistani interests during the rule of General Zia, who provided invaluable help in organizing a successful jihad in defeating the Soviet troops in Afghanistan, while firmly putting Pakistan on the road to Islamization to further fortify his own position. The civilian governments of Prime Ministers Benazir Bhutto and Nawaz Sharif that followed the death of General Zia in an aircrash carried on their own political struggle for self-survival, exploiting the anti-India rhetoric under the watchful eye of the all powerful Army — until the day Prime Minister Nawaz Sharif thought of inviting Indian Prime Minister Atal Bihari Vajpayee in February, 1998 for a dialogue to break the ice between the two neighbours. The re-assertion of power by the Army under General Pervez Musharraf who toppled and exiled Prime Minister Sharif came as no surprise.

All this while the Islamist genie that General Zia had nurtured and let out of the bottle kept on acquiring a power of its own in the name of Islam, Sharia, Ummah and global jihad with a vision of reviving the old Islamic Caliphate which once ruled the world from Arabia to Spain. The jihadis who only a few years ago had helped eject the Soviet troops from Afghanistan now had new targets in sight — India, Afghanistan and Pakistan itself.

General Musharraf in his later years of power increasingly came to be seen as an American agent by the mullah-driven sections of Pakistani society and elements within his own Army administration, resulting in two attempts on his life. The professional and well-off classes on the other hand mounted pressure on him in their pursuit of democracy and actively sought America's help for that objective. An uneasy truce between former Prime Minister Benazir Bhutto and the General failed to save the situation. The assassination of Benazir Bhutto shocked the nation while the exit of General Musharraf following the February, 2008 elections failed to stabilise the situation as his critics had expected.

As the new civilian government of Pakistan headed by Benazir Bhutto's widower, Asif Ali Zardari, struggles to find its feet against the all powerful Army and a sceptical civil society, the Taliban, al-Qaeda and other jihadists have managed to strike lightning blows in Pakistan and Afghanistan.

At the same time the American administration under President Barack Obama has begun to turn the screw on Pakistani establishment which has been reminded that there would be no 'blank cheques' or free lunches. Fresh American aid would be strictly tied to delivery of successful action against jihadi terrorism. That is the stark message of the Obama administration. Its refusal to stop Drone attacks on Pakistani havens for terrorists in hot pursuit actions, violating Pakistan's territorial sovereignty may be a bitter pill for Pakistan to swallow but there is no escape.

The de facto rulers of Pakistan have for long outwitted the US in extracting massive financial and military aid as a terrorism dividend to enrich the defence forces rank and file, as well as to carry on a low intensity war against India in Kashmir. There are genuine fears in India that with or without the American largesse the Pakistani establishment is unlikely to restrain its state or non-state actors from striking at targets in Kashmir and the rest of India. The post-Mumbai infiltration of militants and their skirmishes with the Indian army in the Kupwara forests of Kashmir are pointers to more violence ahead.

Pakistani rulers' recurrent itch against India seems to be unstoppable in their self-survival game, never mind the cost to the country's development and people's well being. That itch has its origin in the 1947 partition of India and the gross misinterpretation of the two-nation theory by the successors of Pakistan's founder, Quaid-e-Azam Mohammad Ali Jinnah. Had Mr Jinnah lived long enough he would not have allowed Pakistan to become a narrow, theocratic Islamist state. He was a modern, secular man whose Islam, like that of the poet, Allama (Sir Mohammed) Iqbal, did not preach enmity towards the followers of other religions. But time was not on Jinnah's side; he died prematurely for Pakistan's stable foundation.

To Prime Minister Attlee and the British establishment that itch looked pretty natural, fore-visioned in the 1909 Separate Electorates legislation of the Viceroy Lord Minto and the 1932 Communal Award of Labour Prime Minister Ramsay MacDonald who had sent Attlee as one of the members of the Simon Commission to find a solution to the Indian problem.

Britain's post-war mad rush to divide India with a cut and run strategy only exacerbated the situation further. Her voluntary pullout from India under Attlee's Labour Party may have been on high moral grounds of the party's democratic ideology and its resolve to extend that ideology to the people of her most prized colony, yet that was not the whole story. There were other factors too which hastened the imperial pullout that became a scuttle of staggering proportions. Britain's parlous economic condition at home was a highly compelling reason for getting rid of the imperial burden at the earliest. The ensuing scuttle had devastating consequences which virtually wiped out the magnanimity of the gesture of voluntary transfer of power.

The loss of at least one million lives and the uprooting of another 12 million people from their hearths and homes in less than three months in the western Indian sector alone in history's biggest population exchange cannot be forgotten or wished away. The role of the top leaders responsible for the decisions cannot escape questioning even long after the cataclysm.

The role of Prime Minister Attlee and Lord Mountbatten of Britain, Pandit Nehru of India, and Quaid-e-Azam Mohammad Ali Jinnah of Pakistan, all great national leaders with a wider world vision but also with their own blind spots, reveals on close scrutiny monumental self-delusion and failure to carry out or translate the partition plan as intended.

Leading the quartet was Mountbatten, Britain's last Viceroy in India, nominally though he was only carrying out Prime Minister Attlee's "instructions". Attlee's original plan for transfer of power to Indian hands by June 1948 was speeded up by Mountbatten so drastically that it let loose forces of hate that he was unable to control despite earlier promises of using all available weapons, including troops, tanks and even aircraft, to nip the trouble, wherever it arose, in the bud.

Muddying the waters for all four of them was Sir Evan Jenkins, the Governor of Punjab, who advised Mountbatten against the idea of imposing military rule in parts of Punjab as demanded by Jinnah and Nehru on 23rd and 24th of June 1947 respectively. The Governor who was administering Punjab under his direct rule (under Section 93) since the resignation of Punjab Premier Sir Khizar Hayat in the first week of March, failed to stop the deterioration of law and order. Adequate police and military strength was available to control the situation but he did not activate the machinery right at the start of the troubles in March or even after Jinnah's and Nehru's suggestion full 50 days before the 15th August transfer of power deadline. He let it slip by taking only half measures like imposing collective community fines at a couple of places and making only token arrests of a few troublemakers. Without any province-wide strategy, he let the situation drift. Clearly he was out of his depth or was convinced in the imperial belief: apre's Pax Britannica le de'luge for India.

Appalled at the continuing deterioration of law and order situation Nehru called for the dismissal of Jenkins and a string of other officials under him, but Mountbatten stubbornly defended Jenkins whose share in Punjab's bloodletting cannot be underestimated.

Mountbatten, who seemed to have secured plenipotentiary powers while accepting the job as Viceroy, virtually devised his own plan and cajoled the Cabinet in London and political leaders in India into believing that partition at the earliest was the best solution. After barely two months of taking up his job in India, he sent his Chief of Staff, Lord Ismay, from New Delhi to London asking him to "make them (the Cabinet) realise that speed is the essence of the contract. Without speed we will miss the opportunity ... I am convinced that in order to have the best chance of obtaining our long term object, the grant of Dominion Status (transfer of power) must take place during 1947 (not June 1948)."

Mountbatten, who was the main author of the 3rd June transfer of power plan, compounded the problem by not having the provision of a common Governor-General for an interim period up to the completion of partition written into the 3rd June plan. He simply assumed that the two sides would accept the idea at his suggestion. India did accept it but Jinnah decided to name himself as the first Governor-General of Pakistan. Mountbatten tried hard to dissuade him but Jinnah was adamant. As a result, the effectiveness of British authority and Mountbatten's own impartiality became utterly questionable.

Mountbatten, who has been widely credited with having taken the right course in the given conditions, is said to have revised his opinion about his performance, according to BBC correspondent John Osman who met him at a Life Guards dinner in Windsor soon after he had returned from covering the 1965 India–Pakistan war. In a letter to London's *Spectator* magazine, Osman said when he got talking to Mountbatten on India he found the ex-Viceroy full of remorse for how he had 'got things wrong'. Osman's letter, which appeared under the heading "The Viceroy's Verdict" in the September 2004 issue, concluded: "Mountbatten was not to be consoled. To this day his own judgment on how he had performed in India rings in my ears and in my memory. As one who dislikes the tasteless use in writing of the dictionary's 'vulgar slang' word, I shall permit myself an exception this time because it is the only honest way of reporting accurately what the last Viceroy of India thought about the way he had done his job: 'I fucked it up'."

The BBC correspondent's version of Mountbatten's own 'verdict' may sound an extreme summation, but for millions of sufferers and their descendents in India, Pakistan and now Bangladesh the rude summation is the nearest to their gut feeling.

Prime Minister Attlee, who was neck deep in trouble on the home front with the economy in a shambles, was only too ready to have the Indian burden taken off his shoulders. Transfer of power by 15th August 1947, as suddenly suggested by Mountbatten, didn't seem to be too soon.

Talking about partition massacres, Attlee though regretful over the loss of life recalls in *A Prime Minister Remembers* with some cold satisfaction: "I can only say that the death toll would have been far higher if we hadn't come out — if we had tried to hold India…"

"We would have preferred a United India. We couldn't get it, though we tried hard. But broadly speaking the thing went off well, I think. That was because we handed over power in India on a definite announced date and they knew they had to take it. That was absolutely essential…the experiment came off and that when we came out of India, we left behind so much goodwill."

Like many others, Attlee also hoped that partition or 'severance' would be temporary.[1]

In India, both Nehru for the Congress and Jinnah for the Muslim League, whatever their feelings, didn't demur or raise any objection to such an early departure date – 15th August 1947.

Nehru and several of his colleagues even deluded themselves by believing that Pakistan would be so unviable culturally and economically that its leaders would soon come back for reunion with India![2] Nehru, though frequently weighed down by pangs of conscience, had mixed feelings as he said in his farewell message to Mountbatten in June 1948: "May be, we have made many mistakes, you and we ... but I do believe that we did try to do right ... the right thing by India."

For Pakistan, Jinnah wishfully thought that once the new country was established old suspicions and enmities would wither away.[3] His famous Karachi declaration in the Constituent Assembly of Pakistan that Hindus and Muslims would "cease to be Hindus and Muslims..." and just be citizens of Pakistan became an early casualty of theocratic extremism even before his death barely 13 months away. Like Nehru he too was unable to stop the communal massacres. Nor was he to know how his country would be undermined by religious fundamentalists and jihadis of later years.

Jinnah had envisaged Pakistan as a modern Islamic republic — not an Islamist theocratic state which it unfortunately became after the almighty push by General Zia-ul Haq. But the battle for the soul of Pakistan is very much in progress. Lawyers achieving the restoration of Chief Justice Iftikhar Mohammad Choudhary, peaceful exit of General Musharraf after the national elections and women demonstrating with 'Go Taliban, Go' banners in Lahore give the nation new hope. Pakistan's civil society may have been down for the best part of 60 years but it's not out. Given cool heads, dialogue and eschewing of denial of saboteurs within, the larger battle for peace in the South Asian region, especially India, Pakistan and Afghanistan, is surely winnable. The alternative is simply unthinkable.

Notes

1. *The Times* (London) report on Attlee moving the second reading of the Indian Independence Bill in the House of Commons on 10 July, 1947: "He (Attlee) earnestly hoped that this severance might not endure, that the two new Dominions they now proposed to set up might in course of time come together again to form one great member state of the British Commonwealth of Nations."

2. Nehru to KPS Menon, 29 April 1947. "I have no doubt whatever that sooner or later India will have to function as a unified country. Perhaps the best way to reach that stage is to go through some kind of partition now."

Nehru to Brigadier (later Field Marshal) KM Cariappa: "But of one thing I am convinced that ultimately there will be united and strong India. We have often to go through the valley of shadows before we reach the sun-lit mountain tops."

Both quotes from *Jawaharlal Nehru — A Biography* (Vol I pp 343–49) by Gopal S.

3. Appendix: V, VI and VII

PART 1

1

India–Pakistan Wars and Peace

The animus born of the 1947 partition has cast a long — over half a century long — shadow on the relationship between India and Pakistan. Mutual distrust which has sparked four overt and covert wars — 1947, 1965, 1971, 1999 — and several major attacks on Indian institutions and cities like the 2001 attack on the Indian parliament and the 26/11 carnage in Mumbai in 2008 boils over from time to time.

While Mumbai 26/11 has come to symbolise the defining moment in Indo–Pak relations, Pakistan's de facto rulers (Army top brass) have suffered a series of quick-fire blows to their authority from erstwhile Islamist allies (Taliban, al Qaeda, Jaish-e-Muhammad, Harkat-ul-Mujahideen, Hizb-ul-Mujahideen, Tehreek-e-Taliban Pakistan and an assortment of jihadis operating under ever-changing names). The post-Mumbai attacks on the touring Sri Lankan cricketers in Lahore and bloody assaults on the police training academy near Lahore, on paramilitary Frontier Constabulary camp in federal capital Islamabad, and on the secret service (ISI) zonal offices in Islamabad and Lahore have shaken the confidence of people at home and abroad in the ability of the rulers to contain the Taliban element or fundas, as Islamist fundamentalists are known by another name in the country.

Whether Pakistan has reached the tipping point in the battle against home grown state or non-state actors, aided and even armed by the quasi-official agencies over long years to fight India in Kashmir and to extract more money from the United States under the pretext of fighting al Qaeda, is a moot point. But the moment seems to have arrived for the de facto rulers to make a decisive choice between a backward Talibanised society and a modern polity. The popular myth that the rulers could control and use the genie they had long kept in the bottle has been exploded.

President Barack Obama of US, who completed his first 100 days in office in May 2009, virtually read the riot act to the Pakistani rulers urging them to push back the advancing Taliban forces which had reached Buner, barely 60 miles from national capital Islamabad, after wresting control over Swat Valley in the North Western Frontier Province in a disastrous 'peace deal'. The Pakistani military duly obliged by launching a full scale offensive, using for the first time helicopter gunships, on Taliban holdouts. At stake was American and international aid to Pakistan, as well as the very survival of the Pakistani state. The surrender and re-capture of Swat Valley marks a new chapter in Pakistan's military history.

Obama told the world press: "I am gravely concerned about the situation in Pakistan, not because I think that they're immediately going to be overrun and that the Taliban would take over Pakistan. I am more concerned that the civilian government there right now is very fragile and don't seem to have the capacity to deliver basic services — schools, health care, rule of law, a judicial system that works for the majority of the people."

An alarmed Obama, though somewhat confident about the security of Pakistan's nuclear arsenal, said that the Pakistani army recognised the dangers of weapons falling into the wrong hands. He also expressed the hope that Pakistan's army had begun to realise that home-grown militants and not India posed the biggest threat to its stability.

Mr Obama is entitled to his fond hope. That still leaves Pakistan's de facto rulers with another well-practised option: whether to continue selectively using some of the armed fundas like the UN proscribed Lashkar-e-Tayyeba, renamed Jamat-ud-Dawa/Falah-e-Insaniyat Foundation, against India in Kashmir and elsewhwere. The muffled gloating with which Lahore High Court's order releasing Hafiz Muhammed Saeed, chief of the UN proscribed

Lashkar, has been greeted by those in power in Pakistan remains an unhappy signal for India and a sad commentary on Pakistan's commitment to act against men behind Mumbai's attackers.

The Mumbai carnage which claimed the lives of 173 people, including 33 Muslims, besides over 300 injured, has brought India and Pakistan to the brink — not of active conflict — but to the brink of collapse of the bilateral dialogue so painstakingly sustained through the previous ten years. The 10-year-old peace process began on a high note with the 1998 bus ride to Pakistan by former Indian Prime Minister Atal Behari Vajpayee at the invitation of Pakistan's then Prime Minister Nawaz Sharif. But Sharif had not taken into account the strength of the Army without whose "permission" nothing, not even a dialogue with India, could move. The power struggle that ensued saw Sharif toppled and exiled to Saudi Arabia by the army strongman General Pervez Musharraf, who later dealt a knock-out blow to the peace dialogue with his high altitude covert war in the Kargil region of Kashmir in 1999. The second knock-out blow was delivered with the December 2001 attack on the Indian parliament by the so-called "non-state" elements of mixed identity, including Indian agents or collaborators. The third knock-out came in November 2008 with the attack on Mumbai's top hotels, sites and a Jewish retreat, again by so-called "non-state" actors from Pakistan, completing a hat-trick of major terrorist strikes.

The origin and instigation or inspiration of the Mumbai 26/11 attackers, as in earlier instances, were vehemently doubted and dismissed out of hand by Pakistani authorities for full 42 days when the country's National Security Adviser, Major-General (retired) Mahmud Ali Durrani, let the cat out of the bag by admitting that the lone surviving member of the 10-man terror team, Ajmal Amir Kasab was indeed a Pakistani national. Durrani, for his pains, was summarily sacked by Prime Minister Yusuf Reza Gilani for 'irresponsible behaviour' (giving the county a 'bad name' by speaking the truth). Durrani said he had cleared his statement to the *Dawn* newspaper with President Asif Ali Zardari, but that was not enough to save him in the confused power equations in Pakistan where the Army and

Inter-Services Intelligence hold powerful cards. Durrani's statement was later corroborated by Information Minister Sherry Rehman and others.

Kasab's identity, first confirmed by London's *Observer* newspaper and reconfirmed by Pakistan's own Geo Television channel, continued to be denied by the Islamabad establishment as it could open the floodgates to the identity of the other attackers whose bodies Pakistan didn't wish to claim, even for burial in their home surroundings. The identities of the attackers could also lead to the identities of their handlers and hideouts in Pakistan to which Kasab's evidence and other sources pointed.

Former Pakistan Prime Minister Nawaz Sharif also came out against the establishment's cover-up of the identity of the perpetrators of the Mumbai carnage. He specifically questioned why Mumbai's lone surviving attacker Kasab's home village of Faridkot near Dipalpur in Okara district of Pakistan had been cordoned off and journalists and others prevented from meeting the villagers and Kasab's parents. Under obvious pressure from the Army and the popular frenzy that had been whipped up against India, Sharif was reported to have somewhat back tracked. His apparent change of tack seemed in line with President Asif Ali Zardari's about-turns on so many counts since (Zardari) assuming office. The Army appeared to have simply muzzled the political voices. But to clear his stand a few days later, Sharif urged the ruling establishment to "seriously" consider the evidence provided by India and to keep the communication channels open to avoid "misunderstandings" between the two countries.

Civil rights groups of Pakistan have spoken out about the dangers of the denial policy. A joint statement issued by the Human Rights Commission of Pakistan headed by Asma Jahangir and the South Asian Free Media Association led by Imtiaz Alam and delivered in Amritsar at a meeting with Indian dialogue promoters called for "judicious prosecution" of the Mumbai 26/11 culprits. Without mincing any words, the statement underlined: "After passing through a denial mode, Pakistan has accepted the truth that those who attacked Mumbai were from Pakistan.

"Following this admission which should have come earlier, India must eschew its anger and get Pakistan to engage in negotiations on the basis of what has been revealed about Pakistan's involvement in the Mumbai attack." For his troubles, Alam was subjected to a physical attack a few days later in Lahore, apparently for making an "unpatriotic" call to the authorities to come clean on the affair without further delay.

Right from the start of the Mumbai attack, India and several other countries, notably the USA, had been urging Pakistan to take action against the handlers of the attackers. But all this to no avail, even after India provided a detailed dossier of evidence through the US and others and also directly to Pakistan.

Whichever way Pakistan's internal power struggle plays out, Pakistan has been reluctant to abandon the denial mode about the involvement of its state, 'non-state' or 'state-less' operators from its soil. The halting and hesitant admission of Kasab's identity puts question marks over the long term intentions and tactics of Pakistan's de facto rulers. The exhaustive dossier of evidence, including satellite phone intercepts, was dismissed by Pakistani authorities as mere 'information' rather than 'proof' worthy of action.

Persistent stonewalling tactics run the risk of worsening the chances of peace or even the resumption of the composite dialogue.

There have been excesses in India too like the 1992 demolition of the 16th century Babri mosque complex and the 2002 Gujarat pogrom by Hindutva zealots aided, abetted or at least unstopped by the right-wing state government. They stick out as "kalanks" or black marks on India's secular image.

While in India there has been widespread condemnation of the Hindutva attacks by large sections of majority-Hindu population and state and federal political parties, Pakistan's rulers have been in near total denial as if they can't do any wrong or can't see any wrong being hatched under their very nose. Blaming India for media scares, knee-jerk reactions and lack of evidence has become their pet ploy. The dramatic assaults like the attack on the Indian Parliament, the Indian embassy in Kabul and the Mumbai carnage seen vividly on world television screens are evidence enough for anyone willing to see the naked horror. Asking for yet more "proof" in the face of such open evidence seems beyond all comprehension. It's like saying the Holocaust perpetrated by the Nazis never took place!

The enormity of the carnage perpetrated in Mumbai is too grave to be obfuscated by denials, subterfuge or soft promises of action against law breakers. The frequent bleeding of India through low-level localised proxy attacks cannot go on any longer. As the Indian Foreign Minister, Pranab Mukherjee, said at a joint press conference with the then US Secretary of State, Condoleezza Rice in New Delhi that in 2008 alone six Indian cities had been attacked with various skills and kills extinguishing 350 lives.

Mukherjee has repeatedly reminded Pakistan in unambiguous words that the issue could not be brushed under the carpet and Pakistan's shifty and shifting tactics won't do. India's disenchantment with Pakistan was total and all options had to be kept open if Pakistan failed to dismantle its terror network on its soil. The Indian Congress party president Sonia Gandhi's warning that India was capable of giving "a befitting reply" only reinforced India's resolve to fight terrorism.

Faced with persistent denials by Pakistan, the Indian Prime Minister Manmohan Singh had no choice but to tell Pakistan in clear words that it was utilising "terrorism as an instrument of state policy" against India. While declaring that "war was no solution", he had earlier hoped that "better sense would prevail over the leadership of Pakistan and heed the demands of civilised countries and bring to justice the perpetrators of the Mumbai attack.

The ground reality in Pakistan is such that the key to any peace with neighbours or any meaningful war against jihadis in Afghanistan or elsewhere, or even maintaining law and order at home lies in the hands of the Army.

And the key to exerting any real influence on Pakistan lies in the hands of Saudi Arabia and the USA, in that order. Saudi Arabia, which has both moral and financial influence, needs to persuade Pakistan to act against al-Qaeda and all its affiliates in a determined fashion, both in the western sector adjoining Afghanistan and in the eastern sector adjoining India, including Kashmir, as they pose a threat not only to India or America and the West but also to Saudi Arabia and Pakistan itself. Playing soft in either sector cannot work. Nor would shifting forces from western to eastern borders act the policy of blessing overt or covert action on the eastern side against India needs to be abandoned if any dialogue with India is to prosper.

Saudi Arabia itself needs to be persuaded by its American and other allies that the funding of over 22,000 Pakistani madarsas or seminaries, mainly by Arab charities, needs to be redirected to convert them into modern schools. For the madarsas are the hotbed and recruiting grounds of al-Qaeda and future suicide bombers. The textbooks of these schools need to be revised and the mullahs (priests) in schools and mosques need to be watched to stop the spread of fanaticism. Other financial aid to Pakistan also needs to be watched and seen to be used for social and economic development for which it is granted.

Likewise America too needs to monitor how its aid is actually utilised by Pakistan. The Pakistan Army has had too much money and weaponry showered on it by the Bush administration over eight years in the name of the Afghanistan war against the Taliban and al-Qaeda. The earlier US administrations had their own excuses and reasons for arming and financing Pakistan for nearly 50 years. Quite a lot of that American largesse has been deployed against India in the low-intensity "proxy war" in Kashmir and several Indian cities.

In a policy corrective, the US President Barack Obama, who had already said during his election campaign that it was no use throwing money on the table (of Pakistan's military rulers), has devised a new strategy to help Pakistan save itself from the Taliban, al-Qaeda and bankruptcy. Unfortunately some powerful elements within the Army still see the mullahs and the Taliban as spiritual allies. Not for nothing was ex-President General Musharraf known for his Military Mullah Alliance (MMA)! Musharraf may have gone, but the MMA spirit is still alive, even after the eight-day siege of the Red Mosque that cost 106 lives in July 2007 and the September 2008 bombing of the Marriott hotel in Islamabad, and the 2009 happenings in Lahore, Islamabad, and Sharia-ruled pax Talibana badlands of Swat and other Pakistan areas bordering Afghanistan.

The Army in Pakistan has to be persuaded that riding the (mullah) tiger is never a safe option. The mullah-driven suicide bombers who destroyed Marriott Hotel would not have hesitated even if the Army generals had been present in the hotel at the time. Rather they would have been too glad to have some star-studded victims.

For long, too long, Pakistan's rulers have used the fundamentalist forces against India. The animus against India and the baggage of the last few decades may not be easy to shed but it must be done as there is no alternative to peace.

Brave efforts at capping the old animus have been made over the years in the face of grave odds and obstacles. Such efforts have not gone unnoticed by peace forces on both sides of the divide. One of the first salvos for peace was launched as early as April 1950 when Indian Prime Minister Pandit Jawaharlal Nehru and Pakistan Prime Minister Liaquat Ali Khan signed an agreement in New Delhi to try to chart out a new path of tolerant neighbourliness between the two nations. The tragic assassination of Mr Liaquat Ali Khan in Rawalpindi the following year put paid to that effort which held out a flicker of early hope.

The next big effort at a rapprochement was undertaken during Sher-e-Kashmir Sheikh Mohammed Abdullah's 1964 visit to Pakistan where the idea of a loose confederation of India, Pakistan and Kashmir was broached before the then Pakistan President, Field Marshal Ayub Khan. The Sheikh's idea, which was not well received in New Delhi, got a definitive thumbs-down from Ayub Khan, though the hope of a Nehru–Ayub meeting was soon held out. But the hand of fate extinguished that hope with the sudden death of Nehru on the last day of the Sheikh's visit to Pakistan, and with that another rapprochement bid consigned to oblivion.

The ascendance of military rulers — with nominal civilian prime ministers and presidents — after Liaquat Ali's assassination kept the anti-India pot boiling. Kashmir or "liberation of Muslims from the Indian yoke" became a handy tool to divert public attention from the underlying political, economic and social challenges at home.

Appeals with Islamic slogans became de riguer for every leader, civilian or military, seeking power. American and Saudi help — military and financial — came in handy. The US administrations sucked Pakistan into pacts like SEATO (South East Asia Treaty Organisation) and CENTO (Central Treaty Organisation, first known as the Baghdad Pact) in the great game of keeping the Soviet bear at bay, while the Saudis funded the expansion of the hardline Sunni/Wahabi Islam in the entire Indian sub-continent.

American arms and Saudi money through charities fed the fundamentalist tiger against India. Years later, riding the tiger is proving disastrous, as it always does. For nearly five decades, the civilian and military rulers of Pakistan appeared to be in full control and enjoying the tiger ride. However, the sixth decade was to unsettle that dream ride. The tiger began to bite the hand that fed it. Two attempts on the life of President General Musharraf and the assassination of former Prime Minister Benazir Bhutto in the 60th year of independence brought the nation and its ruling classes face to face with the challenge from within.

The 1947 covert war over Kashmir was followed by the 1965 overt war against India. Both wars turned out to be inconclusive as outside mediation through the United Nations and the Soviet Union respectively produced truce, however uneasy and temporary.

The 1971–72 conflagration over Bangladesh produced a conclusive victory for India, though largely the result of Pakistani rulers' coercive policies and refusal to abide by democratic rules for power sharing. Large sections of Pakistani public opinion, though, continue to blame India for the emergence of Bangladesh as an independent breakaway nation. The surrender of 93,000 Pakistani soldiers was followed by the Simla Agreement between Pakistan Prime Minister Zulfikar Ali Bhutto and Indian Prime Minister Indira Gandhi. It was the same Mr Bhutto who had earlier pledged himself to a thousand years' war against India. Notwithstanding the Simla accord, bitterness in relations continued over the next quarter of a century and more.

The Kargil (Kashmir) conflict of 1999 was waiting to happen even though Indian Prime Minister Atal Behari Vajpayee had made his famous bus journey to Lahore earlier on February 20, 1999 and once again reassured the Pakistani establishment of India's full acceptance and recognition of Pakistan by visiting the Minar-e-Pakistan, honouring the foundation of Pakistan flowing from the 1940 Lahore Resolution of the Muslim League party under Quaid-e-Azam Mohammad Ali Jinnah. Mr Vajpayee's words, however, failed to satisfy the military establishment of Pakistan under Commander-in-Chief General Pervez Musharraf who was preparing for Operation Kargil. Mr Vajpayee's homage at the Minar-e-Pakistan (Column marking the founding principles of Pakistan) raised hackles of some of his own Bharatiya Janata Party leaders at home and most demonstrably of Pakistan's Jamat-e-Islami and other fundamentalists, including military ranks.

His visit to the Minar-e-Pakistan was fraught with doubts and suspicions among his own party faithful at home: "But some people were of the view that if I went to the place it would mean that I had put my mohar (seal) of approval on the formation of Pakistan. I asked what all this meant. Is Pakistan dependent on my approval? Pakistan has its own mohar (stamp) and it is in operation. It is true that we (India) did not want partition… (Nevertheless) the country was divided and new provinces and separate countries were formed. This has hurt us and although the wounds have healed the scar has indeed persisted. But the scar reminds us that we have to live together and living together requires that we march together."

Mr Vajpayee's recognition of Pakistan's own stamp or mohar has come to acquire seminal importance in removing long embedded suspicions among Pakistani, hearts even though in the immediate instance it failed to win over Pakistan's military top brass who under General Musharraf surprised India with the Kargil incursion in Kashmir barely three months after Mr Vajpayee and host Prime Minister Nawaz Sharif broke bread together at the Lahore Fort banquet. Mr Vajpayee's ability to pursue the entente cordiale later with President General Musharraf's regime has deepened the feeling of trust among people of Pakistan and remains a source of strength unaffected by the changes of political regimes in both countries.

In the short run, though, Vajpayee's bus journey's bonhomie failed to prevent the Generals from conspiring to launch a covert attack on India in the name of Kashmiri freedom fighters.

Pakistan's three armed service chiefs, notably General Pervez Musharraf, had deliberately absented themselves from the reception to the Indian Prime Minister at the border, giving rise to reports in Pakistani newspapers next day that the service chiefs were against the bus diplomacy and all it sought to promote. The militant Islamist groups like the Jamat-e-Tulba, the student youth wing of the Jamat-e-Islami, called for a hartal or shutdown against the Indian Prime Minister's visit and even attacked cars of foreign diplomats and guests travelling to attend the banquet in honour of the visiting Prime Minister. The Pakistani military chiefs, though, made a belated yet calculated diplomatic gesture of offering a salute to the visiting Prime Minister at the reception at the Government House in Lahore so as not to fully reveal their hand in advance. The well laid plans for the Kargil adventure in Kashmir, an invasion of the Indian controlled territory across the line of control by supposedly civilian faith soldiers or Mujahids, were carried out in the inhospitable Kashmir mountain terrain (altitude 14,000–20,000 ft) with a surprise attack on Indian positions. The resultant toll on both sides and claims of victory by both sides is history.

One important detail of calling a halt to the conflict was the intervention of US President Bill Clinton who persuaded Pakistan Prime Minister Nawaz Sharif to ask his military chiefs to step back to the status quo and stop the conflict from turning into a bigger war with graver consequences. However unpalatable it was to General Musharraf, even he must have realised that the cost of the adventure was much more than he had bargained for. The confrontation ended with a face saver for both sides, each in its own turn deceiving domestic national audience by calling it a victory! The public on both sides had been fooled, though fairly large sections remained skeptic of official claims.

However bitter the conflicts, they produced border or line of control agreements of lasting resilience.

The Simla Agreement, though signed between a victorious India and a vanquished Pakistan following the Bangladesh war, had its lighter moments too. Simla signatory Pakistan Prime Minister Zulfikar Ali Bhutto's daughter Benazir, then a teenager and later herself a Prime Minister for two terms, recalled the rather hilarious progress of drafting of the agreement. Lodged on the upper floor of the main mansion where the agreement was being signed, she was kept informed of the final stages of the drafting process. Several drafts were attempted by the officials of the two countries and it was decided by the Pakistani draftsmen that an unsuccessful draft would be signalled to her with the words 'Ladki hai — it's a girl' while a successful and agreed draft would be called 'Ladka hai — It's a boy'. So after several Ladkis or girls, finally a Ladka or boy was born. Young Benazir protested how chauvinistic the whole thing was but she said "nobody was listening". She even missed witnessing the signing of the agreement as she could not push her way through the press crowd gathered around the door to the signing chamber.[1]

The uneasy truce that followed the Kargil war retained high tension undercurrent for nearly four years. The withdrawal of Pakistani troops to status quo ante after Kargil war did not appear to have produced any change of heart or strategy. The military regime under President General Musharraf launched a diplomatic offensive asking India to come to the negotiating table to discuss what it called the core issue of Kashmir and other bilateral problems. India's refusal to accept the Kashmir issue even as a 'dispute' and her insistence on Kashmir being an 'atoot ang' or integral part of India not open to question seemed to put India in the diplomatic dock for perceived rejectionist attitude to any peace overture. Not to be seen as a 'rejectionist' party, India agreed to hold talks with Pakistan to discuss all bilateral issues including Kashmir and terrorist attacks by infiltrators from PoK (Pakistan Occupied Kashmir) in a 'composite dialogue'.

Meanwhile, US President Bill Clinton's visit in March 2000 to the Indian sub-continent proved an eye-opener for the western powers who seemed to have dismissed India's security concerns arising from terrorist training camps and attacks from across the 'Pakistan Occupied Kashmir' or 'Azad (Free) Kashmir' as the territory under Pakistani control is referred to by the two sides. The evening before President Clinton's address to Indian Parliament in New Delhi, thirty-five Sikh minority community members of Chhatisinghpura in Indian controlled Kashmir were gunned down by allegedly Pakistan inspired terrorists to draw the attention of the US President to the "freedom struggle" in Kashmir. But President Clinton seemed to think otherwise saying: "You cannot expect a dialogue to go forward unless there is absence of violence and a respect for the Line of Control."

However, without officially taking sides over the Chhatisingpura incident President Clinton in his address over Pakistan Television (PTV) after his New Delhi visit told his Pakistani hosts in clearest words that 'you cannot change borders with blood'. There was no official comment from the military regime in Pakistan but the message could not have gone un-noticed.

President Clinton's forthright remark was certainly a reminder to Pakistan's military rulers that there was no room for any Kargil-style adventure to redraw the borders (in Kashmir).

Nevertheless, without giving up the tactic of proxy war in Kashmir, Pakistan President General Musharraf intensified his diplomatic offensive culminating in the bilateral Summit at Agra, the historic Indian city, in July 2001, under the composite dialogue concept which allowed the entire gamut of issues to be discussed including Kashmir, the central issue for Pakistan, and terrorist raids in Indian controlled Kashmir from across the Pakistani controlled Kashmir territory. Each side had a different — almost exact opposite — focus in the 'composite dialogue'. The much-hyped Agra Summit collapsed precisely because of each side's insistence on making its own perceived central issue (Kashmir liberation solution for Pakistan and India's demand for end to cross border raids) as a kind of pre-condition for further progress.[2] The draft agreement which was about to be signed, as claimed by General Musharraf in his autobiographical account, *In the Line of Fire*,[3] and again in his highly paid New Delhi lecture (fee of 10 million rupees) in 2009, never saw the light of the day. Nor was it ever confirmed by Indian Prime Minister Atal Behari Vajpayee.

The two leaders, fortunately, left the dialogue open for another day. (General Musharraf's implicit offer to manage a reduction of cross border raids in Kashmir as a quid pro quo for reduction of Indian troops in Kashmir has always been totally unacceptable to India and it has indeed taken a long time for the Pakistani military and civil establishment to comprehend the Indian insistence on at least a recognition of de facto status quo. Troops pullout was never a bargaining counter for India. Troops reduction in Kashmir only when India's internal security deems it so, not because of any Pakistani demand. It has been an open secret that the Line of Control in Kashmir was to be treated as a sort of a border as had been orally agreed as part of the 1972 Simla accord signed by Pakistan Prime Minister Zulfikar Ali Bhutto and Indian Prime Minister Indira Gandhi. However, spoken words have no place in the affairs of states. General Musharraf's claim of a draft nearly agreed (but not actually agreed) with Prime Minister Vajpayee at Agra belongs to the same category. Yet the encouraging part of the long search for an accord was that the dialogue continued.

Then occurred the truly bombshell event of 9/11 (11 September 2001) attack by Bin Laden's al-Qaeda Islamist jihadis on the twin Trade Towers in New York besides an attack on the Pentagon and another diverted by passengers to a Pennsylvania airfield. For the first time the Western powers understood the meaning and impact of fundamentalist menace in the name of Islam of which India had long been a victim. Even then General Musharraf thought he could join the US and the West against Islamist al-Qaeda and in exchange ask for help in putting pressure on India to help resolve the Kashmir issue according to his light. "We can tell India to lay off…" said the General to his domestic audience that joining America and the West could help the struggle against India.

But it was not so easy to translate on the ground. The Americans and the West too played along for some more time, perhaps giving General Musharraf time to allow recalcitrant Pakistani civil and military leaders to fall in line.

Then came the attacks on India's Kashmir Legislative Assembly and the Indian Parliament by terrorists covertly yet unambiguously aligned with fundamentalist Islamist forces covertly blessed by Pakistan's Inter-Services Intelligence (ISI). At least that is the unshakeable view of most Indians. Pakistan under General Musharraf in a first reaction even suggested that the attacks could have been stage managed by the Indian government to deflect people's attention from domestic problems and that the attacks had nothing to do with Pakistan. But condemnation by world leaders forced General Musharraf to offer his cooperation and promise of action against any individual or group with the rider that India provided proof or evidence of involvement in the attacks.

India, naturally, had no time for such words of cooperation. The government of Prime Minister Vajpayee put its troops on high alert all along the Indo–Pakistan border and the Line of Control in Kashmir. Blaming Pakistan squarely for aiding and abetting terrorism, voices in India were heard about using the option of "surgical strikes" on terror bases or camps across the Kashmir Line of Control.

In the highly charged atmosphere of mutual suspicion, India recalled her envoy to Pakistan, cancelled all bus, train and air services to Pakistan, while on her part Pakistan replied in tit-for-tat style, sending all talk of a dialogue into the deepest limbo.

The Indian army's strike formations including tanks and heavy artillery were moved closer to the Pakistan border as Pakistan did the same. It was an eye-ball to eye-ball formation ready for confrontation any moment. The Indian Prime Minister talked of an "aar-paar" moment, a time for decisive action and a probable fight to the finish. The world was alarmed at seeing the two nuclear armed neighbours on the brink of impending disaster. The United States and her allies in particular were alarmed at the prospect of a nuclear war and a massive setback in their fight against the Taliban and al-Qaeda in Afghanistan. Mediation diplomacy moved into double-quick speed to pull the warring nations back from the brink of a possible nuclear war.

President General Musharraf was persuaded, ostensibly by the United States and Britain, to announce that "no individual or organisation would be allowed to indulge in acts of terrorism (against India) in the name of Kashmir". That was the declaration (12 January 2002) to mollify India. Yet in the same public address he told his domestic constituency that there could be "no compromise on the Kashmir issue".

So the stand-off continued unabated. India refused to pull back its troops from the borders until General Musharraf delivered on his promise with firm evidence of action to stop cross-border raids and dismantling of terrorist bases, madrassas and camps, on its side of the Line of Control. The Western powers pressed on with their efforts for de-escalation by both sides. But there was no let-up among the armed rivals. The Independence Day (August 14 and 15, 2002) speeches by Prime Minister Vajpayee and President General Musharraf pandered to respective domestic audiences. General Musharraf denounced elections in Indian controlled Jammu and Kashmir as a farce while Prime Minister Vajpayee retorted by asking the General to desist from giving lectures on democracy and look within to set his own house in order. American Ambassador to India, Mr Robert Blackwill, hailed Jammu and Kashmir (J&K)

elections as truly democratic. The Indian government's bilateral invitations to Iran and several other countries for observers for the elections seemed to have paid off in winning the diplomatic and publicity round.

The two leaders' performance at the UN General Assembly's annual gathering in September brought out more vitriol with General Musharraf accusing India of tarnishing Pakistan's image by harping on terrorism and Prime Minister Vajpayee accusing Pakistan of nuclear blackmail.

The eye-ball to eye-ball stand-off continued into the 10th month when both countries seemed to blink under Western pressure and the unbearable cost of maintaining such a large number of troops on action ready alert for such a long time. New Delhi, weighed down by the internal military advice over damage to troops morale during an overlong alert and its financial cost, suddenly decided on 16 October 2002 to pull back troops from forward positions on the international border. Pakistan, for whom the costs were crippling and Western pressure even more compelling, lost no time for a reciprocal pullback.

The long stand-off coupled with increasing Western pressure appeared to be the turning point in changing the mindset of the then Pakistani establishment under General Musharraf against a military solution and reduced low-cost proxy operations by jihadi guerrillas.

The composite dialogue launched between India and Pakistan in 2004 was beginning to yield results — until the Mumbai sabotage of the peace process in the last quarter of 2008. Mercifully even in the lowest depth of distrust between the two countries, the two countries exchanged lists of their nuclear installations on the first day of the new year in 2009, as part of an annual exercise since 1991. The Agreement on Prohibition of attacks on Nuclear Installations and Facilities, which was signed in 1988, has been faithfully observed since its ratification in 1991. The two countries also exchanged lists of each other's citizens, mostly fishermen straying into each other's waters, lodged in their prisons in a six-monthly exercise under another agreement. A much older and inspiring bilateral agreement, the

Indus Water Treaty signed in 1960, which covers sharing of waters flowing from the Kashmir region remains in place despite frequent differences.

Notwithstanding all deflections and mis-adventures, the two countries cannot afford to stop looking at the advantages of non-belligerence and peace because there is no alternative to it if the wishes and prosperity of the vast majority of people on both sides are not to be jeopardised.

2

Kashmir : Paradise Valley and Jihadi Noises

Gar Firdaus Bar-Roo-aye Zameen Ast
Hameen Ast, Hameen Ast, Hameen Ast.

—Persian couplet on Kashmir Valley

(If there is Paradise on Earth
It's here, It's here, It's here.)

Kashmir, the Switzerland of the East and once known as the land of the Hindu and Buddhist rishis and sages and Muslim Sufis, has been in the news for the wrong reasons over the past few decades since 1947. Independence from the autocratic rule of the Maharaja and the departure of British rulers from the sub-continent after the creation of two new dominions of India and Pakistan in 1947 has turned Kashmir into a mountainous punch bag in the middle.

The battle for the state of Jammu and Kashmir started right in 1947, just a couple of months after the partition of India. Ever since then each side has claimed the state as an integral part of its own country. The new state of Pakistan laid claim to it as an extension of the two-nation theory on the basis of the Muslim majority of its population. Secular new India, which never accepted the two-nation theory but accepted partition, said the majority of Jammu and Kashmir population, although Muslim, had cast its lot with India under the undisputed leadership of Sheikh Abdullah, a staunchly secular Muslim who had rejected the two-nation theory long

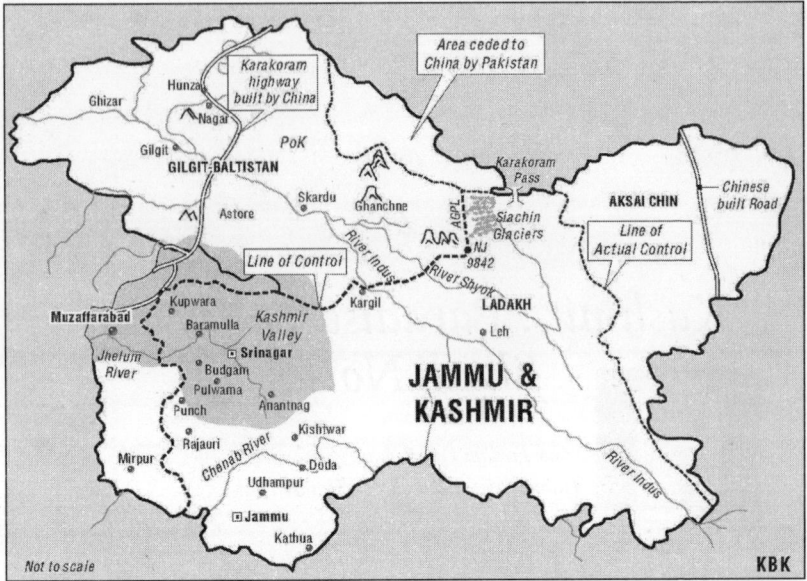

before the partition of the sub-continent. New India also buttressed its claim with the constitutional fact that the ruler of the state, Maharaja Hari Singh, had signed accession to India in line with the outgoing British rulers' policy of leaving the rulers of the princely states free to join either of the two new Dominions of India or Pakistan.

Pakistan, under its leader and Governor-General, Mohammed Ali Jinnah, refused to accept the fait accompli and launched (or blessed) an invasion of Jammu and Kashmir by the so-called tribesmen from the North West Frontier Province and elsewhere in aid of the breakaway rebel Muslim groups from parts of the state adjoining the new dominion of Pakistan. The repulse which the tribal invaders suffered at the hands of the vast majority of Kashmir's Muslims under the leadership of Sheikh Abdullah and Indian armed forces is an historical fact. So is the intervention of the United Nations following a complaint by India and the consequent ceasefire which resulted in the de facto division of the state into two parts — the Indian-controlled part stretching from Jammu to Ladakh regions including the Kashmir Valley with Srinagar as capital and the Pakistan-controlled western and northern parts with Muzaffrabad as capital. The ceasefire line which

was later christened Line of Control has survived four India–Pakistan wars
— 1947, 1965, 1971 and 1999 — besides innumerable violations.

For ready reference, as things stand since late 1947, India controls
roughly half (three sixths) of the pre-1947 state of Jammu and Kashmir,
including the Kashmir Valley which constitutes about one-sixth of the state.
Another two-sixths comprising northern parts like Baltistan, Gilgit Agency
and western areas including Muzaffrabad are controlled by Pakistan. The
remainder, a little more than one-sixth, in the north-east — Aksai Chin — is
controlled by China along with a portion of about 5,000 sq km area in the
Korakurram range ceded to Beijing by Pakistan in 1963. All the hullabaloo
in the world is in reality about the Valley which is often confused with the
whole of Jammu and Kashmir state.

The 1949 United Nations Resolutions vis-à-vis India and Pakistan
calling for a free and fair plebiscite after the removal of all outside (Pakistani)
armed elements or forces remain unimplemented 60 years on for want of
timely fulfilment of required conditions. Both sides have, from time to
time, talked of the irrelevance of those Resolutions and even of the Line of
Control, but have failed to resolve the issue so far.

On the non-legal but emotional front, each side has laid claim to the
state as an integral part of its own being, raising it above just territorial
considerations. Neither side considers it as just a matter of land grab or gain
or loss of geographical territory. For Pakistan it has been a matter of 'faith'
and a fight for the 'rights of Kashmiri Muslim brethren'. For India it is a
matter of the secular soul of the Muslim, Hindu and other people of the
state and the country as a whole and rejection of the theocratic, separatist
ideology, which has spawned self-righteous 'jihad', suicide bombings and
terrorising of opponents with death threats and actual elimination.

Worst of all, starting in 1989 the Islamists perpetrated ethnic cleansing
of the Pandit or Hindu minority from the Kashmir Valley. The expulsion of
nearly a quarter million Pandits and 25,000 Muslims, who dared to support
their Hindu friends, is a standing proof of the lethal blow dealt to Kashmir

by the Hurriyat — literal equivalent freedom or Azadi, in practice theocratic separatism — (full name: All Parties Hurriyat Conference, a conglomeration of 13 or more factions brought under one banner with the encouragement of Paksitan's Islamist military ruler General Zia-ul-Haq and Roben Raphel, the then US Ambassador in Islamabad, both of whom died in an aircrash in Paksitan 1988). The Hurriyat, which has fitfully claimed dominance in Kashmir Valley for nearly 20 years since 1989, has tried and succeeded in good measure, thankfully not completely, in imposing a theocratic regime. Its aim, outwardly peaceful and Islamic, is an Islamist Kashmir. Mercifully the fundamentalists, after enough blood on their hands, have been on the back foot after the 2008 Kashmir elections, and the flame of Kashmiryat, the centuries old ethos of Kashmir, is no longer in danger of being blown away so easily.

The 2002 state elections in Jammu and Kashmir on the Indian side of the Line of Control, when the ruling National Conference party led by Farooq Abdullah and his son Omar was defeated by a Congress and People's Democratic Party alliance, saw the assassination of 99 candidates and their supporters for the 'sin' of participation in elections which were declared 'Haram' or 'anti-Islam' by the separatist demagogues. Democratic elections are anathema to Islamists because they could expose the hollowness of their claims to represent the people. As in Pakistan where they have never been able to emerge as a majority party in any of the provinces, the Islamists of the Hurriyat brand have always shunned elections for fear of being overwhelmingly rejected by the electorate.

Despite all their separatist and theocratic shouts, the series of Assembly elections held across the Indian-controlled part of the state reveal an undeniable political facet of the people of the state. The nine elections from 1962 to 2008 — the first four held after every five years and the last five after every six years under new rules — recorded a voter turnout of more than 60 per cent in all but two exercises. While every election was routinely dismissed by the fundamentalist and pro-Pakistan elements as irrelevant and fraudulent, yet the people of the state came out to vote again and again. No amount of boycott dictat by mullahs (priests), separatists, agent provocateurs and gun wielding terrorists could stop the people from voting in such huge numbers. Every election has been a victory for democracy, no matter what the mullahs preach from the pulpits or their 'blessed' militants' mayhem through the barrels of their guns.

The 2002 and 2008 elections have a telling story to tell. The urban concentration of capital Srinagar has long been flush with arms and money from foreign sources (Pakistan's ISI, Saudi and other Arab charities and American agencies especially during President Bush's term). Well heeled fundamentalist leaders also dexterously exploited Indian television and newspapers besides foreign media like the UK's BBC in the name of democracy and freedom of the press which portrayed them as militants and freedom fighters rather than theocratic bigots. The fear of the gun and the sweetener of money coupled with boycott calls from the pulpit, which have dominated Srinagar from time to time, turning it into a jihadi pocket of sorts, successfully kept large numbers of city voters away from exercising their franchise. As a result, only about four per cent voters were able to cast their vote in Srinagar in the 2002 elections. Outside the capital the people were out of the easy reach of the fundamentalist slogans, threats and gunshots. And they voted with their hands and feet.

The US ambassador to India, Robert Blackwill, hailed the 2002 elections as a free and fair democratic exercise, though Pakistan stuck to its habitual rejection of the democratic process and branded Blackwill's observations improper. The fundamentalists within the state, funded, inspired and armed by Pakistan's intelligence agencies and other groups, chanted their anti-Indian slogans and called for a boycott of the entire election process. They tried to enforce their boycott call with the gun and actually killed 99 candidates and their supporters who defied their dictat. Despite all the terrorist mayhem, 43.7 per cent voters out of a total electorate of 6.17 million cast their ballots and put the Congress–PDP alliance in power.

Six years later in 2008, despite the humungous noises by the jihadi fringe, the people came out in droves, trudging long distances through wind and snow to cast their ballots in open defiance of the fear of the gun and stamped a thundering turnout of over 60 per cent. Even the jihadi pocket of Srinagar recorded nearly 20 per cent turnout — five times that of 2002.

Elections in Jammu and Kashmir on the Indian side of the Line of Control have been summarily dubbed 'fake' by successive regimes in Pakistan in their well-orchestrated propaganda campaigns, deliberately ignoring the dynamics of an internationally recognised democratic exercise and all that it embodies. While the 2002 election was applauded, among others, by American Ambassador Robert Blackwill as a fair and free exercise, the 2008 election drew applause from his successor, David Mulford.

The mere fact of a large turnout time after time and the rise and fall of political parties reflecting the verdict of the people underscores the legitimacy and vibrancy of the democratic system. A look at just two elections — 2002 and 2008 — speaks for the intrinsic strength of the electoral process and the power of the people to retain or change their rulers. The 2002 elections, which were thrown open to observers from several countries, including the Islamic Republic of Iran, saw the rejection of the National Conference ruling party led by Farooq Abdullah and its replacement by a combination of the People's Democratic Party and the Congress party. The PDP led by Mufti Muhammed Saeed and the Congress led by Ghulam Nabi Azad entered a novel power sharing pact with Mufti's party ruling for the first three years and the Congress ruling the state for the second half of the six-year term. Barring differences that occasionally cropped up, the pact worked out fairly well for the best part of five and a half years and functioned orderly even during the strained last six months.

The 2008 elections proved even more dynamic, giving diverse parties a substantial share and voice in the Legislative Assembly. The National Conference led by the son and grandson of the late Sher-i-Kashmir (Lion of Kashmir) Sheikh Abdullah emerged as the largest party with 28 seats in the 87-seat Assembly. The party drew its strength (and seats) from all parts of Jammu and Kashmir, thus demonstrating its sway as a pan-Kashmir grouping.

The PDP, the second largest party, saw its power base confined to the Kashmir Valley even though it increased its share of seats from 16 in 2002 to 21 in 2008. Led by the father and daughter duo of Mufti Muhammed Saeed and Mehbooba Mufti, the party's campaign plank of self-rule for the state (with special appeal to the fundamentalist separatists), dual currency and and loosening of the Line of Control for free-er flow of goods and people paid off with more Assembly seats, but kept it hemmed in the Valley.

The Congress emerged as the third largest party with its power base spread over most parts of the state but with its number of seats reduced from 20 in 2002 to 17 in 2008.

The Hindutva Bhartiya Janta Party came fourth with its Assembly seat share soaring from just one in 2002 to 11 in 2008. But its power base remained severely restricted to the Hindu-majority Jammu region. Yet even there the secular parties like the National Conference and Congress retained some of their 2002 seats, denying the BJP any claim to represent all Hindus in the state.

The eventual permutation and combination of coalition politics after the 2008 election led to the formation of a government led by National Conference Chief Minister, Omar Abdullah, 38-year-old grandson of Sheikh Abdullah, in a power sharing arrangement with the Congress party. Both parties, by and large, have a pan-Kashmir image. In the process the Congress abandoned its 2002 alliance with the PDP and joined the National Conference, an older ally in several earlier elections.

The devil in the 2008 elections was the allotment and cancellation of an 100-acre plot of land for seasonal use by pilgrims on their way to the Hindu shrine (snow lingam or phallus symbol of fertility) and rock temple of Amarnath. The Muslim fundamentalist and separatist lobby whipped up the issue as an attempt at permanently locating a base for the Hindus and thereby changing the demography of the Muslim majority area of the state. All attempts at explanation and clarification by the Congress government which was in power in the second half of the six-year term failed to pacify the protesters. The PDP took the opportunist route to increase its vote bank among the Jamaat-i-Islami followers opposing the land allotment in the coming 2008 elections. It cynically broke ranks with its Congress partner on the issue, though technically keeping the partnership alive.

The cancellation of the shrine land allotment by a panicked Congress government led by Ghulam Nabi Azad had a noticeable effect on the outcome of the 2008 elections with BJP, the Hindutva party, polarising the electorate in Jammu region in its favour and increasing its strength in the new assembly to 11 seats from just one in the previous assembly. The PDP, which acquired the undeclared support of the fundamentalist Jamaat-i-Islami followers, also increased its strength in the Muslim majority Valley from 16 to 21 seats. But both outfits unambiguously attracted the communal tag despite their denials to the contrary.

The older devil of separatism which has cast its shadow over several elections maintains its presence on the political chessboard of Kashmir, making its opportunist moves but never winning the game. Nonetheless its declared aim of Azadi continues to cast its spell, rising or falling in sporadic bubbles. Its proponents, the Hurriyat Conference of 13 or more factions, the Coordination Committee with cross-border (Pakistan) links and a myriad other name-changing splinter support groups, have deliberately avoided defining their concept of Azadi or freedom, though apparently united on a break with India. Whether Azadi means Kashmir as an Islamic republic independent of both India and Pakistan or it means Kashmir becoming part of Pakistan has been kept intentionally unclear. Clearly the separatist lobby is afraid of clarifying its aim and objective of Azadi as that could cost it the support a substantial section of the majority of Muslim population of the Valley. However strong the theocratic Islamic bond, the Muslim majority of the Valley is in no mood to be absorbed and subjugated by Pakistan.

Equally, stand-alone Azadi or independence is not a practical option, many realise this though perhaps as many wish for it.

Yet despite the overwhelming rejection of the boycott call by the voters, separatist sentiment manages to survive. It may be down but it is not out, thanks to a clever confusion created by non-definition of the concept of Azadi.

In the end any resolution of the Kashmir issue would ideally need the cooperation of both India and Pakistan. Despite all the separatist noises, Kashmiri identity remains part of the Indo–Pak cultural ethos.

At stake is this common heritage of which Kashmiryat is the jewel being covered of late in jihadi shroud. The roots of Kashmiryat go back to centuries and are too deeply imbedded in the people's psyche to be destroyed by the jihadist bigotry.

It was Kashmir from where, before the dawn of Christianity, Buddhist monks and Hindu scholars travelled in all directions — to parts of India, Central Asia and the Far Eastern island countries such as Indonesia. One of them, Guna-Verman, introduced Buddhism in Java before moving on to mainland China.

The advent of Islam in Kashmir in the 13th and 14th centuries brought not just Muslim rule but a wave of Sufi thought which intermingled with the old established Shaivism or the cult of Shiva and brought forth the flowering of the Hindu-Muslim composite culture called Kashmiryat. The flame of Kashmiryat has been burning bright since the days of Zain-ul-Abidin, the 15th century ruler also known by his Hindu title as Budh Shah, followed by the Mughal rulers from Akbar to Prince Dara Shikoh who made their summer salies from the hot plains of India to the cool Valley of Kashmir, just like the British used to move their durbars (secretariat) every summer to Simla from the searing heat of New Delhi three centuries later.

Come the 1947 Partition of India, that flame of Kashmiryat began to be buffeted, rather severely, by the winds of separatist radicalism in the name of Islam. Thankfully that flame of composite culture still survives and the message of Sufis like the poetess Lal Ded or Lalleshwari and her nephew Noor-ud-Din or Nund Rishi still reverberates the valley and fills the hearts and minds of its people. Their Hindu-Muslim sufi faith is the fount of

Kashmiryat. No wonder even today lots of Kashmiri citizens have names like Salim Pandit.

The enthusiastic reception given to Junoon, the rock band with Pakistani lead singer Salman Ahmad in the summer of 2008 was a hearty answer to the Hurriyat's separatist ideology. Young and old Kashmiri fans of the band enjoyed the same music which is loved by the people across the subcontinent. Junoon's ever popular numbers — Sayonee, Ya Ali and Khudi Ko Kar Buland Itna — filled the air on a Sunday evening in May on the banks of Dal Lake in state capital Srinagar and touched the heart beats of the Kashmiri audience, giving a lie, if one was ever needed, to the Hurriyat and Jehadi separatist doctrine. In fact the United Jihad Council (UJC) and Hizb-ul-Mujahideen, umbrella organisations of militant groups on both sides of the Line of Control between India and Pakistan, had called for a boycott of the concert and warned against participation in it. The UJC chief, Syed Salahuddin, and Hizb chief Muhammad Yusuf Shah had asked the Pakistan government to stop the band from visiting India. Similar advice had been issued by Hurriyat factions in Srinagar. Luckily to no effect. Salman Ali, the Junoon band leader who had played to audiences in several Indian cities over the last 10 years, in a brief message asked militants to join him in his "musical jihad for peace".

Truly stuck in their separatist grooves, the Hurriyat leaders, Jehadis and their fellow travellers organised a seminar on a synthesis of a different kind in the same city of Srinagar on the same day as Junoon was beaming its musical message of unity of humanity. The Hurriyat seminar was titled "Kashmiri sentiment, sacrifices and realism—A synthesis". The only "synthesis" it presented, as seen in the long website report of an online newspaper, was a reiteration of Azadi or freedom from India, by speaker after speaker. However, some were more anti-India and anti-all things Indian, including elections held later in the year, than others.

Unlike Syed Ali Shah Geelani, the veteran hardline Islamist leader, some of the speakers at the Hurriyat seminar seemed prepared to consider, even accept, current "realities" and called for the formulation of new strategies to deal with the changing situation. Hurriyat's "moderate" and younger chairman, Mirwaiz Moulvi Muhammad Farooq, though not calling for an outright boycott of the 2008 elections, nevertheless thought they were "not a substitute for any peace process". Afraid of elections, the self-styled makers of public opinion have been blowing their own trumpet to hog the limelight.

Most of them generally share the wavelength of official and un-official voices from Pakistan, though some factions have occasionally denounced some of Islamabad's moves, both during and after President Musharraf's rule. Pakistani journalists' tour of Indian-controlled Kashmir and the Indian journalists' tour of Pakistani-controlled Kashmir organised by SAFMA journalists in 2004–2005 were dismissed out of hand by Hurriyat and their fellow travellers on both sides of the divide. So has been their rejection of peace overtures — like the Junoon rock concert in Srinagar and Pakistani cricketers' participation as members of Indian teams in the Twenty-20 Indian Players League (IPL) series. The cricket extravaganza was blessed or at least unhindered by the newly elected civilian government of Pakistan and by the Indian government of Prime Minister Manmohan Singh. However, the Mumbai 26/11 carnage has put a question mark on all that.

Despite protestations of Islamic peace and religious tolerance, the militant influence of the Hurriyat, Hizbul-Mujahideen, United Jehad Council, Lashkar-e-Tayyeba, Harkat-ul-Jihad Islami (HUJI) and their sympathisers have tried to force the closure of cinema halls, women's salons or beauty parlours, liquor shops, bars, besides imposing boycott of dance and music and ordering a dress code for women. Fortunately, they have lost in good measure, though not completely.

Recalling an incident just a week before the Junoon concert, Kashmiri journalist Praveen Swami described how a dream holiday tour of students from Anantnag Women's Degree College turned hell. The girls, while on a tour of parts of India happened to visit Goa where they danced to the tunes of a rock band one evening at a beach restaurant. They were dressed in nothing more immodest than full length trousers (Indian style salwars) and long shirts.

But all hell broke loose on their return home when a video recording of the harmless fun was leaked by the shop owner who was given the job to transfer the tape to compact discs as holiday mementos. Islamist leader Hilal Ahmed War alleged "the girls had been made to dance in night clubs outside the State (Kashmir)" and that it was "shameful and shocking that our sisters are being exploited and taken to dance clubs and bars in different states of India under the garb of educational and cultural tours." Mirwaiz Umar Farooq, chairman of the Hurriyat and head of Srinagar's biggest mosque, chimed in with allegations of India's "cultural aggression to keep the younger generation (of Kashmiris) away from religious and moral values."

The anti-Indian, and occasionally anti-Pakistani, chants and slogans of a section of the community led by people bearing the standard of the Hurriyat have failed to extinguish the flame of Kashmiryat, notwithstanding their high profile media propaganda. Hurriyat has been preaching the message that the Kashmiris (people of Kashmir Valley) have a persona or identity separate from the rest of the people of India, and from the people of Pakistan too. The Hurriyat doctrine of Azadi or freedom presupposes the separateness of Kashmiri people from the cultural ethos of old Hindustan, now India and Pakistan, as if they are a species apart. Hungry for power and position, the Hurriyat leaders have forgotten that in all essentials the Kashmiris are not a people different from those of India or Pakistan and that their destiny is linked with the people of the sub-continent as it has been through the known history of the land. They may quibble about India or Pakistan but there is no getting away from their common destiny. They are not culturally independent, alien or separate. As things stand, political independence is out of the question. An independent Kashmir is a non-starter as it would only degenerate into a cockpit of Jihadi and international mischief.

Post-1947, even going by the 1949 UN Resolutions on a plebiscite in the whole of Jammu and Kashmir there were only two options — joining India or joining Pakistan. And those two options died for non-fulfilment of the plebiscite conditions, specifically the withdrawal of Pakistani armed elements and uniformed troops, something implicitly recognised by former

President General Musharraf who repeatedly described UN Resolutions as being outdated.

The third option of stand-alone independence was never there under the UN Resolutions.

Fortunately a fourth option of a pre-1947-style Greater Kashmir is still on the horizon if both sides work on the concept of converting the Line of Control into a soft border and recognise de facto control of Pakistan and India as de jure reality in their respective areas. Such a Greater Kashmir with free movement of people and goods is eminently achievable. A start had been made in 2008 just when Mumbai 26/11 happened. The people-to-people contacts and trade can be revived and must be revived for the greater good of Kashmir, India and Pakistan.

Some of the possible routes out of the Kashmir quagmire can be found in the European Union models of cooperation between former arch rivals like France and Germany or the United Kingdom and the Republic of Ireland. Speaking at the Indian newspaper *Hindustan Times* leadership conference in 2004, nearly three years before her assassination by Taliban-style fundamentalists, former Pakistan Prime Minister Benazir Bhutto had put forward her vision saying: "I am looking at two soft borders. One is the Line of Control (in Kashmir), and one is a soft border over the whole of the Indo–Pak gamut. Since India and Pakistan are divided (on) the solution (issue) of territory, we have suggested that this be looked at later. Let us instead look at how we can socially unite the people of Jammu and Kashmir, how we can culturally and economically unite the people of Srinagar (capital of Indian-controlled Kashmir) and Muzaffrabad (capital of Pakistan-controlled Kashmir) without going into the issue of whose territory it is."

Looking at similar possibilities, the contemporary Northern Ireland peace process offers a helpful model. The Ulster or Northern Ireland issue between the United Kingdom and the Republic of Ireland, a legacy of the 1922 partition of Ireland and the 'Troubles' of the preceding 300 years, has been fraught with much greater complexity and historical baggage than the

Kashmir issue. Yet given the determination and goodwill of leadership on both sides, the border between the two parts of Ireland has become irrelevant after the 1998 Good Friday agreement, after a long but dogged dialogue. Free flow of people and goods is already there and a working partnership between the two sides is gradually taking hold. Just as Ulster continues its peace process and finds further hope under the European Union umbrella with its common Euro currency and other cross border conventions and facilities, India and Pakistan, including the two sides of Kashmir, can move forward under the SAARC umbrella, once the Mumbai 26/11 damage is repaired.

Even a cooperative management and demilitarisation of Indian-controlled Kashmir and simultaneous dismantling of terrorist/militant (Jihadi/Azadi) camps and infrastructure in Pakistan-controlled Kashmir can be verily achieved as has been done in Northern Ireland — but after a lot more of confidence building measures and in later stages, requiring immense patience and determination. After all, Northern Ireland's 1998 Agreement has taken more than ten years to achieve a semblance of implementation after so many half starts. The last of de-weaponisation of forces loyal to one side or the other is still working out eleven years after the Agreement. India and Pakistan, in sharp contrast, haven't even reached the starting point of a basic Irish-style agreement!

A four-way consultative process among the governments in Delhi, Islamabad, Srinagar and Muzaffrabad from the two parts of Kashmir should kick-start the cooperative venture towards a stage by stage agreement and its gradual implementation over five or more years. Damage done over 60 years can be repaired but only with patience.

Notes

1. Bhutto Benazir, *Daughter of the East*, pp. 57–58, (Hamish Hamilton, London, 1988).

2. Katyal KK, *Journey to Amity*, p. 95 (Har-Anand, New Delhi, 2006).

3. Musharraf General Pervez, *In the Line of Fire*, pp. 112–17 (Simon & Schuster, London, 2006).

4. Persian couplet attributed to Mughal Emperor Jahangir.

3

Samjhota (Rapprochement) Sabotage SAARC Setback

The India–Pakistan peace process, or what remains of it after the Mumbai carnage of 26/11, 2008, owes a lot since 1998 to two top path-breaking organisations — SAARC and SAFMA — one governmental, the other non-governmental. SAARC, the inter-governmental South Asian Association for Regional Cooperation, and SAFMA, the South Asian Free Media Association, have been key players in bringing eight South Asian nations on a common platform, so vital for the region's development. The biggest achievement of SAARC (born 1985) and SAFMA (born 2000) has been the building up of a broad range of confidence building measures (CBMs) or steps for reduction of trust deficit, initiatives seriously damaged by the Mumbai misadventure by elements out to sabotage the peace dialogue between the region's two biggest countries.

The 26/11 carnage perpetrated by state or non-state actors from Pakistan put paid, at least for an unaffordable interregnum, to the immense goodwill that had been so painstakingly created over the previous decade. Not just India and Pakistan, the entire SAARC region suffered a setback whose ramifications will take time to unravel.

SAARC itself may have been a slow moving elephant and may not have delivered on its promises of peace and development since its birth nearly a quarter of a century ago, yet it has served as a useful platform for talks between mutually suspicious neighbours like India and Pakistan. The sidelines of SAARC summit conferences have afforded unexpected opportunities to the leaders of member countries to discuss thorny bilateral problems which are banned for discussion at the official summits under the association's constitution. This constitutional provision of a ban on raising bilateral issues at the official level has been both a boon and a bane for peace efforts among member nations.

The process launched in 1998 in earnest by the then Prime Minister Nawaz Sharif of Pakistan and India's Prime Minister Atal Bihari Vajpayee and carried on in fits and starts by successive leaders on both sides has had many ups and downs.

The sharp, warlike differences between India and Pakistan, for instance, would have killed SAARC as an organisation long ago but for this ban on bilateral issues being raised at the summits. Yet the summit sidelines have provided the safety valve without which the association would have remained a mere talking shop. Substantial sections of people in the entire region, with ample justification, still believe it to be a talking shop. The attacks on Jammu and Kashmir legislative assembly (2001), the Indian parliament (December 2001), the Indian embassy in Kabul (2008) and Mumbai landmarks (November 2008), to name only a few, have done nothing to reassure doubters and realists.

The biggest casualty of the Mumbai 26/11 carnage that took a toll of over 166 lives and left another 300 people injured was the people-to-people bonhomie when literally hundreds of people from the two Punjabs (of India and Pakistan) crossed the border and enjoyed huge rounds of reciprocal hospitality. (Personally I was one of the beneficiaries of that breakout of peace in 2004 when I visited my old hometown across the border after 57 years and was treated like the prodigal son come home by the town folk.) People crossed the border in hordes, on any excuse from a cricket match to a Punjabi music or literary gathering. They included the curious young ones too who had been born in the post-partition era and who wanted to discover the 'other side' personally rather than through the official and media filters which had often coloured the picture pretty darkly.

Scores of goodwill visits across the dividing line suddenly stood cancelled. Pakistani poets and writers like Intezar Husain, Kishwar Naheeed, Asif Farooqui and Asghar Nazi Syed who had their tickets and visas ready to attend a gathering at the invitation of New Delhi's Ghalib Academy (named after Urdu language's greatest poet) were forced to cancel their plans at the last moment. Renowned ghazal singer Ghulam Ali too had to cancel his shows in Kolkata and other Indian cities.

The Indian cricket team's 2009 tour of Pakistan, a long awaited spectacle of the year, was the most visible casualty of the post-Mumbai tension between the two countries. Not just the Indian tour of Pakistan, the worldwide sports fraternity decided to boycott all engagements on Pakistani soil for the foreseeable near future. The Sri Lankan cricket team's courageous visit to Pakistan had to be cut short after the Islamists attacked the visitors in Lahore.

Bilateral trade, the truly substantive promoter of Indo–Pak dialogue, became a straight victim of the Mumbai fallout. Indian commerce and power minister Jairam Ramesh who was to lead a delegation to Karachi had to cancel his visit for the same reasons. The Indian government which had designed a special website to promote Pakistan's exports to India also put on hold the launch of the site. The website which could help correct the balance of trade, hugely in favour of India till now, was put on hold. The hopes of the business communities of the two countries which were looking to enhance their trade from a mere $2.2 billion in 2007–2008 to $10 billion by 2010 were dashed.

At stake is not just the development and prosperity of the two countries but of the entire South Asian region covered by SAARC. The eight-nation group may have been a slow mover and may not have delivered on its promises of peace and development, yet it has served as a useful platform for talks between mutually suspicious neighbours like India and Pakistan. The sidelines of SAARC summits have afforded unexpected opportunities to the leaders of the member countries to discuss thorny bilateral problems.

It was exactly such an opportunity at the 2002 Kathmandu summit in Nepal which President General Pervez Musharraf of Pakistan availed of by going up to Indian Prime Minister Atal Behari Vajpayee for a handshake in full glare of the cameras. Vajpayee, not to be outsmarted, responded with equal aplomb. The handshake started the thaw in the relations between the two countries which had remained frozen since the 1999 Kargil military conflagration between the two nations.

A few weeks later it prompted Vajpayee to offer India's hand of friendship to Pakistan on the occasion of Eid celebrations in the two countries. Any occasion (excuse!) seemed good to further unfreeze relations and none better than Eid, the common Muslim festival in the two nations. And no better place to beam that message from than Srinagar in the valley of Kashmir, the valley over which a thousand skirmishes have been launched between the two neighbours.

Vajpayee's offer was warmly greeted in Pakistan by the then Prime Minister Zafarullah Jamali, setting the scene for a deeper entente cordiale. Watching the scene from the wings, SAFMA journalists came up with their Track II diplomacy by arranging a conference of Indian and Pakistani parliamentarians and other experts in August 2003 in Islamabad. The frank talks which such gatherings spark, set the scene for the 2004 SAARC summit, also in Islamabad.

Again the bonhomie on the summit sidelines proved its usefulness with Prime Minister Vajpayee meeting President General Musharraf and leaving Islamabad with a farewell message: "Aap apni hifazat ka khyal rakhye ga — please take care of your personal security." Vajpayee's gesture of concern for the General's safety after a life attempt by suicide attackers on Christmas day, a few days earlier, pulled the two leaders — and countries — closer still. The joint press statement issued by the two leaders (not part of the summit, yet flowing from its sidelines) was euphoric even though there was nothing concrete to show for it. "History has been made," exclaimed President Musharraf. The two foreign ministers, Yashwant Sinha of India and Khurshid Mehmud Kasuri of Pakistan, were ecstatic. So were Brajesh Mishra, Vajpayee's principal personal secretary, and Tariq Aziz, the chief aide of General Musharraf. Mishra and Aziz had succeeded in drafting a joint statement, when there was not much of an excuse for it, in sharp contrast to the failure of the aides at the 2001 Agra summit between the two leaders when there was so urgent a need for a joint statement. Sheer jugglery of words turned the Islamabad summit into a success against the backdrop of failure at Agra.

History may not have been made. But the peace process was kept going. The foreign secretaries of the two countries revived the composite dialogue based on the model devised several years ago after talks between former Indian Prime Minister IK Gujral and Pakistan Prime Minister Nawaz Sharif and later by Vajpayee and Nawaz Sharif. The composite dialogue's eight-point format meant dialogue on two central issues — Kashmir and security (fight against terrorist attacks) to be conducted at senior (Foreign Secretary) level, while other issues were to be tackled at experts level. Human traffic and drugs would be handled by Home Secretaries and friendly exchanges by cultural secretaries and so on. All issues are under simultaneous discussion but with no time limit for resolution. This composite dialogue format remains resilient, suspended, not abandoned even after the Mumbai carnage.

Just when the Vajpayee–Musharraf trust was gaining real strength, general elections brought a change of government in India. Vajpayee's NDA coalition government was replaced by the coalition government of Prime Minister Manmohan Singh of the Congress led by party president Sonia Gandhi. Pakistan for once feared the Indo–Pak goodwill might become strained under the new administration. The fear was unfounded as India's policy toward Pakistan remained unchanged.

In fact, the biggest CBM (confidence building measure) during recent years has come in the shape of cultural exchanges which lifted travel restrictions and suddenly opened the floodgates of people-to-people contacts. The large scale exchanges between the two Punjabs on the flimsiest of pretexts, like cricket matches, with both chief ministers actively throwing themselves into them, brought out an unprecedented display of goodwill giving rise to widespread optimism that the peace process had become irreversible. However, realistic politicians and observers had rightly cautioned that the bonhomie between the two Punjabs was not to be compared with the union between East and West Germany. All talk of union or federation was misplaced. There was no German parallel. Nevertheless, the goodwill generated was very much worthwhile.

In a way 2004 became the year of the people-to-people contacts and cross-border festivals of togetherness. The popular fervour became infectious, encouraging ministers and bureaucrats on both sides to lower their suspicion guards. President Musharraf and party leaders like Benazir Bhutto and Nawaz Sharif, even from exile, besides Track II diplomacy players like SAFMA and a host of others, vied with each other in promoting the peace dialogue.

Enjoying dictatorial powers, President Musharraf, like a true military man, wanted to resolve the Kashmir issue, the 'core' issue for all Pakistani regimes, during his tenure. He unbundled several initiatives aimed to win popular applause at home and diplomatic support abroad. That is not to detract from his sincere push for an early resolution of differences with India, that have bedevilled Indo–Pak cooperation and economic progress for over half a century. His first salvo in that search was to openly suggest that the 1949 United Nations Resolutions — about a plebiscite in Kashmir as to whether the people of Kashmir wanted to join India or Pakistan — were outdated, something quite welcome in India. That was a departure from the long held views of previous Pakistani regimes and found public expression and media debate for the first time in Pakistan. Not restricting himself to diplomatic or ministerial channels, he laid out his cards on the table at a breakfast meeting with journalists on 18 April 2005, and spelled out three other factors that had been floating around. First that Pakistan could not accept the Line of Control (LOC) in Kashmir being turned into a regular border (even if it might be acceptable to India). Secondly Indo–Pak borders could not be changed, as previous attempts (through wars) had failed, something India had always maintained. Thirdly, Indo–Pak borders could be made irrelevant, allowing people to visit or trade across the borders, which would be welcome on both sides.

Six weeks later, the General came out with another permutation of a possible solution of the Kashmir issue at a meeting of journalists from SAFMA. India, he said, had ruled out re-drawing of boundaries, while Pakistan was against making the LoC in Kashmir as a permanent border. Also, he said, there was a third factor that borders should be made irrelevant (not abolished). Along with these three concepts he rolled out two more on the table: self-governance for Kashmir and its demilitarisation.

To the general public it may have sounded all so very confusing. But not to the General. He was throwing in all such ideas so that some compromise solution based on all such factors could be found.

Quite separately, former Prime Minister Benazir Bhutto, over three years before her assassination in December 2007, while leading the opposition from exile, was voicing not dissimilar ideas. Addressing the Indian newspaper *Hindustan Times* Leadership conference in 2004 in New Delhi, she commended the European Union model for South Asia and cooperation between India and Pakistan on the model of France and Germany, once plagued by historic nationalist conflicts.

"I am looking at two soft borders. One is the Line of Control (in Kashmir), and one is a soft border over the whole of the Indo–Pak gamut. Since India and Pakistan (are) divided on the solution of territory, we have suggested that this be looked at later. Let us instead look at how we can socially unite people of Jammu and Kashmir, how we can culturally and economically unite the people of Srinagar (capital of Indian controlled Kashmir) and Muzaffrabad (capital of Pakistan controlled Kashmir) without going into the issue of whose territory it is…

"It was as a result of my proposal (at the 1988 SAARC summit) to Rajiv Gandhi (former Indian Prime Minister, assassinated in 1991) that we allow judges and parliamentarians to travel without visas to each others' country...

"The way we are placed today is the way Europe was placed fifty years ago. For a European leader to have said that we are going to have a single currency would have jettisoned the idea of a common market. I don't want to jettison ideas and I don't want to hijack from future generations, decisions they may take..."[1]

Leave it to the future generations what you can't decide today was her vision, which appears to be an eminently sound alternative to war. Another leader, Sardar Abdul Qayyum, former Prime Minister of Pakistan controlled Kashmir (known as Azad Kashmir in Pakistan and PoK — Pakistan Occupied Kashmir — in India) strongly urged giving up old positions and even hinted at converting the Line of Control into a permanent border and making it a soft one. That way, he said during his 2007 visit to India, people from both sides would be able to travel and trade across it freely and turn Kashmir into a bridge between India and Pakistan, an aspiration shared by Indians and Pakistanis, as well as by Kashmiris.

The dialogue had been powered by a series of boosters which have become a byword under the acronym CBMs (confidence building measures). SAFMA, the journalists' group, has never stopped emphasising the need for ever more CBMs by underlining the need of constant efforts to reduce the "trust deficit" between the two neighbours. The "trust deficit" had been so large that short of breaking diplomatic relations, the two countries had been playing tit-for-tat games of petty revenge at the slightest excuse. Cricket matches between the two neighbours remained snapped for fourteen years until February 2004. A train service, the poor main's link between the two neighbours which had been running for nearly 30 years, was suspended for a long time till 2004. Poor fishermen straying into each other's waters in Gujarat (India) and Sindh (Pakistan) sectors, who were detained for weeks and months began to be released with lesser delay than before. Come 2004 the old mind-set began to change at a steady canter. Bus and train services linking the two countries were resumed in some areas and launched in other areas, especially in the Kashmir sector. Admittedly the pace of these openings had been slow due to bureaucratic hurdles, especially over visa/travel permit delays. But given the momentum of newly generated goodwill, the people of the two countries felt hopeful of a new era — until Mumbai 26/11 shattered it all.

One of the major CBMs was born out of a shared tragedy when blood was spilled by the nationals of the two countries on a common journey. It occurred in February 2007 when 66 people, Indians and Pakistanis, were killed by terrorists who lobbed two bombs on the Samjhota Express (Friendship train) on its journey from New Delhi to the Pakistan border enroute to Lahore in Pakistan. The fundamentalist enemies of peace succeeded in killing innocent passengers, but failed to kill the spirit of friendship. In fact they redoubled the resolve of the two countries to strengthen the peace venture now sealed with common blood. There was widespread condemnation of the bomb attack in both countries. Nearly all of the victims were Muslims, from both countries, killed by bombers operating in the name of religion.

Foreign observers and newspapers recorded their surprise with headlines like "Old Foes Join in Anger as Train Bombings Toll Rises to 66" (*The New York Times*).

Since the train attack occurred in India, at Diwana near the city of Panipat, the Indian government as a gesture of sympathy paid nearly 50 million rupees to the legal heirs of 33 Pakistani victims of the tragedy in line with payments to the relatives of its own nationals who perished in the attack. The train may have been derailed but the Samjhota Express was back on track. And it was not just a train. Samjhota was a movement propelled by people's support on both sides. But the people hadn't reckoned with the hidden hand of Samjhota saboteurs.

Notwithstanding such attempts at derailment of the peace process (and there have been many — bomb blasts at Varanasi in March 2006, New

Delhi in July 2006, Malegaon in September 2006, Hyderabad in May 2007, Ajmer Sharif in October 2007 and Jaipur and five other cities in 2008) the Indo–Pak dialogue seemed to have acquired a momentum of its own. The process had become so multi-faceted that it was difficult to imagine the future, at least near future, without it. During a visit to Lahore in 2004 as part of an Indian journalists' team, this author was struck by the frank discussion in the open forum. Nothing was taboo. One Pakistani speaker openly reminded his compatriots before an audience of some 300 people that no Indian Prime Minister could change the national constitution and hand over any part of Kashmir to Pakistan. Nor could Manmohan Singh, Prime Minister of India, do any such thing.

So the solution of India–Pakistan problems had to be found some other way. Another speaker jokingly said the problems of the two countries could best be solved by making the secret intelligence services of the two countries to sit together and sort out the differences. Four years down the line something similar did happen. The Indian Institute for Defence Studies and Analyses (IDSA) actually signed a memorandum of understanding (MOU) with Pakistan's Institute for Strategic Studies (ISS) at a meeting of the think tanks of the two sides. Both countries started releasing each other's jailed 'spies' and prisoners taken during the 1965 and 1971 wars. Such reciprocal gestures (2008) appeared to mark the dawn of a new era of Samjhota (rapprochement or friendship) between the two countries — until the Mumbai 26/11 carnage of 2008.

The qualitative change in the Indo–Pak dialogue since 2004 had created a new momentum for the peace process between the two countries. The loud departures from the long held positions as enunciated by President General Musharraf during his tenure as President and C-in-C till early 2008, and by former Prime Ministers Nawaz Sharif and Benazir Bhutto appeared to have imparted a common thrust to the dialogue process over-riding any personal or party-political differences just as India's foreign (Pakistan) policy remained unchanged when Prime Minister Vajpayee's NDA government lost power to the Congress coalition government in the 2004 general elections. In fact the Congress-led government under Prime Minister Manmohan Singh, and party president Sonia Gandhi carried forward the Vajpayee baton of friendship with Pakistan.

The emergence of a broad coalition government of Pakistan People's Party, Nawaz Sharif's Muslim League (N) and Awami League led by Asfandyar Khan from the North West Frontier Province appeared to infuse a new vigour into the Indo–Pak peace process. Guided by Asif Ali Zardari, widower of Benazir Bhutto and bearer of her mantle, the coalition government looked set to take the peace process to a new dimension. Mr Zardari indeed took the peace process a big step further when he boldly declared that Indo–Pak relations should not be held 'hostage' to the Kashmir issue, the sticking point for half a century. The Kashmir issue, he said, "can wait" for resolution by "future generations" in a "mature" way in an atmosphere of "trust" which had been in short supply for a long time.

Speaking to New Delhi based journalist Karan Thapar for his *Devil's Advocate* programme on the CNN-IBN television channel in March 2008, Zardari said: "We have a strong Kashmir Policy. We always had one. But having said that, we don't want to be (held) hostage to that situation. That is a situation we can agree to disagree (on). Countries do, we have positions, you have positions. We can agree to disagree on everything."

"We can wait. We can be patient till everybody grows up further. Maybe the coming generation grows up even further and then let's interact as human beings and come to a position of love."

Asked if his Pakistan People's Party would be willing to put aside the Kashmir issue just as India and China had set aside their border dispute to concentrate on trade and other issues, Mr Zardari replied "Exactly".

No previous Pakistani leader had gone as far as that, though from time to time some had counselled patience and had not insisted on putting any time limit on resolving the Kashmir issue.

But Zardari had not cleared his statements with the de facto rulers of the country. He had to eat his words and suffer climbdowns which few leaders, even by Pakistan standards, had suffered. He managed to become the President of the country but with a severely battered personal image.

Freeing Indo–Pak relations from the Kashmir issue and leaving it to be solved with patience in future seemed a great advance and could have marked another milestone in the peace process fervently cherished by the people of the two countries.

A settlement in future can mean possible new options as have emerged elsewhere in the world. The resolution of the Northern Ireland (Ulster) issue between the United Kingdom and the Republic of Ireland is a recent example to emulate. The Ulster 'Troubles', as the conflict had been known since the 1922 partition of Ireland into the Southern Republic with Dublin as capital and London affiliate Northern Ireland with Belfast as capital, started to ease only with the Good Friday Agreement of 1998 after so many years of bloody clashes between the Republican Catholics and Protestant Unionists (allied to the UK). It took a further eight years to transform the 1998 ceasefire into a power-sharing government. To put the issue in an historical perspective, the 'Troubles' of Northern Ireland go back three centuries to the reign of Britain's King James, 1608 onwards, (some would say even 500 years earlier) when London ruled over the whole of Ireland.

All that historical baggage notwithstanding, London and Dublin governments, helped by the United States, continue to build upon that 1998 agreement. The influence of the European Union of which both Ireland and the United Kingdom are members is increasingly working as an integrating force between the two parts of Ireland. Under the European Union umbrella, borders between Northern and Southern Ireland are loosening — trade, and travel and movement of workers and capital are in a free flow as never before.

A similar revolution embracing member nations of the South Asian Association for Regional Cooperation (SAARC) could transform relations between member countries like India and Pakistan. The full impetus of intra-region trade, tourism and cross-border people-to-people contacts is not yet there but the first stirrings are pretty perceptible.

The idea of SAARC, which took root with its first summit conference in 1985, has come some way, albeit too slowly. By 2002 the seven member states — Bangladesh, Bhutan, India, Maldives, Nepal, Pakistan, and Sri Lanka — had resolved to create a South Asian Economic Union, perhaps like the European Economic Community which has flowered into the European Union. The drive to implement and expand the economic union objectives with gradual steps towards a South Asian Free Trade Area (SAFTA) agreement, an economic and customs union and a common currency and even a South Asian Parliament was beginning to catch the imagination of some of the opinion makers in the region. Afghanistan joined SAARC as the eighth member in 2007. The time for a SAARC union on the European Union model appeared to be not too distant.

The composite dialogue launched between India and Pakistan in 2004 was beginning to yield similar results — until the Mumbai sabotage of the peace process in the last quarter of 2008. Mercifully, even in the lowest depth of distrust, the two countries exchanged lists of their nuclear installations on the first day of the new year in 2009, in an annual exercise since 1991. The Agreement on Prohibition of attacks on Nuclear Installations and Facilities, which was signed in 1988, has been faithfully observed since its ratification in 1991. The two countries also exchanged lists of each other's citizens, mostly fishermen straying into each other's waters, lodged in their prisons in a six-monthly exercise under a more recent agreement. A much older and inspiring bilateral agreement, the Indus Water Treaty signed in 1960, which covers sharing of waters flowing from the Kashmir region remains in place despite all quarrels.

The opening of bus services between Srinagar and Muzaffrabad and between Poonch and Rawalkot across the Line of Control in the Kashmir sector appeared to be a hopeful signal for greater flow of people — until Mumbai 26/11, 2008.

Note

1. *Hindustan Times,* Leadership Initiative, Peace Dividend, pp. 112–17, (Roli Books, New Delhi 2004)

4

Bangladesh–Pakistan

The transformation of East Bengal to East Pakistan to modern Bangladesh is a long and winding journey. The first partition of Bengal into East Bengal (plus some parts of Assam) and West Bengal was executed by the British Viceroy Lord Curzon (1888–1905) and was delivered in 1905 almost as his parting kick in the old game of divide and rule. The stratagem of that first division — separating the Muslim majority area from the Hindu-majority super-province or Presidency of Bengal including Orissa and parts of Bihar — was repeated in 1947.

That first experiment of carving out a Muslim-majority province separated from the Hindu-majority Presidency of Bengal lasted barely six years with massive protests forcing the re-union of the two parts in 1911 when the capital of British ruled India was also shifted from Calcutta to New Delhi. The separatist demand, once blessed and legitimised, could not be kept under the lid for too long. It was revived in its second incarnation in 1947 when the newborn province was christened East Pakistan, though physically separated from West Pakistan by a thousand miles of Indian territory which inevitably put a great strain on the religious (Islamic) or faith union. But the cultural differences between the two parts of Pakistan were to put much greater strain on both. The ethos of Bengali language of the eastern wing could not gel with the dominant Urdu script languages of West Pakistan. (Urdu, the national language of Pakistan, is not the mother tongue in any part of Pakistan, though the Urdu script is common to the spoken languages of all four provinces of Punjab, Sindh, Balochistan and NWFP).

The clash of linguistic cultures eventually took its toll with East Pakistan's explosive severance from West Pakistan and the birth of Bangladesh, though both retain Islam as the underpinning majority faith.

The 1947 partition of the sub-continent may have nominally created two Dominions, Pakistan and India, in reality it soon became clear that it was a three-way partition — India, West Pakistan and East Pakistan. The bonhomie born of a common religion (Islam) between East and West Pakistan proved short-lived. In fact, the first signs of a schism became unmistakably visible after the declaration of Urdu as the national language of both East and West Pakistan by Quaid-e-Azam Mohammad Ali Jinnah during his 1948 visit to East Pakistan.

Bengali students openly protested against Jinnah's speech and demanded national language status for their native tongue.

Four years on in February 1952, police had to open fire to control the demonstrators in the first of many language riots that occurred in East Pakistan's capital Dhaka. Twenty people were killed and scores others injured, though the West Pakistani figures counted only three dead. To this day, February 21 is observed as Shaeed (Martyrs) Day to commemorate the sacrifices of the Bengali youth for their language.

A common factor which bedevilled all three parts of the sub-continent in varying proportions was the treatment of minorities. While the issue of minorities between West Pakistan and India (mainly East Punjab) was settled in less than three months through a balance of unofficial terror, massacres, forced expulsion of the minorities and finally exchange of population, the Bengal sector suffered a slow bloodletting over the coming half century. It was largely a one-way exodus of Hindus from East Pakistan, later Bangladesh, to West Bengal and other adjoining parts of India.

The Hindu population which constituted a 28 per cent minority in East Pakistan/Bangladesh area in 1947 (based on the 1941 census during the British Raj) has been reduced to less than a third (9.2 per cent) as per the

2001 census of Bangladesh without any appreciable two-way exchange of population, official or unofficial. It was an overwhelming one-way flow from East Pakistan to India. On the other hand the Muslim population of West Bengal which stood at about 20 per cent has risen to 27 per cent by 2001, besides registering a similar rise in Assam and some of the other northeastern states of India.

The first couple of years after 1947 witnessed somewhat voluntary migration of East Pakistan's middle and professional class Hindus who, kind of, saw the writing on the wall in terms of lack of promotion or survival chances at the pre-partition level. The Hindus who formed about 70 per cent of the total population (200,000) of the capital city of Dhaka in 1947 were reduced to 5 per cent within two years, emigrating to India's Bengal and other parts after selling their properties and businesses at knock-down prices. The steady migration, largely a result of the pressure of West Pakistani officials based in East Pakistan and supported by home grown Islamists, developed into a mini-exodus by February 1950 after the Meghna (river) Bridge killings when over 200 Hindus were slaughtered and their bodies thrown into the river below.

The Meghna killings sent a shock wave among Hindus throughout East Pakistan, setting off a spurt of panic migration to Indian Bengal where it did produce a counter reaction, fortunately not of original intensity. The situation was quickly brought under control on the Indian side while similar efforts were also made on the East Pakistani side. The flare-up was grave enough to make Pakistani and Indian Prime Ministers, Liaquat Ali Khan and Pandit Nehru, hold peace talks in what came to be known as the Liaquat-Nehru Agreement of April 1950.

The Liaquat-Nehru Pact, officially known as the Delhi Agreement, tried to reassure minorities on both sides and instil confidence in them to stick to their old abodes and not leave their homes or work places. The idea of exchange of population that was effected through a balance of terror between East and West Punjab on the other side of the sub-continent in 1947 was not considered even as an option by both Prime Ministers. Any exchange of population or property was to be strictly voluntary. Those who had already fled in panic were to be helped with restoration of their homes or other property.

Sadly the implementation of the agreement remained an exercise on paper in East (Pakistan) Bengal while authorities wedded to secularism in West (Indian) Bengal made a tolerably satisfactory job of it. The Liaquat-Nehru Pact, however, led to the resignation of two central ministers from the Indian cabinet because they feared that the absence of population exchange provision could turn migration into a one-way exodus of Hindus from East Pakistan. The fear of the resigning ministers — Shyama Prasad Mookerjee and KC Niyogi, both from Bengal and who knew the ground situation — proved true in the years ahead.

A further confirmation of Pakistan's inability or unwillingness to reassure minority Hindus came a few months later (in October 1950) with the resignation of Pakistan Minister for Law and Labour, Jogendra Nath Mandal, the lone Hindu member of the Pakistan central cabinet, alleging the killing of about 1,500 people in his native district of Barisal alone as part of province-wide riots which, he said in his resignation letter, claimed 10,000 lives. Mandal sent his letter to Pakistan Prime Minister Liaquat Ali Khan after migrating to the safe haven of Calcutta in Indian Bengal. This migratory trend continued for the next 20 years and beyond, resulting in an increasingly insecure life for minority Hindus in East (Pakistan) Bengal.

Not just Hindus, a sizeable numbers of Bengali Muslims too felt insecure in East Pakistan which was steadily being dominated by the West Pakistani civil and military establishment. Muslim Bengali nationalist defenders of native culture and language, who were being picked off by officials from West Pakistan, fled for a safe haven in India. The Hindu minority in East (Pakistan) Bengal, of course, was the recipient of double attention — from the West Pakistani officer class as well as from Islamists among the Bengalis.

So this double migration of Hindus and some Muslims from East

(Pakistan) Bengal continued to gather pace right up to the end of 1971 when East Pakistan became Bangladesh.

The 1965 India–Pakistan war over Kashmir which ended with the Tashkent declaration of peace brokered by the Soviet Union signalled the decline of Field Marshal President Ayub Khan's authority. The Tashkent declaration came as a great shock to the people of Pakistan who had been led to expect a great victory. Political party leaders exploited the popular anger to mount an assault on the military rule and called for a return to democracy. Instead of explaining the necessity of the Tashkent compromise, Ayub Khan went into virtual silence and seclusion. Popular anger boiled over and riots broke out in both the eastern and western wings of Paksitan.

In East Bengal the Awami League led by Sheikh Mujibur Rahman once again raised the protest flag with its six-point demands charter. The six-point autonomy manifesto demanded:

1. A federal and parliamentary system of government with elections based on adult suffrage and reflecting distribution of population in the country.

2. The federal government to be responsible for foreign affairs and defence only.

3. East Pakistan and West Pakistan to have separate currencies and each wing to have full control over its financial affairs.

4. Each wing to raise its own taxation and revenue resources, with the federal government funded by guaranteed grants.

5. Each wing to control its own foreign exchange earnings.

6. Each wing to raise its own militia or paramilitary forces.

In West Pakistan, Zulfikar Ali Bhutto resigned his post as Foreign Minister in Ayub's civilian cabinet and floated his own People's Party of Pakistan (PPP) calling for Islamic socialism with a populist promise of Roti, Kapra aur Makan (bread, clothes and a house for everybody). Ayub tried to defuse the situation by calling a national conference of popular leaders but without much success. Nearly 700 people were called but only 21 from the most populous province of East Bengal attended.

Ayub had increasingly become a symbol of inequality, regionally as well as locally in economic terms. His illness in October 1968 and allegations of corruption against his family members further weakened his authority. In poor health and lacking confidence of his fellow Army commanders, he handed over the reins of power to General Agha Mohammad Yahya Khan in March 1969.

Yahya continued Ayub's Martial Law rule in the country but promised, through his Legal Framework Order, to hold the country's first general elections on the basis of adult suffrage. He thought he could blunt the challenge posed by Mujib's Awami League and manipulate election results in the eastern wing by playing various political parties against each other. Yahya, who had unbundled Ayub's unpopular One Unit West Pakistan into the old four provinces, had also discarded Ayub's formula of parity between the country's two wings, unmindful of any possibility of dominance by the majority population of the eastern wing.

Yahya carried out his promise and held the elections in December 1970 after delays and dramatics. His confidence in his ability to manipulate the elections, however, rebounded on him and on West Pakistan. The results gave Mujib's Awami League sweeping victory not only in the eastern wing but absolute majority in the whole of Pakistan. With the Awami League capturing 167 of the 169 seats allotted to the eastern wing in a house of 313 members, it was disaster writ large for the West Pakistani elite whose hold on the reins of power was unchallenged until now. Zulfikar Ali Bhutto's PPP could secure only 80 seats while all other parties put together managed just 59 seats.

The result was shatteringly unacceptable to the West Pakistanis who had grown accustomed to rule the country beyond any thought of morrow. Confronted with such heavy odds, the West Pakistani military and civil forces joined hands to forge some strategy to wriggle out of the bitter harvest of democracy. But there was no room to manoeuvre.

The first session of the newly elected National Assembly or parliament which had been scheduled to be held on 3 March 1971 was postponed to 25 March, provoking a political storm in East Pakistan. Mujib's Awami League, which called the election a referendum on autonomy, now wanted the transfer of power even before the first session of the new Assembly. On hearing of the postponement of the Assembly session, Mujib gave a call for general strike. Protests were met with Army action. The protesters ignored the martial law under which the whole of Pakistan was being ruled since General Yahya Khan's takeover from Ayub Khan in 1969. There was open revolt in East Pakistan.

At the same time Yahya and Bhutto had been holding talks with Mujib in Dhaka apparently to defuse the situation, but their main objective was to gain time. When the talks broke down they flew back to West Pakistan on 25 March. Simultaneously, while the negotiations were going on through March, thousands of troops from West Pakistan were being flown into East Pakistan via Colombo, while Bengali military personnel were being sidelined or relocated to non-sensitive positions. Mujib's Awami League was outlawed and all political activity banned on 26 March. Censorship was imposed in both wings of the country so that people in the West were kept in the dark on what was going on in the East.

The news of the massacre of professors and students at Dhaka University's Jagannath Hall a day earlier spread like wildfire.

Mujib's Awami League proclaimed the Independence of Bangladesh on 26 March. Mukti Bahini (liberaton force), Rakhi Bahini, Shanti Bahini and other independence groups had raised their flags at various centres in the country.

Bengali military units in Chittagong under Major Zia-ur-Rahman, future President, whose widow Begum Khaleda Zia was to become Prime Minister, raised the flag of independence on 27 March, from his army outpost in Kalurghat, Chittagong, and broadcast the famous line 'Ami Major Zia bolchhi…' (I am Major Zia speaking…) from the Swadhin Bangla Betar

Kendra (Independent Bangla Wireless Station).

The paramilitary East Pakistan Rifles mutinied and joined the Mukti Bahini against the Pakistan Army.

A full blown liberation war had erupted. East and West Pakistan were on an irreversible collision course.

The formation of a government-in-exile was announced by Mujib's Awami League on 17 April.

From West Pakistan, Lieutenant-General Tikka Khan, who had arrived in March as Yahya's hand-picked Martial Law Administrator/Governor of East Pakistan and Chief of Eastern Command, put into operation his emergency plan to crush the revolt with a heavy hand. A month later Tikka Khan, known as the 'Butcher of Balochistan' from his earlier campaigns, was ably assisted by Lt-Gen AAK Niazi who took charge of the Eastern Command.

From March 1971 onwards Yahya and his forces in the east were on a mission to re-educate and Islamize the Bengalis whom they considered not Muslim enough. As one West Pakistani commander, Major Bashir, SSO of 9th Division at Comilla, told Karachi journalist Anthony Mascarenhas: "This is a war between the pure and impure. The people here may have Muslim names and may call themselves Muslims but they are Hindus at heart. You won't believe the moulvi (priest) of the Cantonment Mosque here issued a fatwa during Friday prayers that the people would attain jannat (heaven) if they killed West Pakistanis. We sorted the bastards out and we are sorting out the others. Those left will be real Muslims. We will even teach them Urdu (the lingua franca of West Pakistan)."

Mascarenhas, the journalist and author of *The Rape of Bangladesh*, had to quit his job, home and country for revealing the horrors in articles published in London's *Sunday Times*.

For full nine months the West Pakistani forces under Tikka Khan let loose their reign of terror on the Bengali population. The objective was two-fold. To crush the recalcitrant Bengali elements and to reduce the Bengali majority of 56 per cent in the whole of Pakistan to some manageable proportions.

The Hindu minority, staunchly Bengali speaking, was an easy first target. The pogrom against the Hindus was eminently successful.

The six-year campaign between the 1965 Ind–Pakistan war and Bangladesh Liberation War, which saw the biggest exodus of the minority Hindus from East Bengal reached its climax, giving India the strongest palpable reason to join the liberation forces against West Pakistani military forces.

By 25 October 1971, full seven weeks before the end of the Liberation War, 9.54 million (95.4 lakh) people, mostly Hindus but a substantial number of anti-Pakistani Muslims as well, had crossed over to India, according to Senator Edward Kennedy's report to the US Senate Judiciary Committee. The final two months of October and November saw an average of nearly 10,645 refugees fleeing to India every day.

Indian Prime Minister Indira Gandhi, having foretold world leaders about the intolerable refugee crisis and other atrocities, finally declared her hand and ordered Indian troops to help Bangladesh liberation forces and join the war on 3 December 1971.

The very next day — 4 December — the US, which refused to recognise the Pakistani (West) atrocities in East Pakistan and which had long allied itself with Pakistan through SEATO, CENTO and other agreements, introduced a resolution in the UN Security Council calling for immediate cessation of hostilities and withdrawal of Indian troops. India's ally, the Soviet Union, vetoed the US resolution on the grounds that the Pakistani atrocities must stop before Indian forces pull back. Pakistan's other ally, China, opposed the Soviet stand. The Chinese representative, Huang Hua, said: "The question of East Pakistan is purely an internal matter of Pakistan and no one has the right to intervene in it." The Soviet Representative countered that because of the massive influx of refugees from East Pakistan into India caused by Pakistani atrocities, this was no longer an internal issue.

Having lost the diplomatic battle at the UN, the US Administration of President Richard Nixon and his Secretary of State, Henry Kissinger, tried gunboat diplomacy by dispatching a naval task force of 10 ships led by aircraft carrier *Enterprise* of the US Seventh Fleet from South Vietnam to the Bay of Bengal, apparently to signal US support for Pakistan. India had already said that it had no designs on Pakistan. About the same time the Soviet Union also declared it was dispatching two combat ships, a cruiser and a submarine from Vladivostok to join its minesweeper and two destroyers already in the Bay of Bengal. The *Enterprise* task force reached the Bay of Bengal on 15 December by which time the Indian forces had almost finished the job under the overall command of General Sam Manekshaw.

On land, the Indian army led by Lieutenant-General Jagjit Singh Aurora, which had struck with lightning speed, scored a decisive victory on 16 December, forcing Pakistan's Lieutenant-General Niazi to surrender. The Indian forces had won the war in barely 14 days. Over 93,000 Pakistani troops were taken prisoner of war. With the surrender of Pakistani troops Bangladesh achieved its Liberation on 16 December 1971.

Job done, most of the Indian forces pulled out of Bangladesh pretty quickly (last few units out in three months), leaving Bangladesh to manage its own affairs.

Pakistan, of course, has continued to blame India for its break-up as a calculated attack on its unity, though many of her own probes, including the Hudood-ur-Rehman commission of inquiry, point to blunders nearer home.

The cost of Islamic West Pakistan's mis-handling of East Bengal: three million fellow Muslims (Bangladesh official figure) and thousands of Hindus killed, besides nearly 10 million Hindus and thousands of Muslims driven out of East Bengal, taking permanent refuge in India and causing a gigantic demographic upheaval in adjoining Indian states.

After the signing of the Simla Agreement between India and Pakistan in 1972, Pakistan took quite a while before recognising Bangladesh in 1974 and established full diplomatic relations in 1976. Trade and cultural ties followed in 1978, with a more significant breakthrough coming in 1983 when Pakistan foreign minister paid homage to Bangladesh martyrs at a memorial in Dhaka and offered an oblique expression of regret — not apology — for the unfortunate happenings before the Liberation.

Relations between the two countries were strengthened in the 1980s during the tenure of General Ershad Hossain in Bangladesh and General Zia-ul-Haq in Pakistan, with both countries also supporting the US war against the Soviet forces in Afghanistan. Further improvement came with the visit of Bangladesh Prime Minister Begum Khaleda Zia to Pakistan in 2006.

However, relations showed signs of cooling in early 2009 with suspicions of involvement of Pakistani elements and collaborators in the paramilitary BDR (Bangladesh Rifles) mutiny when over 50 army officers, including the chief of the BDR, were killed.

Bangladesh–Pakistan relations remain fluid under the shadow of fundamentalist forces and their extra-territorial links.

*****

One of the saddest legacies of the 1947–71 West Pakistani dominance over the then East Pakistan has been the plight of Urdu speaking loyalists of the western wing who did not want to live in Bangladesh after its independence. They are known as Biharis because most of them had crossed over from India's Bihar province at the time of partition. As citizens of Pakistan they wanted to be resettled in Pakistan for which they had opted in 1947. Pakistan duly promised them repatriation but has failed to implement its promise, leaving the Biharis in limbo ever since 1971.

Well over 300,000 of them have lived miserable lives in some 70 refugee camps spread all over the country since it became Bangladesh. Unwanted in Bangladesh for having sided with West Pakistanis during the liberation struggle, they are unwanted in Pakistan too, for fear of creating demographic and political problems wherever they may be settled in Pakistan. Having had a difficult relationship with the other Urdu-speaking migrants known as Muhajirs from the United Provinces of old India, the Pakistani establishment is said to be wary of yet more Urdu speakers. Old loyalty to the idea of Pakistan doesn't seem to count any more. In fact, it hasn't counted ever since the creation of Pakistan, according to embittered Biharis and Muhajirs.

Nearly four decades on a new generation of Biharis, born and bred in Bangladesh camps, has come up to challenge parental loyalties to Pakistan. Gathering under the banner of Stranded Pakistanis Youth Movement (SPYRM), they launched a court battle to seek Bangladesh citizenship. And they won it in the High Court. "Our people do not have access to government jobs, our children cannot go to school. We cannot even open a bank account, let alone take a loan. Why should we go to Pakistan? We don't belong to Pakistan," a youth movement leader said after the court battle in May 2008.

But the older generation of parents and grandparents have other views. For reasons more practical than old loyalist considerations, they want to remain Pakistani citizens, as it guarantees livelihood with free rations in the camps run by the United Nations High Commissioner for Refugees and Bangladesh government. Pakistan government once again promised to look at the repatriation issue with sympathy. But so far there hasn't been even tea! Dhaka home ministry officials, however, offered the hope of Bangladeshi citizenship to the younger generation of refugees, who constitute nearly half of the 300,000 camp population. But the ground situation has not changed even after another year and more.

So the luckless Biharis continue to subsist on hope, desperately clinging to their Urdu language saying: *Duniya ummeed pe kaim hai — The world is built on hope.*

5

Bangladesh–India

It is ironic that India and Bangladesh have been so cool towards each other for such a long time in spite of the fact that the national anthems of both countries — *Amar Sonar Bangla* and *Jana Gana Mana* — are written by the same poet, Rabindranath Tagore!

Bangladesh has been an unlucky country. The Sonar Bangla (Golden Bengal) dream of its people has been dealt cruel blows again and again. From mid-August 1947 to mid-December 1971 when it was East Pakistan, the eastern province of the new Islamic state of Pakistan, it was the victim of both natural and man-made disasters. Its demand for autonomy and self-governance invited unprecedented repression from brotherly Islamic rulers of western Pakistan, resulting in a genocide that claimed three million lives (Bangladesh official figure) and drove out millions more into neighbouring India.

Liberation came towards the end of 1971 after a bitter war and for the best part of the next four decades Bangladesh has witnessed turmoil on a pretty disturbing scale. The years since 1991 have seen two ladies, Begum Khaleda Zia, the widow of former President Ziaur Rahman, and Sheikh Hasina Wajed, the daughter of the first president and founding father of the nation, Sheikh Mujibur Rahman, pitted against each other. They have alternated as Prime Ministers — Begum Khaleda Zia from 1991–96 and 2001–2006, and Sheikh Hasina from 1996–2001 and 2009 onwards.

Right or wrong, the two Begums, as the two ladies are popularly known, are said to have polarised Bangladesh society into opposing camps. Both have impeccable patriotic credentials. Sheikh Hasina of the Awami League inherits the mantle of her martyred father and leader of the Liberation struggle Sheikh Mujibur Rahman. Begum Khaleda Zia of the Bangladesh Nationalist Party is the widow of Major (later General and head of the country) Ziaur Rahman, who joined the independence struggle by raising the Liberation flag from his army outpost in Kalurghat, Chittagong, in 1971.

The rivalry between the two Begums goes deeper than mere personal or political opposition. It has family antecedents. The granting of virtual indemnity to the killers of Sheikh Mujib by his successor, Khondokar Mustaque Ahmed as President, and continuation of that indemnity by General Ziaur Rehman is said to have poisoned the relationship between the two ladies beyond repair. But repair they must — for their country's sake! The trial of Mujib's killers and 1971 war criminals remains a burning issue nearly 40 years on.

Party political confrontation on everything from allocating seating berths in parliament to opposition rivals by both Begums when in power to non-participation in each other's iftar gatherings during the Islamic holy month of Ramadan damages both parties. In the 2009 round, the virtual boycott of parliamentary proceedings, including the budget debate by Begum Zia's BNP, the main opposition party, undermines the country's faith in democracy.

The BNP's failure to send two of its MPs for the all-pary delegation to assess the implications of the construction of Tipaimukh dam upstream in India, rejecting the idea out of hand in line with the its old rejection of any cooperative venture with India, does little credit to the party. The level of bickerings has sunk to much smaller issues wich must be stopped by both parties. Both Begums owe it to the nation by showing mutual accommodation, even generosity, to each other to give peace and stability a chance.

The country has seen several coups d'e'tat since its liberation and narrowly escaped one in February 2009 when a determined band of men from its paramilitary border defence force known as the Bangladesh Rifl es (BDR) staged a bloody mutiny against officers (drawn from the regular army) and killed 52 officers, including Major-General Shakil Ahmed, the chief of the BDR. The toll included another 24 people besides scores others injured.

The mutiny was a baptism of fire for Prime Minister Sheikh Hasina who had been elected less than two months ago. The mutiny story, apparently over pay, perks and promotions, is still unfolding with heavy suggestions of the involvement of Islamist elements who have never accepted the secular polity and Liberation from Pakistan. Like the trial of the alleged killers of founder president Sheikh Mujib, the role of Islamist forces remains a burning issue well into the fourth decade of Liberation.

But on to India–Bangladesh relations. India's role in Bangladesh's liberation war is well documented and so is her speedy pullout of troops after the 14-day successful campaign. Not to be mistaken for any conquistador intentions, the Indian Army deliberately began to thin out of Bangladesh within a week of the Pakistan Army's surrender on 16 December 1971. The 14-day intervention of the Indian armed forces won the hearts of all (except the pro-Pakistani elements) in Bangladesh which could be heard in the chants of Joy Bangla, Joy India and Joy Indira Gandhi by Dhaka crowds greeting Indian soldiers.

Both Indian Prime Minister Indira Gandhi and Bangladesh's founding father Sheikh Mujibur Rahman repeatedly let it be known that the Indian forces were in Bangladesh at the request of Bangladesh and would leave the moment Dhaka wanted them to go. The last of the Indian soldiers left in three months. In fact, the Indian army's stay, for this period, was dictated by the need to protect the 93,000 Pakistani prisoners of war from the revenge and fury of Bangladeshi nationalists who had been brutalised over the past 25 years and subjected to genocidal violence in the final nine months from 27 March 1971 to 16 December Liberation Day.

Sheikh Mujib, the architect of Bangladesh's independence, suffered several spells in Pakistani jails during, 25 years since 1947 in a political struggle that culminated in his call for independence on 26 March 1971, moments before he was arrested (for the last time) and bundled out on a plane to prison in the then western wing of Pakistan. His homecoming to Dhaka via London and New Delhi after he was freed (following nearly 10 months of internment) on 10 January 1972 has since become a national day of celebrations.

But the challenges of the war ravaged economy and near breakdown of law and order compounded by famine conditions at home were too onerous to leave any time for well-earned celebrations. The launch of a new constitution based on the four pillars of "Nationalism, Socialism, Democracy and Secularism" as the "Fundamental Principles of State Policy" and the conduct of elections for a new parliament had to be managed despite the prevailing turmoil. But as the first Prime Minister he soon felt that things were too chaotic to be managed in a parliamentary system of government. So he switched to a presidential form of government, assumed power as president and imposed emergency rule, which critics have branded as dictatorship.

Bangabandhu (Friend of the Bangla nation), as he was popularly known, persevered with his experiment, hoping for a turnaround. His trust in his people was total and he fervently believed the country would soon turn the corner. Little did he know that within Bangabhaban (the Presidential Palace) some junior army officers were plotting to do him in. On 15 August 1975, barely three and a half years after the Liberation, they struck with lightning speed and ruthlessness, killing most members of the family, including three-year-old son Russell, who happened to be in Dhaka. Only two members, daughters Sheikh Hasina and Sheikh Rehana who were abroad in Europe, were the lucky survivors. Nearly 25 years later Hasina was to become Prime Minister the first time from 1996 to 2001 and again in 2009 to carry on the fight for the ideas for which her father lived and died.

The next 15 years after Mujib's assassination saw a number of coups d´e´tat and the rise and fall of two somewhat lasting military governments, first under General Ziaur Rahman (as Chief Martial Law Administrator and President) from November 1976 to May 1981 and then under General Hossain Mohammad Ershad from March 1982 to December 1990. General Zia was shot dead by army rebels in Chittagong while General Ershad was ousted from power after mass protests by civilian political parties led by Mujib's daughter Sheikh Hasina of the Awami League, General Zia's widow Khaleda Zia of the Bangladesh Nationalist Party, and other disparate groups.

Both General Zia and General Ershad, however, saw fit to garner popular support by what critics describe as the Islamization of polity. Within six months of his assumption of power General Zia by Proclamation dropped the word "secularism" from the first Constitution, (and replaced it with amendment declaring "Absolute trust and faith in the Almighty Allah shall be the basis of all action)." Article 8 of the first Constitution (brought in by Mujibur Rahman) said: "The principles of Nationalism, Socialism, Democracy and Secularism...constitute the fundamental principles of State Policy." General Zia's Proclamation (amendment) said: "The principles of absolute trust and faith in the Almighty Allah, Nationalism, Democracy and Socialism...shall constitute the fundamental principles of State Policy."

General Ersham took it a step further by declaring Islam as the State religion in June 1988, but it proved a bit too late to save his government form the onslaught of popular protests that resulted in his ouster from power in December 1990.

One party that clearly gained strength from the changes in the Constitution was the Jamat-e-Islami, if not in absolute voting strength and number of seats in parliament but certainly as a powerful alliance partner of the Bangladesh Nationalist Party of Begum Khaleda Zia, who became Prime Minister in the February 1991 elections and again in 2001.

The intervening years between Begum Khaleda Zia's two terms as Prime Minister saw the arrival of Awami League's Sheikh Hasina as Prime

Minister. Sheikh Hasina also became Prime Minister for a second term in the December 2008 elections. The two Begums (Ladies) have thus been alternating as prime ministers in successive general elections since 1991, except for nearly two years (2007–8) when a military backed caretaker government was in power before holding its promised general elections that brought Sheikh Hasina to power for a second term.

The rapid Islamization of the country after the 1975 upheaval leading to the declaration of Islam as the State Religion of the Republic under the Eighth Amendment of the Constitution in 1988 led to the rejuvenation of the Jamat-e-Islami and the rise of splinter groups like Jamat-ul-Mujahideen Bangladesh (JMB) led by Sidiqul Alam, better known as Bangla Bhai. The Islamist fear let loose by Bangla Bhai across the country was so pervasive that the US President Bill Clinton thought it fit to cancel the second leg of his Bangladesh tour in 2000 over security concerns. Bangla Bhai was later said to have been the man behind a wave of simultaneous bombings at sixty towns and cities across the country in 2005. His apologists even suggested that he was a fictional creation of the anti-Islamic media and propaganda. Finally he was caught in flesh and blood, tried and executed during the rule of the caretaker army backed regime in 2007. It is also suggested that his supporters among the BDR avenged his death during the 2009 mutiny against army officers involved in operations against Islamists. The JMB is even alleged to have links with Pakistan's ISI (Inter-Services Intelligence) agency whose hand in the BDR mutiny is being widely suspected in Bangladesh.

Intermixed with all this is the highly emotional issue of the trial of 1971 war criminals (who collaborated with the Pakistani forces) and the killers of Sheikh Mujib who was assassinated in 1975, creating an interminable gulf between Bangladesh and Pakistan.

The Islamization policies under some of the leaders had the effect of legitimising fundamentalist parties like the Jamat-e-Islami which have kept the anti-India pot boiling. It would be naive to deny the support the Jamat and its allies have received over the years from powerful external forces, chiefly the Inter-Services Intelligence of Pakistan. Opportunistic alliance with Jamat by both major parties — the BNP and Awami League — gave fundamentalist forces a position from which it is difficult to dislodge them.

No wonder, fired by the Jamat propaganda, the list of Bangladeshi grievances, suspicions and prejudices against big neighbour India has become well-entrenched. The construction of the Farakka Barrage on the river Ganges is at the top of that list. Blaming India for withdrawal of water upstream at Farakka and depriving lower riparian Bangladesh of its share of the nectar of life, the Barrage is also said to adversely affect the world heritage Sundarbans forests and coastal region. With just an extra 10–20% withdrawal of water, the Barrage could, according to India's detractors, pose the threat of turning "much of the area in Bangladesh into desert".[1]

The Joint Rivers Commission set-up since 2003 to address the river waters problem seems to have made little impact so far. Sharing of waters of more than 30 other rivers and tributaries remains deadlocked in this hostile climate of mutual suspicion.

Not mere suspicion, but a kind of antipathy ingrained in the psyche seems to have taken hold of a certain section of opinion leaders in Bangladesh. India's support to the 1971 Bangladesh liberation struggle is even viewed in such quarters as 'primarily determined by its (India's) aspiration to overcome its geo-strategic weakness vis-à-vis Pakistan'.[2]

Such a sweeping simplification of India-Bangladesh and India–Pakistan relations is followed by rumours of the Indian army's involvement in plundering of Bangladesh's material resources before the army's withdrawal from Bangladesh. All this easily gells in with the portrayal of India as the wily Big Brother or Hegemon of South Asia.

Far more significant is the trust deficit created between the two countries by such elements. It is this deficit that bedevils normal bilateral relationship. Speaking at the Shimla conference of the eight-nation SAFMA journalists in 2007, former Indian finance minister and BJP leader Yashwant Sinha pointed out that Bangladesh's exports to China in 2005 amounted to US $46.33 million while her imports from China stood at $1,824.02 million, leaving a trade gap of US $1,777.39 million. In the same year, Bangladesh exported goods worth US $118.88 million while her imports from India totalled $1951.25 million — showing a trade gap of $1,832.37 million, almost similar to China's. "Yet the deficit with China is not an issue in Bangladesh while the deficit with India is a huge emotional issue. China is not considered a threat to Bangladesh, India is."[3]

From time to time India has relaxed its tariff regime and lowered trade barriers to relieve the burden of Bangladesh and other less developed countries in the region. Perhaps India could do more in that direction. In the final analysis, however, the ground reality must prevail and the two countries must learn to live with that reality. Even huge imports from India cannot be all that bad for Bangladesh which may have to import the same goods from a distant country at, inevitably, a higher cost. Given the goodwill on both sides the imbalance can be substantially cushioned, if not abolished. Unfortunately as things stand 60 years after the 1947 Partition, the 'trust deficit' between the two countries remains far more worrying than the trade deficit.

Perhaps, the most striking case of Indo–Bangladesh trust deficit in recent years has been the failure of negotiations over the $3 billion project by India's industry giant Tata group to set up fertilizer and power plants in Bangladesh. Even a revised Tata offer for the purchase of gas to run the plants, at least in the initial years, failed to find acceptance. Rejection or acceptance of deals, even after prolonged negotiations, is part of the game. But the lurid propaganda let loose during the negotiations by some people in certain influential quarters took the Indian public quite by surprise, further entrenching mutual suspicion and prejudice. Some of the speakers at a domestic 'dialogue' among Bangladeshi business and trade leaders alleged that the Indian Tata group "wanted to loot the natural resources of the country in the name of investment."[4] Economist Dr Anu Muhammad told fellow participants at the National Press Club 'dialogue' in Dhaka in

February 2006 that the deal was not just 'destructive', the foreign investors wanted to "rob" Bangladesh of its natural resources. He criticised the Bangladesh government's energy adviser for saying that the country had gas reserves for 50 years. Giving his own estimate Dr Anu Muhammad asserted: "Bangladesh has gas reserves for 7–8 years, what Mahmudur Rahman, government adviser, said is based on a mere possibility."

Another speaker at the same 'dialogue', Badiul Alam of the Bangladesh Steel Mill Owners Association, feared Tata's investment might 'destroy' the local small industries as Tata had not clarified in 'black and white' what kind of steel products it would produce. Instead of seeking details from Tata, the steel mill owner merely chose to brand the Tata group as a 'destroyer'.

A couple of months later the Tatas made a revised offer to the government. Some of the leaders of the Federation of Bangladesh Chambers of Commerce and Industry (FBCCI) also criticised the Tata offer but were more restrained in their language, only sounding a note of 'caution' before finalising any deal. FBCCI president Mir Nasir Hossain told reporters after a meeting with Tata group representatives: "The government should go ahead with the Tata's multi-billion investment proposal cautiously so that the country does not lose anything substantially during implementation of the project."

Perfect caution. Perhaps more persistence in negotiations could have done the trick! Alas, a huge Confidence Building Measure (CBM) between the two countries had been lost, at least till the possible next round of negotiations.

Re-opening of pre-1947 transit facilities which could prove a win-win proposition for both countries has remained bogged down in the climate of distrust. Bangladesh, under some governing regimes, has for long been averse to the idea of Indian or Burmese gas pipelines to pass through its territory, not gratis but for a fee, for onward passage to energy starved Indian states. Similarly a pre-1947 restoration of some of the rail links from West Bengal to north-eastern states of India across Bangladesh territory could halve the travel times for people and goods between the two parts of India, besides benefiting the Bangladesh economy. Despite all such obstacles, Indian Prime Minister Manmohan Singh announced duty free access for Bangladeshi goods to India in 2007 at the 14th SAARC Summit without any reciprocity requirements under a wider South Asian trade (SAFTA) gesture to all less developed countries (LDCs) of the region. The former Indian Foreign Minister Pranab Mukerjee offered to look at more such facilities during a visit to Dhaka in 2009, days before the country was rocked by the BDR mutiny. A ray of some hope on the transit issue also appeared to be on the horizon but was lost in the dark clouds of the BDR turmoil.

Barring a few outbreaks of warmth and cordiality during some periods, a kind of cold war has characterised relations between the two countries for most of the 60 years since the 1947 partition. The Ganges water treaty and the prospect of Teen Bigha accord with India providing a corridor to link parts of Bangladeshi areas did raise some hopes for a broader entente but the optimism proved woefully short-lived. In fact Indo–Bangladesh relations have been in a long freeze since the India–Pakistan war of 1965 when East Bengal was still East Pakistan.

Nevertheless, signs of renewed cordiality were witnessed in 2008 with the revival of a passenger train service between Dhaka, the capital of Bangladesh, and Calcutta, the capital of Indian (West) Bengal, after a break of 43 long years since the 1965 India–Pakistan war.

Called Moitree Express (Friendship Express) the train was launched on the Bengali New Year (14 April), a day celebrated by both Bengals. Under this rail agreement each country will operate one train a week carrying about 400 passengers, covering a distance of 538 km in about 14 hours. Goods trains between the two countries had been revived in 2001 after a gap of 35 years. The revival of the passenger train has sparked renewed optimism for a lasting thaw between the two neighbours.

Signals of substantial co-operaion with a real change of mindset have been on the horizon during 2009 which saw a brick and mortar (literally) building of ties with Bangladesh exporting 400 million bricks worth $40 million to neighbouring north-eastern Indian state of Tripura, a shouting distance over the border. Speaking after the brick export launch, president of India–Bangladesh Chamber of Commerce, Abdul Matlub Ahmad said that given the renewed optimism Bangladesh exports to India could rise to $1 billion by 2011 and correct some trade imbalance. Until 2009 Indian exports stood at about $3 billion while Bangladesh exported goods worth a mere $40 million.

Bangladesh Commerce Minister Faruk Khan, who addressed the gathering at the launch ceremony, went even further by saying that India could use the Bangladeshi port of Chittagong, if there was spare capacity, opening a new trade link between north-eastern Indian states and the rest of India after a gap of 60-odd years since 1947. He told an Indian reporter: "The day is not far off when you will be able to use Chittagong as your port. In this globalised world, one will not call it my port or your port. It is our port."

In fact, bilateral relations had started improving during the administration of the caretaker military backed government of Bangladesh (which took power in January 2007). A process of engagement with India, exploring the possibility of cooperation in defence and border affairs, had been set in motion. The Bangladesh Army Chief, General Moeen U Ahmed, paid a week long visit to India when he visited some of the Indian military establishments and discussed possible training facilities for the Bangladesh Navy and Air Force personnel in India.

Joint Navy exercises were also mooted. In a symbolic gesture, the first of its kind since the Bangladesh Liberation War of 1971, the visiting General presented a replica of the war medal of the Bangladesh Armed Forces to the Indian Army Chief, General Dipak Kapur.

Recalling the 1971 cooperation, General Moeen said the relations between India and Bangladesh were founded in the battlefield. India's General Kapur, who hosted a dinner in honour of his Bangladeshi counterpart at the

Battle Honour Mess, also recalled his active participation in the Bangladesh Liberation War.

In another gesture the Bangladesh Army invited 10 Indian Army veterans of the 1971 Bangladesh Liberation War to a commemorative ceremony. The Indian veterans were led by Major-General JFR Jacob. It was a "reunion" of comrades in arms, said General Jacob who recalled with nostalgia the memories of battles they fought together. The Indian team was invited to the Independence and National Day celebrations in Dhaka, a first since 1971, marking a renewal of warm relations and an end of the long cold spell.

The two-way Army visits also coincided with border talks between the chief of Bangladesh Rifles, Major-General Shakil Ahmed, and the Director-General of India's Border Security Force, Mr AK Mitra. The BDR chief's visit to India and his assurances on some of the thorny issues reflected a thaw in the bitter border relations between the two neighbours which have been marked with quite a few bloody skirmishes over the years.

Addressing a joint press conference with Mitra, his Indian host, General Ahmed said that the Indian rebel Paresh Barua, leader of the United Liberation Front of Assam (ULFA), was 'no longer staying' in Bangladesh, implying that Barua was indeed operating from Bangladesh at some time. The visiting General also said that Bangladesh would not hesitate to hand over anti-Indian rebels if they were found on Bangladesh soil. On his part, the Indian border chief who submitted a list of 117 hideouts/camps of Indian insurgents in Bangladesh, said India had handed over seven Bangladeshi criminals who had fled to India.

The meeting between two border forces chiefs was marked not with a litany of old accusations and denials but with goodwill and pledges of future cooperation in curbing trafficking in women and children, drugs and arms smuggling and other activities. [A sad fact for the record: Bangladesh border force chief Major-General Shakil Ahmed was killed, along with his wife Nazneen, in the February 2009 BDR troopers' mutiny.]

The arrest of the former Bangladesh National Security Intelligence (NSI) chief, Shahabuddin Ahmed, by Dhaka authorities in May 2009 on charges of involvement in a 2004 ULFA arms smuggling case marked further cooperation between the two countries. Ahmed was arrested in Chittagong for his alleged role in transporting 10 truckloads of weapons for ULFA militants holed up in north-eastern India. The weapons included 27,000 grenades, 150 rocket launchers, 1.1 million ammunition rounds and 1,100 submachine guns.

Apart from the security issue, the single most thorny problem from India's standpoint remains the steady flow of Bangladeshi migrants, not just minority Hindus but Muslims as well, before and after Liberation into India. Once again the problem is a legacy of the 1947 partition.

While the issue of minorities between West Pakistan and India (mainly East Punjab) was settled in less than three months through a balance of unofficial terror, massacres, forced expulsion of the minorities and finally exchange of population in 1947, the Bengal sector suffered a slow blood letting over half a century and more. And it was largely a one-way exodus from East Pakistan, later Bangladesh, to West Bengal and other adjoining parts of India.

Hindu population, which constituted a 28 per cent minority in East Pakistan/Bangladesh area in 1947 (based on the 1941 census during the British Raj) has been reduced to less then a third (9.2 per cent) of the 1947 level as per the 2001 census of Bangladesh without any appreciable two-way exchange of population, official or unofficial. It was an overwhelming one-way flow from East Pakistan to India. In the other direction the Muslim population of West Bengal which stood at about 20 per cent in 1947 has risen to 27 per cent by 2001, besides registering a rise of varying proportions in north-eastern states of India and metropolitan cities across the country.

The demographic change caused by illegal migration from Bangladesh, before and after the 1971 Liberation war, has undoubtedly caused huge problems in Indian states at the receiving end. Varying estimates put the number of such migrants at between 12 million at the lower end to the lurid figure of 22 million by some of India's Hindutva parivar groups. It is conveniently forgotten that more than half of the immigrants are Hindus for whom there is plenty of sympathy. For Muslims there is only anger and occasionally violent antipathy. The consequences for them have been horrifying — from the 1983 Nellie massacre to the continuing fear of daily harassment by police and other authorities despite protection by some of the politicians who use them as their vote banks.

There are no quick fixes to manage this migration problem which must be recognised as a human problem and dealt with humanely. In a constantly changing world we are all migrants. Our ancestors came from some place to settle somewhere else, maybe from the next country, next state or next village. Ninety nine point nine (99.9) per cent migrants everywhere are economic refugees even if that definition may be disputed by legal experts and jurists.

The United States of America is one of the biggest recipients of economic refugees from all parts of the world, especially from Mexico and other Latin American countries. It has fenced hundreds of miles of its southern border and erected watch towers to keep off the hungry hordes from the South. Yet they keep coming to earn a tolerable living, suffering exploitation for years before getting some respite. Every ten years or so the US absorbs the "illegals" by declaring an amnesty and the refugees, legal and illegal, gradually become the loyal citizens of their adopted country. Even in the interim period they are not hounded out or harassed unless the odd few individuals indulge in some criminal activity. When caught they are treated like other home grown deviants.

India too needs to take a larger and generous view of the very human problem of migrants from Bangladesh. Dubbing every migrant a criminal in a fit of anger is an easy option, which is the politician's first weapon. India may not be as rich or geographically as big as the US, but for the Bangladeshi migrants it is a magnet of prosperity. We all move from village to village or city to city. India's diaspora abroad, of which we are so proud, are also migrants in different countries. A generous vision of our neighbourhood won't render India much poorer. An American-style one-off amnesty for Bangladeshi migrants won't make things any worse. Let's be real. Those who are already in India cannot be wished away. Instead of criminalising them, India should set them free — free to move from demographically disturbed Assam, Nagaland, Tripura or West Bengal to new pastures. Once set free from fear of detection, detention and even the humiliating need to change religious identity for a pitiful existence, they would move to less pressurised parts of India, and like the Mexicans of America, become normal, even proud, citizens of their adopted land.

A fanciful vision? Not if some people were to stop wearing their darkening glasses.

People of the region must think of South Asia as a whole, not just as nation states. And the day must come when SAARC, like the European Union will have no visas or work permits for its larger family. India already has such arrangements in place with Nepal and Bhutan. Bangladesh could be the next. Others can join the visa-free club when they are ready. Let a core group of two or three SAARC nations make a start. European Union started with six members and has been expanding ever since. Europe has achieved such a visa-free vision, can SAARC afford to lag behind?

Notes

1. *South Asian Journal*, No. 5, July–September 2004, Bangladesh–India Tussles by Lailufar Yasmin, paragraph 1

2. *ibid.* paragraph 9.

3. Address by Yashwant Sinha, former Indian Finance Minister, at South Asian Free Media Association Conference, Shimla, June 2007.

4. *New Age*, Dhaka, February 9, 2006, seminar.

6

Hometown re-visited after 57 years

It was a dream come true. It was a visit to my old childhood town Pakpattan, once called Ajodhan on the banks of the River Satluj — like Ayodhya on River Saryu in northern India. Our sub-continental history is stronger on myth than on any convincing fact. Take your pick where lies your holy town. What is definite is that long after Ajodhan became Pakpattan Sharif, it has been known as the town of Baba Farid, the sufisaint whose mazar (mausoleum) lies on the upper part of the town variously called Utaar or Dhakki.

The little gate to where Baba Farid is laid to rest is known as Bahishti Darwaza or the heavenly gate which opens only during the Urs time, marking the birth of Baba Farid. Thanks to the khadims (servants) of the shrine who were kind enough to bestow Dastarband or wrapround robe on a wandering son of the town come home after fifty seven years of the country's partition.

Let me begin at the beginning of my two-week visit to Pakistan as a member of South Asia Free Media Association (SAFMA) which made my homecoming to Pakpattan possible. Our 70-strong contingent of Indian journalists was paying a return visit to SAFMA's Pakistan chapter led by veteran journalist and SAFMA secretary general Imtiaz Alam of Pakistan's *Jang* and *The News* group. After five days in Lahore, our first port of call, I was delighted to get my visa extended for a week to visit Pakpattan which I could not get on my earlier visits to Pakistan.

I had my bags packed ready in Lahore and clutching my freshly arrived visa extension papers I set off for Niazi bus adda (stand) for the coach to Pakpattan. I had no address to go to, having lost all contact with my childhood friends and acquaintances during the past half-century. But I knew the town's landmarks and was sure to find my way despite inevitable bewildering changes that have transformed every town in the sub-continent because of population explosion and the equally explosive urbanisation. A fellow passenger on the bus suggested a hotel he knew for the night's stay and even took me to the place as we landed at the Pakpattan bus stand.

It was about an hour after sunset as I put my bags in the hotel room. After a little rest and fresh-up I stepped out of my hotel. Fixing my whereabouts in my mind (small towns don't have local maps or street signs) I ventured to take a brisk walk up one of the half-lit streets leading to the Badr-Dewan Masjid. It was in this vicinity where I used to know a sweets and milk shop owned by Mian Qutab Shah, the father of one of my old schoolmates, Hussain Shah.

Finding the alley-ways a bit too circuitous, I asked a couple of men for directions to the Badr-Dewan mosque, named after the son-in-law of Baba Farid. Asif the younger of the two men and his companion offered to accompany me to the place on finding that I was an old citizen of the town, now on a visit from Delhi.

Our banter grew more and more affable as we walked the streets and saying our customary salaam or greetings to one and all of Asif's acquaintances on the way. We reached the mosque and after a short halt we stepped out towards the triangular street junction where my old school friend Hussain's father had his milk shop. The shop used to be the masjid quarter's most popular hub and gossip junction. But now the place was shut and boarded up. The milk business had long ceased with my friend Hussain having left this world for the next a few years ago. The shop premises had only recently been sold for a paltry sum of Rs 15,000 (fifteen thousand rupees — about $300). The whole area looked run down — a sign of the changing times. It was well past midnight that Asif and his friend accompanied me back towards my hotel. Instead of going straight into my hotel I offered to accompany my new friends part of the way towards their homes — another customary courtesy typical of old world small town leisurely life.

When alone I remembered suddenly that in my excitement I hadn't eaten anything since breakfast in Lahore. Spotting a wayside eatery I asked for a meal if it wasn't too late. It was around one o'clock in the morning or thereafter but the owner was obliging enough to fry up a couple of pieces of fish. He asked his assistant to fetch a couple of hot rotis (bread) from a nearby place to go with the fish. After tucking in the meal I went straight to my hotel room a couple of hundred yards away and fell asleep pretty quickly.

Next morning after an unsatisfactory couple of cups of tea and no toast, I decided to go into the town and move into a better looking hotel. And there at Mehran Hotel on Baba Farid Shahrah (Road) began another round of friendships which I shall cherish forever. Young Abrar Hussain urf Zafar, one of the five brothers who own the Mehran, and I struck an instant dialogue cordiale discovering each other's background.

Zafar's family had been driven out of the Ferozepore area of India to Pakpattan while my family had been ejected from Pakpattan and driven in the opposite direction by Partition in 1947. But it hadn't embittered the people on either side against each other. Murder, rape and mayhem that accompanied the Partition was not visited upon communities by local town or village folk but by the lumpen gangs of outsiders. The locals, in fact, invariably protected the life and limb of their long time friends and neighbours who were being driven out into the unknown. Thousands handed over the keys to their homes to neighbours, fondly hoping to return after a few days or weeks. Hindus from Pakistan left their belongings in the safe custody of Muslim neighbours while Muslims from East Punjab left theirs in the custody of Hindus, hoping to return soon to their ancestral abodes.

Reports of Hindu and Muslim refugee caravans travelling in the opposite direction and attacking each other are certainly over-exaggerated. Rather they commiserated with each other over their common plight. Likewise, Zafar and I recounted to each other cross-country perceptions, reaffirming the people's desire to discover or rediscover cross border relationships. That is precisely what I discovered in kind abundance during my four-day ziarat or sojourn to Pakpattan.

Riding pillion on the scooters of Zafar and my new found local journalist friend Mohammad Ali, I saw wide eyed my old town in its post-Partition incarnation. The empty spaces that I used to traverse as a child while walking from my house to school at the other end of the town had all been filled with people, houses and shops. The old town hall had vanished, giving place to shops and homes. The sugarcane fields and tall trees and greens opposite my father's office and house had all given way to concrete homes and colonies as far as the eye could see.

The old rajwaha or rivulet on way to the local courts where my father used to appear as a lawyer in cases defending his clients had been reduced to a dry gutter, though I was told by a wisened old tobacco seller sitting by his wheel barrow that water does flow through it during the summers. The old law courts had been converted into an extension of the local police station while the bar room had given way to a new mosque, the courts having moved to spanking new premises at the other end of the town.

The decay, disappearance or replacement of buildings is part of the sweep of time which takes its inevitable toll. But memories and landmarks do linger a while longer, sometimes lot longer. One such landmark which has withstood this challenge at least for a couple of centuries is the town's Kachcha Burj, a sizeable tower made entirely of soft earth. It had nearly 100 steps up which as a child I had climbed several times for the top view of the town. The steps and part of the tower have crumbled. So has the upper storey of the house bang opposite which was once my ancestral home. The new occupants were gracious enough to take me and my friend Zafar into the house and up the stairs for a view of the surrounding dwellings.

Hidden at the end of the narrow street by the side of the tower (Androon Kachcha Burj as it is called) lay another set of my childhood memories. A colony of carpenters — more artists than traditional furniture makers — producing colourful lattoos or tops, even bangi or whistling tops, lampshades and other décor items, used to live there. To my joy they or their descendents still lived there, though their art and craft had yielded way to other professional trades.

I knocked at the main door of the colony when a bearded man emerged. I asked whether Uncle Sultan or Muhammad Yaar or any of their children including my playmate Niaz still lived there. To my sorrow, but not too much surprise, the man replied they had all passed away, the uncles several years ago and Uncle Sultan's son Niaz a few years later.

Scratching my head I asked about another playmate called Laddi. With hands raised and face puckered with laughter he said: "I am Laddi." "Then I am Cuckoo," I replied. With moist eyes we fell into an ecstatic embrace and trance.

Needless to say we hugged and laughed. His sister overheard and invited us in. Old family stories tumbled out over cups of tea. Laddi even remembered how my mother used to play sitar. He and his brother-in-law had now turned to new trades as masons and house builders while I told them about my life as a journalist. Thus Cuckoo and Laddi had met after more than half a century!

As the word about my arrival (a Pakpattan journalist come home) spread in the town, Hotel Mehran became the meeting point and mini-hub of old remembrancers and promoters of Sanjha (shared or common) Punjab, embodying common heritage and culture beyond borders. I was invited for dinners, lunches and teas. Sadly I managed only a few during my short stay of four days, hoping to make it another time. It was fascinating to hear stories from a couple of old Marxists and critics of the British Raj as well some who had fond memories of the Raj days.

One of the stories related to the rise of the Tiwana clan that produced two prime ministers of the old Punjab besides other rich and famous landlords.

The Tiwanas started as keepers of mules, the only transport for the English Sahibs and their Memsahibs at hill stations during the early Raj days. They used to hawk their rides by shouting "Two anna, two anna, two anna per ride." The British Sahibs and their wives rewarded the mule men not only with two annas, a goodly sum in those days, but also with vast tracts of land, making them the future landed gentry of Twoannas or Tiwanas! Later I came to know that the Saxenas and Asthanas of today's India were once similarly "Six anna and Eight anna" beneficiaries of the Raj.

The visit to my childhood alma mater — Government High School — was another high point of my sojourn. Muhammad Ali, the Pakpattan correspondent of the Lahore-based daily *Khabrain* published in Urdu, Punjabi and Sindhi, took me round to my old school. A short introduction with the new headmaster sahib in his office was soon followed by a meeting with some of the teaching staff and even a round of couple of classrooms where the old schoolboy and journalist from India introduced himself to new schoolboys and shook hands with some of them. It was a touching experience. As my tribute, I presented a copy of my book, *India and Britannia — An abiding* Affair, for the school library. The headmaster sahib called for the old register bearing my name and roll number as a candidate appearing in the matriculation examination in March 1947. Very kindly he handed me a photo copy of the long and broad page, affixing his signatures and stamp on it. It was a certificate extraordinaire! I felt so humble and proud.

The love and affection showered on me by old and new residents of the town was indeed limitless. Sadly, my last day of stay in Pakpattan was upon me. I had to catch a bus back to Lahore where other journalist colleagues were arriving after their tour of Kashmir on the Pakistani side of the Line of Control.

After farewell salams and handshakes with people at the hotel I stood by the pay desk to clear my bill for the wonderful stay and rounds of tea and eats. Zafar and his brother proprietors wouldn't accept a single paisa.

I was stunned. My attempt to offer some payment was instead met with hugs and more handshakes. Khalid Sahib, another friend devoted to Sanjha Punjab and author of a book on the town's history, specially brought his car to take me to the bus stand which was only a few yards away. At the bus station, after yet another round of tea and biscuits, the bus owners wouldn't accept the fare to Lahore. A memorable ride to Lahore and indeed to Pakistan.

SAARC
Member Countries

Turkmenistan Tajikistan Tajikistan

AFGHANISTAN

Iran

PAKISTAN

China

NEPAL

BHUTAN

INDIA

Myanmar

BANGLADESH

Arabian
Sea

Bay of
Bengal

SRI LANKA

MALDIVES

INDIAN OCEAN

Map not to scale

7

The SAARC Horizon

The South Asian mutual cooperation idea, which was first mooted by General Ziaur Rahman of Bangladesh in 1977, has been coming a long time. It took nearly eight years for it to come into being as SAARC, the South Asian Association for Regional Cooperation,[1] when the leaders of seven member nations held their first summit conference in 1985. And nearly a quarter century on it is still coming as an institution with any substantial record of delivery on promises made at its summits over the years.

It has certainly established a permanent secretariat in Kathmandu, Nepal, and some mini-headquarters at national centres for some of its programmes. But so far it hasn't ignited the imagination of the people of the region which is home to a fifth of the humanity on planet Earth. SAARC has the potential and capability to chart its way out of the abysmal poverty that stalks the region, which is also home to a quarter of the world's poor.

The region's elite has the intellect and brain power to think out plans and strategies for a new future so solemnly voiced at summit after summit.

The vision is there. But SAARC lacks delivery because it is too diffused. Its roving eye has all things in sight but is focused on none. The South Asian elite in all its diversity represents a galaxy of talkers, scholars and analysts. But they all seem to falter when it comes to delivery on the promised vision. Promotion of democracy, human rights, gender equality, economic equity (roti, kapra aur makan) and a South Asian Free Trade Area (SAFTA) with economic union and common currency are all excellent objectives.

But how do we achieve any or some of these objectives. Through political agreements at the summits or through economic instruments of trade or through people-to-people contacts? Unfortunately the people-to-people contacts, highly popular though they are, can be snapped at a stroke by political masters of the day whenever they so wish. The India—Pakistan people's friendship tap has been turned off peremptorily umpteen times by the powers that be. It seems some of the governments are afraid of people-to-people contacts. Even a straight forward and simple initiative of making newspapers of member nations easily and speedily available across the region has failed to take off despite numerous joint declarations over the last quarter of a century. European newspapers are available almost the same day in most EU member countries. But not so in SAARC nations. National newspapers of the region seldom catch the daily flight across neighbouring borders. Stationing of correspondents in each other's country requires endless bureaucratic clearances. Intelligence agencies, foreign ministry and interior ministry officials all seem to revel in preventing the free flow of people and ideas. Information technology and internet has provided some chink for a few professionals, but the internet is no substitute for newspapers and first hand people-to-people get-togethers. Barring the odd exception, political leaders and cabinet ministers from presidents or prime ministers down the line swallow bureaucratic advice hook, line and sinker and are rendered totally helpless in breaking the logjam and opening up the region. Trade perhaps is the most potent key to regional cooperation. It holds the promise of profit and most political, even military, leaders would think twice or at least hesitate before killing the golden hen or goose, although sometimes they are known to have coldly discarded even the profit principle for personal or party political survival. Nevertheless, the trade and profit route remains the best instrument as it has more lasting strength than any other strategy.

That has been the tried and tested course (strategy/weapon) of groupings like the ASEAN[2] and the European Union. The EU, for instance, started purely as a coal and steel community, dedicated to managing just two commodities for trade and peaceful uses before it expanded its horizon to encompass a wide range of objectives among the core six member nations while the rest of Europe looked on. It has taken a long time for others to join in but the EU has come to stay because it concentrated on economic or trade cooperation for the first three decades when it called itself European Economic Community and Common Market before diversifying into other laudable objectives like a common social charter, a common non-visa regime with free movement of citizens and workers, common currency and a European parliament. Even after 60 years it still has many headaches to overcome — the financing of the Common Agricultural Policy being the oldest and most stubborn of them. A common view on foreign affairs, if not foreign policy, a common defence strategy and a highly controversial European constitution still remain to be tackled. But the EU has gloriously delivered on its greatest promise of peace among member nations by concentrating first on economic cooperation. France and Germany, the two original pillars of the EU, boldly set aside their 150-year-old history of wars and conflict for peace — through trade.

The task before SAARC is much easier (a mere 60 years of India–Pakistan confrontations) than that of the European Union. It also has only eight members compared with EU's 27, with more to come.

The SAARC leaders, who have often held EU as a model for cooperation, can walk a similar path by concentrating first on the key instrument of economic cooperation in the fight against the common scourge of poverty that afflicts the entire region. It can do it by honing SAFTA which it has already identified and even made some preliminary progress in that direction.

Like SAARC, SAFTA (South Asia Free Trade Area) too has been a slow mover. Its predecessor SAPTA (South Asia Preference Trade Area) also took a fair while to get moving. Even there India and Pakistan are still far from fully cooperative. Pakistan, which was granted MFN (most favoured nation) status for trade by India in 1990, has not been able to reciprocate over the best part of two decades. SAFTA itself was expected to become operational by 2005, then by 2008 and then again by 2010 in the silver jubilee year of SAARC. But that objective looks rather distant.

The biggest factor holding back most SAFTA and SAARC initiatives is the India–Pakistan unending mutual distrust, bordering on a kind of congenital incompatibility, degenerating into actual armed conflagrations a la 1999 Kargil war and Mumbai 26/11, 2008 by operatives from Pakistan.

Not to be held back by such factors, India decided to extend some of SAFTA facilities to neighbours like Bangladesh, Nepal, Bhutan and Sri Lanka, willing to trade on a bilateral basis. The move has been interpreted by Pakistan as a step to isolate it, prompting suggestions that it might counteract by having similar bilateral arrangements with countries like Sri Lanka. In fact, Pakistan is reported to have entered into a free trade agreement with Sri Lanka, starting 2009. All very good. Pakistan should also create enough trust with its immediate neighbour Afghanistan for bilateral trade. Formation of an AF–Pak sub-bloc need not be considered detrimental to SAARC as a whole as long as it does not stop other SAARC members (read India) from forging similar trade ties with Afghanistan.

In fact the two sub-blocs — with Indian and Pakistani initiatives — can later come together when the circumstances are conducive.

Indian efforts to spread the SAFTA message among such a sub-bloc of nations who are prepared to join in have been too often branded as Big Brother dominance over smaller nations. Some of the inspired writers have even called it India's Monroe doctrine even though their own establishment's agencies have for long tried to keep Afghanistan as an area of strategic depth. Clearly such emotional hype is typical India-bashing and nothing but diplomatic blackmail. All of which sows the seeds of discord in SAARC and is disruptive in its entirety. India may have 70 per cent of SAARC's population or the biggest land mass, economy or GDP but that is no reason to demonise it.

Promotion of a free trade area in the whole of SAARC region or in a sub-region does not mean any carte blanche open door for flooding a smaller nation's market. Free trade also includes the very effective mechanism called "negative lists" of commodities to be barred from entry. Every nation has the right to slap its "negative list" to protect its core markets. India does not send fabricated clothes or tea to Bangladesh and Sri Lanka for exactly the same considerations. There is always room for caution against trade imbalance among trading partners. Ways must be found to get round this imbalance rather than shut the door on trade with near neighbours and switch to markets further afield. Trading with far off partners will naturally be costly in terms of transport and time.

Intra-SAARC trade, sagging at a mere 4 per cent of the region's world trade, could have doubled from about $7 billion in 2006 to $14 billion by 2010, according to an Indian estimate.[3] But ground reality remains stubbornly lower. Internal trade via SAFTA can indeed be a vital instrument, not just for cooperation but for peace in the region. Friction between India and Pakistan, or Nepal and Bhutan, can be substantially reduced by trade which is the key to peace through business-to-business and people-to-people contacts. Insistence on resolution of political differences first is simply putting the cart before the horse. India and China have humungous border disputes but the two neighbours have opened trading doors in recent years, reaping a win-win harvest in both directions.

Power may flow through the barrel of a gun but peace flows through the trade pipe. Keep the trade pipe open, peace and resolution of toughest questions, like the Indo–Pak Kashmir issue, will follow through.

Give SAFTA a chance and make SAARC a peace bloc on the global chess board. If the European Union with much bigger problems can achieve peace and political stature through economic cooperation, SAARC too can realise its vision of peace, prosperity and a place on the world stage.

Overshadowing everything else in SAARC is mass poverty, the mother of all problems afflicting the region which has a population of nearly 1.47 billion or a quarter of our planet Earth's total.

The region also has the largest pool of people below the poverty line (BPL), nearly 25 per cent of the total at a conservative guess based on various official estimates which are notoriously non-credible. At least another 25 per cent are hovering perilously above or close to the poverty line. More than half of the region's poor live in rural areas and are battling literally for subsistence, quite unlike European or American poor who suffer from huge inequalities but not from lack of two square meals and a roof over their head. In sharp contrast poverty in South Asia has its own definition and bleakest reality, starkly visible in rampant malnutrition among young mothers and children between birth and five years of their life. Lack of micro-credit for people around the poverty line is the core issue of the region and unfortunately not enough attention has been paid to the issue over the quarter century of SAARC's existence. Nor is it because of the lack of a way out of this darkness. The success of Bangladesh's Grameen Bank pioneered by Nobel laureate Muhammad Yunus has shown the way out of this morass of poverty. Lot of lip service has been paid to the Yunus model but no concrete reform of the lending system has been undertaken. The old Western or World Bank style commercial lending system must be jettisoned or supplemented with a new banking system, if the poorest of the poor have to be helped. The Yunus model has no place for the compound interest lending system which has often led to suicides or worse — bonded slavery, despite all legal banning. Nor does it demand any collateral or joint guarantee. Repayment of a thousand rupee (a little over $20 dollars) loan can never go beyond double the original thousand rupees. And the beauty of this micro credit model is that there are virtually no defaulters. Over 98 per cent of the borrowers honour their debt.

Not until the regional leadership can create a Yunus-style micro credit system for the poverty line people of member countries can SAARC do anything meaningful for its peoples. National finance ministries of the region need to be revamped with the addition of pretty substantial micro-credit sub-ministries or wings under deputy ministers with independent charge of the new departments and officered by specialists in rural economics. India has made a good start in a variant of the idea with its NAREGS (National Rural Employment Guarantee Scheme) venture since 2006, but it has a long way to go and still needs to be sharpened and finely honed to deliver payments and micro-credit facilities to the poor at their door in the village.

For SAARC as a whole a permanent economic commission should be established with dedicated funds for micro-economic issues and with chief advisers like SAARC's own Nobel laureates Muhammad Yunus and Amartya Sen, who have done pioneering work on the economics of poverty. Rebooting of SAARC to make it fit for the purpose is the need of the hour as the group approaches its 25th jubilee year without any discernible silver lining for the poverty-stricken peoples of the region.

Notes

1   SAARC member countries: Afghanistan, Bangladesh, Bhutan, India, Maldives, Nepal, Pakistan and Sri Lanka.

2   ASEAN member nations: Brunei, Cambodia, Indonesia, Laos, Malaysia, Myanmar, Philippines, Singapore, Thailand, Vietnam.

3   FICCI (Federation of Indian Chambers of Commerce and Industry) report, 2006.

Prime Minister Indira Gandhi

Indian Prime Minister Indira Gandhi flanked by Pakistan Prime Minister Zulfikar Ali Bhutto and his daughter Benazir Bhutto during the Simla Accord signing, 1972

Sheikh Abdullah

Bangabandhu Sheikh Mujibur Rahman

BDHC, New Delhi

Lt-General Jagjit Singh Aurora at the signing of the Document of Surrender by Pakistan's Lt-General AAK Niazi in Dhaka, 1971

Ministry of Defence

dialogue ...

dialogue ...

dialogue

PART 2

SEED PLAYERS :
DIVIDE AND RUN

Lord Mountbatten, the last Viceroy with (anti-clockwise) Congress leaders Pandit Nehru, Sardar Vallabhbhai Patel, Acharya JB Kripalani, Sardar Baldev Singh, and Muslim League leaders Sardar Abdur Rab Nishtar, Mr Liaquat Ali Khan and Quaid-e-Azam MA Jinnah on the eve of the Partition announcement in New Delhi.

Press Information Bureau

Lord Mountbatten announcing the Partition plan on 3 June 1947 over the All India Radio.

Field Marshal Sir Claude Auchinleck, C-in-C India 1943-47 and Supreme Commander (India and Pakistan) till 30 November 1947, who stopped what could have been the first open war between India and Pakistan in early Novemebr 1947 by dissuading Pakistan Governor-General M.A. Jinnah from sending armed forces to Kashmir (otherwise he would have to issue 'stand down' orders to all British Army Officers).

Press Information Bureau

Walking together but worlds apart, Pandit Nehru and Mr Jinnah in Simla a year before the Partition.

Carrying the burden of Partition ...

Fleeing with their lives, refugees perched on the roof of a packed train at Ambala, East Punjab, scramble for a ride to safety on the other side of the border.

Press Information Bureau

Lady Edwina Mountbatten, the last Vicereine, walking through a burnt out street in Multan, West Punjab.

Nehru Memorial Museum & Library

Braving the elements after a long day's trudge, a refugee caravan camps out under the open sky.

Press Information Bureau

No (Independence) celebrations for Mahatma Gandhi, instead he walks away to douse the flames of Calcutta's communal cauldron and becomes, what Mountbatten called, the 'one man boundary force' for peace in Bengal.

UK 1947 — *annus horribilis...*

THE INTRUDER
"This thing's always turning up."

Punch, 1947

REHEARSAL
"Everything under control?"

Punch, 1947

THE UNBALANCED LEDGER

Punch, 1947

VICTIMS OF THE FLOOD
[Contributions now urgently needed for the relief of homeless familes should be sent to "The Lord Mayor's National Flood Distress Fund, Mansion House, London E.C.4."]

Punch, 1947

WINTER REVELS
The Minister of Food roasts a potato whole on the Thames.

Punch, 1947

THE FANCY OF FALSTAFF
"Let the sky rain potatoes."—*The Merry Wives of Windsor, Act V.*

Punch, 1947

"I LAUNCHED HER, CHUM. YOU SAIL HER"

(Outgoing Viceroy Lord Wavell in Army fatigues to the last Viceroy Lord Mountbatten in Naval fatigues)

The Hindustan Times

8

UK 1947 — *annus horribilis*

While 1947 was the year of make and break — independence and partition for the people of the Indian sub-continent, for the British it turned out to be the year of the new 'Battle of Britain'. This new battle came in the shape of the spillover cost of the victory over Nazi Germany and Japan which had brought the country to the brink of financial ruin and bankruptcy.

To make matters even more difficult came the unexpectedly severe cold spell from the heavens above. The first two months of the year saw the worst winter spell on record since 1881. Pigeons started dying in London 's Trafalgar Square. Villages across the country were cut off by icy conditions. London remained below freezing point and in continuous frost for a whole week.

'Lights Out at the Dogs', said a *Daily Express* news item on January 7 informing its readers of the loss of their favourite sport of dog racing.

Fuel supplies were critically low and when available, difficult to deliver where needed because of icy roads. Scores of factories had to remain shut for days because coal stocks could not be delivered there.

Power supply, or current as it was called in those days, was spasmodic. Electricity or power cuts were the order of the day in London and other cities.

A month later on February 8, *The Daily Express* came out with a banner headline across all eight columns on its front page:

BRITAIN SWITCHED OFF

A subsidiary headline across 5 columns by 3 columns said 'Over 2,000,000 will be out of work', followed by another 3-column headline saying:

MOVE FOR EMERGENCY DEBATE

The story under the headlines informed:

"Between 2,000,000 and 3,000,000 people are likely to be out of work when electricity for nearly all industries in half of England and Wales is stopped on Monday. Essential services will be exempt ..."

Another explanatory news item by the paper's political correspondent, Guy Eden, told the readers:

THIS IS WHAT YOU
HAVE TO DO

His report bluntly began: "If you are a domestic consumer you may use electricity when it is available. If you are an industrialist consumer your supply may be cut off."

The details followed in a long list of 'Dos' and 'Don'ts' in Question/ Answer (Q & A) style.

Further down came a double-column headline saying:

HOSPITAL WORKS BY
CANDLE LIGHT

The story accompanying the headline said:

"Most of St Pancras Borough was totally blacked-out for 15 minutes from 8.25 last night by a break-down at Pratt Street power-station, Paddington, W.

"Telephone exchanges had hundreds of calls from householders asking what had happened.

"The Great Ormond Street Hospital for Children carried on by candle light, but said the matron: A lot of OP treatment was being given at the time and it was interrupted.

"The BBC Light Orchestra playing in the Light programme at the Camden Hippodrome could not continue and gramophone records took place.

"Cafes and public houses lit candles, and old stoves used in the blitz days were brought out in many café kitchens.

"Cinema audiences were entertained by organists till the light was restored."

As if to rub salt into cold wounds, an American Senator suggested in a widely reported news item that in view of Britain's financial/industrial paralysis, the country should become a part of the United States. The single column front page headline of the deeply hurt *Daily Express*, Britain's Empire flag waving and top selling paper of the time with a circulation of over 3.75 million, said on March 3:

'ENGLAND
CAN BE
STATE *49*'

The news story by *Express* staff reporter underneath read:

"ATLANTA Sunday. Senator George Russell, Georgia Democrat, says in an interview with the Atlanta newspaper, *Constitution* :—

"The British Empire is likely to break up and be unable to carry out commitments.

"England, Scotland, Ireland and Wales should become the 49th, 50th, 51st and 52nd States of America. Each should have two Senators and two Representatives.

"The King and Queen could retire on their incomes. The King could, if he wished, run for the Senate as could Winston Churchill.

"The rest of the Empire should consider some form of association with America."

The news item ended with an anguished reminder from the bottom of the heart of the *Daily Express* thus:

"MEMO to Senator Richard Russell — Georgia and other Southern States still owe Britain £61,000,000 borrowed during the American Civil War (1861–1866)."

The Senator's joke was a downright insult from across the Atlantic.

At home, it was a classic winter of discontent with Tory and even Liberal opposition having a field day. War hero Winston Churchill called for setting the country free from what he called a typical social mismanagement. But the little man, Attlee the Prime Minister, held his nerve and pulled off the miracle of survival.

Early March saw more snow and blizzards. As *The Manchester Guardian* headline of 6th March 1947 caught it:

BLIZZARDS CUT ENGLAND
IN TWO
Roads to South Closed

MANCHESTER—SHEFFIELD RAIL
LINKS SEVERED
Vain Efforts to Keep Lines Clear

"After blizzards had been raging for more than 24 hours in parts of the North and in the Midlands and Wales, an official of the Automobile Association said last night that England was virtually cut in two, with no north to south route that could be called serviceable. Stafford is among the places isolated by road, on the railway, both LNER and LMS direct routes between Manchester and Sheffield are blocked by snowdrifts. Conditions in

Derbyshire are described as the worst ever known.

"The Air Ministry's forecast for today is that there will be a considerable snowfall over a large part of England and Wales."

SNOWSTORMS "BLOTTING OUT EVERYTHING"
Plight of Derbyshire Villages

"Winter has struck with renewed ferocity at the North, the Midlands and Wales, and reports from correspondents last night told of blizzards still raging after 24 hours, of trains snowed up, roads made impassable again, and towns and villages alike suffering hardship unsurpassed at any time in the present bitter weather.

"'The snow is like a moving curtain blotting out everything', said a villager at Earl Sterndale..."

"Miss Hannah Morgan (68), of Bron-y-Dre, Greenland Meadows, Cardigan, was found dead in a car yesterday... The car, which was covered in eight feet of snow, was found yesterday evening..."

SNOW DEFEATS THE RAILWAYMEN

"The railways had a hard fight with the weather yesterday when trains were buried, lines blocked, and time-tables had to be abandoned. Both LNER Woodhead route and the LMS Hope Valley line between Manchester and Sheffield were closed last night.

Another set of headlines the same day ran:

TURKEY AND BEEF
FROM US
Keeping up Ration
STOCKING GRAIN
FOR WINTER '

The Washington dateline report under the headlines said: "The United

States is to send meat to Britain this spring to prevent a cut in the rations and to help Britain to build up stocks of grain for the winter..."

As Britain faced battering by blizzards, the Punjab in far off India was beginning to receive battering of a different kind — inflicted not by nature but by man himself. Communal killings were beginning to take hold of the southern (Multan) and north western (Rawalpindi) areas of the province as the civil administration suffered paralysis of security forces' inadequacy or inaction.

In Britain, by mid-March blizzards and snow abated and instead of the steady thaw the snowmelt turned into floods of furious proportions — the like of which were witnessed again only 60 years later in 2007. A double column report in *The Manchester Guardian* of 19 March 1947 recorded:

FLOODS INVADE THIRTY
COUNTIES
Many Rivers Still Rising
SEVERN MAY SURPASS 1886
RECORD LEVEL
40,000 More Acres Threatened in Fens

"The rivers were still rising last night in nearly all the areas suffering from disastrous floods which have now spread into at least thirty of the 40 counties in England .

"At many points along the Thames the hitherto record flood levels of 1894 have been passed but yesterday was expected to see the peak. The Severn is threatening to turn Shrewsbury into an island — only one road into the town was usable last night — and position at Worcester was stated to be "very grave."

The outlook in the Fens is still critical.

Another report of the same day referred to Prime Minister Attlee's action plan to meet the challenge:

SURVIVAL BY
OUR
OWN EFFORT
Premier's Appeal
to The Nation
WORK TO A PLAN

In a wide ranging broadcast dealing with coal, power, steel, agriculture and other sectors the Prime Minister roused the nation with the battle cry for determination and hope for survival and better standard of life.

"Some people abroad are suggesting that the day of this country is over, some of them thought so in the war, but they discovered their mistake... We shall win in peace just as we did in war..."

"We are short of workers and of raw materials. We must then use our limited resources in the best way. This is where the plan comes in ..."

Coal, power and transport were the foundations on which the plan was built, said Mr Attlee. They were to be nationalised because the Government believed that this was the most efficient way to deal with them.

"Victory in the battle for coal will be a decisive factor in our campaign for national prosperity. The justifiable demands of the miners for better conditions have been met. Management and workers today are friends — they have not always been friends in past years...

"Finally we are very short of workers. We just have not enough people to do all we want. We are getting some help from foreign workers, but that is not enough...

"The moral is clear. All who can work should work. There should be no waste of labour..."

Throughout the winter, spring, summer and into the next season austerity ruled all spheres of life, particularly the food sector both in terms of quality and quantity of food available. Even restaurants were constricted in what they could offer to customers. The five shilling limit on a meal at any restaurant provided a sobering snapshot of the food situation. The Caterers' Association of Great Britain called government plans to boost tourism nothing short of "lunacy". Keep the tourists away till next year (1948) was the considered advice of the caterers to the British Tourist and Holidays Board. A caterers' conference report datelined Fleet Street in the *Manchester Guardian* of 12 April, 1947 carried double column headlines:

BRITAIN "NOT YET READY FOR TOURISTS"
Caterers Say They Would Not Come Again

Quoting the vice-president of the association, the report said:

"It is lunacy to send gentlemen round the world asking tourists to come to this country this year. Caterers cannot possibly cope with an influx of foreign visitors until next year at the earliest, and we will earn ourselves £50,00,000 (fifty million sterling) worth of ill-will if we take them before we are ready".

A cartoon in the same paper 12 days later caught the mood with the following sketch:

HOLIDAY HOTEL
NO ROOM AT THE INN

Months later in its issue of 10th December, the Punch Weekly joked:

"An American visitor having his first meal in a London restaurant complained of the lack of variety in the hors d'oeuvre. He complained still more when told that that wasn't the hors d'oeuvre, it was the meal itself."

Troubles on the economic front seemed to be unending. The crisis gripping large swathes of the economy won't just go away. As *The Times* of August 7, 1947 headlined it:

CUTS ALL ROUND TO MEET
THE CRISIS

SUBSTANTIAL REDUCTIONS IN
FOOD PURCHASES

LESS PETORL FOR TRANSPORT

The subsidiary headlines said:

LONGER HOURS AND LIMITED
CONTROL OF LABOUR

NEW BATTLE OF
BRITAIN
APPEAL TO THE NATION

DRAIN ON DOLLAR
RESERVES
MR STANLEY AND HELP
FROM US

There were cuts across the board along with a call to raise production of coal, steel and other goods as outlined by Prime Minister Attlee in the House of Commons on 6th August.

FOOD — A reduction of £12 million a month to be made in food purchases from hard currency areas. Restrictions on eating in restaurants.

DEFENCE FORCES — The total strength will be reduced to 1,007,000 by March 31, 1948.

PETROL — Basic allowance for private motorists to be reduced by 33.3%.

TIMBER — Imports to be cut by £10,000,000.

INVESTMENT — Tighter controls over public and private capital investments.

Coal, steel and agriculture production to be stepped up by longer working hours and other measures.

The Prime Minister appealed to the nation: "We are engaged in another Battle of Britain. It cannot be won by the few. It demands a united effort by the whole nation."

In the Opposition's view, the Government seemed to be teetering from crisis to crisis. The dollar trouble was perhaps the severest of all. The US was the chief lender and recommended, almost demanded, convertibility of Sterling after all the measures seemed to be failing. The prescription was too strong but there was no running away from it. Sterling was made convertible on 15 July 1947 and rapidly proved disastrous beyond all fears. Convertibility had to be abandoned in less than 40 days by 20 August 1947.

New cuts were on the way, signifying yet another bout of severe crisis. A Government statement on the dire situation in the *Manchester Guardian* of August 28, 1947 said:

FOOD, FOREIGN TRAVEL
AND MOTORING
Government's Economy Cuts

MEAT RATION REDUCED : POINTS
GOODS TO BE READJUSTED
Basic Petrol Abolished from October 1

The official statement issued from 10 Downing Street, among various things, said: "During the past two weeks the Government have been reviewing the economic programme which they announced in the debate in the House of Commons on August 6 and 7. The broad aims of this programme have not been affected by the sudden increase in the drain on our dollar resources which led to last week's decision to limit the convertibility of Sterling... As a result the Government have now decided to bring the following measures into operation at once." The list included meat and tea rations besides hotel, foreign travel and petrol restrictions.

Meat — The meat ration will be reduced from 1s. 2d. to 1s. from September 7.

Tea — The tea ration will not be increased beyond the present reduced level of 2 oz a week.

Hotels — From September 14 the period for which the guests may stay in hotels without surrendering ration books will be reduced from four nights to two.

Luxury Foods — The import of certain luxury foods will be prohibited.

Foreign Travel: It was announced earlier in the month that, as from October 1, 1947, the allowance of foreign currency for pleasure travel would be reduced from £75 for 12 months to £35 for 14 months and that the proportionate allowance for a child would be reduced from £40 to £20. The Government have now decided that the reduction should take effect at once instead of October 1, 1947.

Petrol — Petrol ration by 33⅓ per cent from October 1. In the new situation they have now decided that the basic petrol ration should be abolished altogether from October 1.

While the period leading to August and following thereon was a cruel time in India marking bloodshed, massacres and mass migration within Punjab , for the Attlee government it was one of crippling blows to economy. For Attlee personally it was a testing time of plots and revolts within the cabinet. Inciting colleagues to plot a coup was none other than the trusted and ablest — Sir Stafford Cripps. Hoping to take Attlee's job himself, Cripps reportedly asked Herbert Morrison, Ernest Bevin, Hugh Dalton and other ministers to go together to Attlee and ask for his resignation, apparently to make Bevin the new PM. But all except Cripps wriggled out of the proposed clique at the last moment, leaving Cripps alone to pursue his plans. Undaunted, Cripps went alone to Attlee urging him to resign in favour of Ernest Bevin. Attlee is said to have picked up the scrambler (phone) and said

to Bevin: " Ernie, Stafford is here. Do you want my job?" Bevin's instant
reply was 'NO' which put paid to the plot, leaving Attlee unchallenged.
Bevin's comment to Arthur, the PM's principal private secretary: "What
a man. He plucked victory from disaster. I love the little man. He is our
Campbell Bannerman..."[1]

Attlee's Government and Attlee himself as Prime Minister bravely
survived in 1947, which clearly was the year of almost total absorption in
internal affairs. India, Burma, Palestine, Egypt all were not much more than
irritants. The prospect of Mountbatten taking care of the Indian subcontinent
appeared to be wholly satisfying. Nothing like it. Attlee was well rid of that
burden. A few hundred thousand people killed in the process didn't seem
to bother him much in 1947 — nor in 1954 as he seemed to imply in
his memoir. "We would have preferred a United India. We couldn't get it,
though we tried hard. But broadly speaking the thing went off well, I think.
That was because we handed over power in India on a definite announced
date and they knew they had to take it. That was absolutely essential... the
experiment came off and that when we came out of India, we left behind so
much goodwill."[2]

It is almost beyond belief that Attlee, the leading architect of the
British welfare state and champion of the poor of his country, could chiefly
remember the 'goodwill' left behind in India, almost forgetting the millions
of shattered lives that were also left behind.

Notes

1   Harrris Kenneth, *ATTLEE,* p. 350, Weidenfield and Nicolson,1982.

2   Attlee C.R., *A Prime Minister Remembers — Interviews by Francis Williams,*
     Heinemann, 1961.

9

Mountbatten's Double Scuttle

B ritish Prime Minister Clement Richard Attlee's first major brush with India occurred about 20 years prior to his 20 February 1947 declaration which resulted in the partition of the country. Then better known as Major Attlee and Labour Member of Parliament for Bethnal Green constituency, East London, he was sent to India by Labour Prime Minister Ramsay MacDonald as a member of the Simon Commission which toured India twice — 1927–28 and 1928–29 — to study and report on the 'Indian problem'. Major Attlee was one of two Labour MPs chosen by MacDonald to act as the party's eyes and ears on India and the Commission's work. His contributions to the Commission's report, especially its second part, left a lasting impression which influenced his thinking on India during his years as war time Cabinet member (1939–1945) and chairman of its India Committee, and as Prime Minister after the war.

"When I was a member of the Simon Commission, nearly 20 years earlier, I remember hearing of Pakistan, a Moslem State, composed of the Punjab, Sind, Kashmir, Balochistan, the North-West Frontier Province and Eastern Bengal, but it was talked of then as the idle dream of a communal enthusiast; but now it had taken shape (in the 1940s) and Jinnah was its prophet. Congress on the other hand, had always talked of Indian nation and of a State embracing the whole of the peninsula. Nehru hated the idea of a Confessional State...

"My colleagues and I saw all the difficulties of a division of India into two States — Hindu and Moslem — for any such partition would necessarily leave minorities in both States. We doubted also whether Pakistan, with an important unit geographically separate from the real centre of the new State, was viable. My Cabinet colleagues (1946 Cabinet Mission) and the Viceroy, therefore, spent many hours seeking to get a solution which would satisfy both communities. The difficulty did not lie with any unwillingness of Britain to part with power, but with arranging for the succession. Finally, they returned home, frustrated, though having accomplished much in the creation of good relations, for Indians realized that the Labour Government was in earnest in seeking to implement the promises made by Britain."[1]

So, Attlee's Labour Government set the time table for withdrawal from India by June 1948, about 15 months after 20 February 1947. No surprise, the defenders of the Empire in both Houses of Parliament denounced the plan as unworkable, thoughtless and a rash gamble. Joining the issue in the Upper House on 25 February 1947 Tory Lord Templewood reminded the House that transfer of power, though widely agreed, had to be effected on condition that it would be orderly, that it would be based on a broad measure of agreement (among Indians) and that it would take full account of 'our obligations' (towards depressed classes, minorities and rulers of Princely states). But by a sudden stroke of the pen without any previous consultation with the Opposition, the transfer was to be made without any of these three conditions being retained. The Government, he said, was making 'a gambler's throw' which might come off but equally might do irreparable damage to India. "We believe the Government are morally wrong. It is impossible to make this gigantic transfer in an orderly fashion in 15 months."

Lord Newall also called it 'a gamble — a rash gamble' without due consideration being given to its possible results. Lord Scarborough foresaw chaos and confusion in India: "What would hit many people very hard was the consciousness that after all Great Britain had failed in India… What was needed at this time was not action but pause. There should have been a delegation of all parties (another Simon Commission!) to make one final attempt to persuade the Indian leaders to reach an agreement, and if it failed, "we should have carried on our administration for another ten or twenty years."

Joining the battle with Sir Stafford Cripps who opened the India debate in the House of Commons, Sir John Anderson said that the fixing of the date of withdrawal was an utterly irresponsible step. It was an act of folly to lay down a fixed period in which anything so complicated as the framing of an Indian Constitution has to be accomplished, even for the Central Government of a United India. Much more, it was folly to attempt it when it may possibly mean handing over power to a number of Governments. The only justification for a fixed date he could feel was the possibility of preserving the unity of India. But he regretfully declared his belief that the chance of its doing so was so slight as to be negligible. In short it was "a gamble."

"I greatly fear and I say it with the most profound sorrow that what should stand out as a great act of self-abnegation may go down in history as a surrender and a betrayal," concluded Sir John.

For the Liberals, Mr Clement Davies supported Sir Stafford Cripps' argument that the Government's policy was the only course left open to it. He did not deny that it was fraught with great risk but the risk had to be taken since there could be no standing still, nor a rollback.[2]

Opening the resumed debate in the Commons, Mr Winston Churchill, the Leader of the Opposition, enumerated a long list of denunciations of Attlee's proposal starting with the Government's departure from the 1942 Cripps Mission declaration in three major aspects. The elimination of the stage of Dominion status was the first mistake while "total abandonment" of responsibility for carrying out pledges to the minorities, depressed classes and the princely rulers constituted the second failure. No less great was the third departure. The essence of the 1942 Cripps declaration, he reminded the House, was that there should be agreement between the Indian communities, namely the Moslems and the Hindus. Another mistake, he pointed out, was the dismissal of eminent Indians in the Viceroy's Council and the handing

over of the Government of India to Mr Nehru and others. "In handing over
the Government of India to these so-called political classes, you are handing
over to men of straw of whom in a few years not a trace shall remain,"
thundered Mr Churchill.

Comparing the Government's attitude to India and Palestine with
time limit for one and none for the other, Churchill said to loud cheers and
laughter that "two bottles of medicine had been prepared but given to the
wrong patients."

After making a wild suggestion of considering the option of referring
the Indian problem to the United Nations, Churchill delivered his *piece de
resistance:* "It is with grief that I watch the clattering down of the British Empire
with all the glories and services it has rendered to mankind. (Opposition
cheers) Many have defended Britain against her foes but none can defend
her against herself. We must face the evils that are coming upon us. We
must do our best in all the circumstances and neglect no expedient which
will avert the ruin and disaster which will follow upon the disappearance of
Great Britain as a power in the East. Let us not add by shameful flight, by
premature and hurried scuttle, to the pangs and sorrows which many of us
feel the taint and smear of shame". (Loud Opposition cheering continued
for several minutes after Mr Churchill had resumed his seat)[3]

Winding up the debate, Prime Minister Attlee reminded the Leader of
the Opposition: "I hate to be dogmatic or prophetic (as Mr Churchill was
about calling Indian leaders as men of straw of whom not a trace would
be left in a few years) as to what may happen in India. I differ in this from
Mr Churchill. His practical experience in India was some fifty years ago."
(Laughter and Government cheers) "He formed some very strong opinions
then — I might also say prejudices — and they have remained with him
ever since. I have heard him reiterate those views over a period of years with
a constancy which completely ignores the march of events." (Government
cheers) Attlee closed his reply (to loud cheers): "I am quite sure the whole
House will wish God-speed to the Viceroy (Mountbatten soon to take charge

in India) in his great mission. It is a mission, not as has been suggested of betrayal on our part, but a mission of fulfilment."

And it was this invocation — no less — to Mountbatten, cousin of King George VI, which seemed to have saved everybody's bacon without any sense of victory or defeat and loss of prestige for all sections of the two Houses. Churchill, however inimical to the "clattering down of the Empire", must have been somewhat mollified, at least for some short periods, by Mountbatten's clever choice of General Hastings Lionel (Pug) Ismay, wartime aide of Churchill, as his Chief of Staff. The choice of Sir Eric Charles Mievelle, assistant private secretary to the King, as the Viceroy's principal secretary must have gone down equally well in the Tory and Labour sociopolitical circles.

For Mountbatten it was not so much a mission as ambition to succeed where others had failed. He had accepted the job to score a success in the political field where Cabinet members and stalwarts like Sir Stafford Cripps and Lord Pethick-Lawrence had failed. Writing about Cripps' offer to help him in his new job by flying to India, Mountbatten told his cousin the King: "I don't want to be ham-strung by having to bring out a third version of Cripps' offer !!!"[4] Although he paid lip service to the efforts of Cripps both when he was on a solo mission to win over Indian leaders in 1942 and as a member of the 1946 Cabinet Mission (Cripps, Pethick-Lawrence and AV Alexander), he seemed to have decided quite early on that he was not going to try the old failed formulations of Cripps, Cabinet Mission and others, including that of his predecessor as Viceroy, Lord Wavell who had been dismissed by Attlee. Wavell had recorded the event in his journal : "Just after lunch I had a letter from the PM by special messenger, dismissing me from my post at a month's notice. Not very courteously done."[5]

Almost within three weeks of his arrival in India on 18 March 1947, Mountbatten had come to the conclusion that united or federal India solutions adumbrated by the likes of Cripps and Pethick-Lawrence were not going to work. He routinely presented old formulations to Indian leaders knowing full well that they had already rejected them and there was no chance of reviving the dead horses. Nevertheless, he did make a show of it.

Mountbatten made no secret of his own views. In pretty clear terms he wrote to Pethick-Lawrence in mid-April that "partition is probably inevitable."[6] In his personal weekly report to Prime Minister Attlee and his cousin the King he dwelt at length on riots in Punjab and the North West Frontier Province saying that his talks with Indian leaders had convinced him of the necessity to "make up our minds".

By early May Mountbatten indeed seemed to have made up his mind. As he wrote in his report to the PM and the King : "I will then (after meeting Indian leaders around mid-May) make one final determined effort to secure some compromise on the basis of the Cabinet Mission plan. I shall have to fire my last shot in the shape of our announcement of partition."[7]

Mountbatten sounded so original with his plan of firing his 'last shot' of partition to solve the Indian problem. Yet actually he was not half as original as he claimed. For after all he followed the Wavell formula of dividing India on religious lines in creating two Muslim majority areas — Western region Pakistan and Eastern region Pakistan (later Bangladesh) — and leaving the rest as Hindu-majority India. The contemporary cartoonist, Ahmed, of *The Hindustan Times,* was spot on with his caption to a sketch of a ship with Wavell in Army fatigue telling Mountbatten the sailor: "I LAUNCHED HER, CHUM. YOU SAIL HER!"

Wavell's misfortune was that he was viewed by the post-war Labour Cabinet as an old fogey in the Tory mould while Mountbatten symbolised a breath of fresh air acceptable to all — Labour, Tories and the Royalty. Mountbatten the charmer had won the day. But he also symbolised impatience — with all its consequences that were to unfold later.

Pethick-Lawrence, who was feeling increasingly frustrated at Mountbatten's refusal to listen to his pleas to slow down, resigned.

Attlee, the cold operator that he was, replaced Pethick-Lawrence with young Earl of Listowell as Secretary of State for India. He had been parliamentary under-secretary of state for India for a couple of years. The old, experienced objector out of the way, Mountbatten found in young Listowell a pliable minister who readily accepted and promoted whatever he suggested — the partition of India, as well as the partition of Punjab and Bengal.

Mountbatten was lucky in his choice of having Lord (Pug) Ismay as his chief of staff who, with conviction and skill pushed his (the Viceroy's) agenda. He had sent Ismay to London as his own emissary to convince the Cabinet of the need to speed up operations and win its approval for the partition plan he had devised. "You must make them (Cabinet) realise that *speed is the essence of the contract* (italics added). Without speed we will miss the opportunity… I am convinced that, in order to have the best chance of obtaining our long term object, the grant of Dominion Status must take place during 1947." For acceptance of Dominion Status by both emerging countries would be the hall mark of Mountbatten's success. It would also ensure continued defence cooperation in pursuance of British military and economic interests in South Asia, including Afghanistan, and the Middle East, besides cementing British relations with the new Dominions.

In India, the 'bombshell' objection to Mountbatten's plan came from Nehru who feared 'balkanisation' of India as its consequence. Mountbatten quickly re-jigged his plan by mid-May. At the same time he turned down Cripps' offer to fly out to India to help him. Instead he himself flew to London claiming that he had the acquiescence amounting to an acceptance or almost an agreement in the bag. Given the Cabinet's approval, he could pull it through. The Cabinet, minus Cripps who chose to stay silent at the last moment, led by Attlee was only too ready to have the Indian 'problem' out of the way. The decks were cleared for Mountbatten's finest hour (with the British establishment) with the 3rd June 1947 announcement for India's partition and independence.

Lord Ismay's occasional briefings to his old boss Churchill over the same period must have played a considerable part in keeping Churchill's anger under control and winning his approval of Mountbatten's 3rd June 1947 plan. *The Times* recorded its parliamentary correspondent's report of the 3rd June 1947 proceedings of the House of Commons with the headlines:

ANXIETY TURNS
TO OPTIMISM
MPs and the Plan

APPROVAL FROM
MR CHURCHILL

Part of the report said: "We have reached the stage of trembling when Mr Churchill gets on his feet to speak on India. But what were we hearing? The Leader of the Opposition was saying that the Plan as disclosed by the Prime Minister fulfilled the two main conditions of the Cripps Mission of 1942 — that there should be agreement between the Indian parties and a period of Dominion status in which India or any part of it might decide to remain within the British Commonwealth or to leave it."

What a cop out, one might say, but it provided Mr Churchill enough fig leaf to accept the inevitable. He quickly promised on behalf of the Opposition that it would not oppose the plan and the ensuing independence legislation. "Nor was this the end of Mr Churchill's generosity." *The Times* went on: "He praised the work of the Viceroy (Mountbatten) to whom great credit would be due if the hopes were realised. That credit would extend, Mr Churchill added, to the Prime Minister who had advised the King to appoint Lord Mountbatten."

Once Churchill's approval was in the bag, the Attlee–Mountbatten plan moved through both Houses with record speed. Mountbatten's royal blue blood had charmed everybody. Yet original charges of 'scuttle' and 'gamble' remained, though conveniently forgotten — at least for the time being.

Stalwarts of the Opposition camp, who had been critical of Attlee's 20 February 1947 statement, were going round and round the old circle and pointing to one obstacle or the other which would only have succeeded in postponing the transfer of power to some unspecified date, month or year. Their approach, if anything, would have dangled before the Indians yet another cheque on a never-never bank. Their arguments would have led to a repeat of the 1942 Cripps Plan which dangled the possibility of self-rule not in a time bound manner at the end of the war, as demanded by Indian leaders, but would have ended up as a vague, undated promise. The Indians, especially the Congress leaders, had seen it all before. No wonder Gandhi had called the Cripps offer as a "cheque on a crashing bank."

The result then was the "Quit India" call by the Congress to the British rulers. And it came smack in the middle of the Allied war against Hitler's Nazi Germany and Hirohito's Japan. Any further dithering by the British would only have produced an even tougher Indian reaction against the British Government, already reeling under the post-war crisis.

Yet Attlee's 20 February 1947 gamble (statement) was better than no gamble at all and it did produce an acceptance or rather a compromise agreement, however unsatisfactory to both sides in India, and even to Britain. The Congress had to accept the poison pill of partition, Mr Jinnah's Muslim League had to accept a truncated, "moth-eaten" Pakistan with no corridor linking West and East Pakistan; the British had to leave India not as a united country, which they had created after long years of hard work, but as a divided land, with a divided army to boot.

Nevertheless, it was a tripartite agreement with which Attlee seemed to have plenty of reason to feel satisfied not only in the short run in 1947 but even long afterwards. Yet the Prime Minister patently went wrong when he allowed Mountbatten to shorten the revised pullout period from 12 months (June 1947–June 1948) to a mere 10 weeks (3 June to 15 August 1947).

Attlee's own pullout schedule was 'scuttle' enough but his blind acceptance of Mountbatten's 10-week schedule was double scuttle with tragic consequences for the Indians and Pakistanis.

The squeezing of the 12-month period to 10 weeks was the biggest blunder. It was a mega scuttle which left no time to plan for details vital for even a semblance of orderly administration. The extraordinary speed of the scuttle paved the way for mob rule and mass murders on both sides of the Punjab dividing line.

The British troops and other civil administration personnel were boarding ships to Blighty as Punjab went up in flames. Mountbatten's 'advice' and Armed Forces Chief Sir Claude Auchileck's stubbornness to exclude British military from any law and order duties except specifically to protect British lives and interests prevailed. Probably Auchinleck feared loss of British lives as it happened during the 1857 Mutiny. In the event, not a single British life was lost in the partition turmoil. The Government in London seemed to have washed its hands of the Indian problem. Cabinet ministers and other leaders were congratulating each other over the goodwill retained with the Indians and Pakistanis. In fact the goodwill was more a credit to the Indians and Pakistanis rather than to the British who were engaged in a cut and run operation. It was a success for the British and disaster for the Indians and Pakistanis. The British leadership was content with leaving India, while putting the entire onus for chaos on the Indians and Pakistanis.

Amazingly, Attlee and Mountbatten continued patting themselves for the job done even years after the partition holocaust, though Mountbatten is said to have revised his opinion in later years, according to former BBC reporter John Osman. In his interpretation of the ex-Viceroy's remorse, Mountbatten had "fucked up" his Indian job.[8]

By any yardstick, the gamble went horribly wrong for the Indians and Pakistanis who went through the holocaust and massacre of 200,000 to one million people, whichever estimate you take, and the uprooting of over 12 million people from their homes and hearths in the western Indian sector alone in the first onrush, with more in the eastern Indian Bengal sector, though slowly but steadily. Yet it need not have gone so wrong but for the redoubled scuttle — thanks to Mountbatten's advice in which Attlee had put total faith. Attlee's original pullout limit of 15 months (Feb 1947 – June 48) reduced to 12 months with the acceptance of 3rd June 1947 partition plan was short indeed. But Mountbatten's reduction of 12 months to 10 weeks (3 June – 15 August 1947) made the scuttle immeasurably worse.

The acceptance of the 3rd June 1947 plan by all three sides — the British, the Congress (Indians) and Muslim League for Pakistan — was done without thinking through its details. Mountbatten for instance, assumed that he would stay on as the Governor-General of both new Dominions till the partition plan was implemented. The inability to visualize that Mr Jinnah himself would become the very first Governor-General upset all calculations for an orderly transfer of power. The first mistake, of course, was made by Attlee himself by not drawing out the details of the transfer of power. Had Attlee said in the first place in his 20 February 1947 Statement that power would be transferred after 15 months of rule (up to June 48) under a common Governor-General, a common Armed Forces Chief and the existing common federal structure, the Indian sides would have accepted the conditions willy nilly. But Attlee gave a virtual *carte blanche* to Mountbatten and accepted whatever the Viceroy said. 'Accept Viceroy's proposal', he told his private secretary Sir Leslie Rowan who sounded visibly surprised at the mention of 15 August date announced by Mountbatten.[9]

And not only Attlee, the entire British establishment was swept off its feet!

In an effort at minimizing the tragedy and in self-justification, Mountbatten claimed in November 1947 during a visit to India House in London that 'only' a hundred thousand (one lakh) people had died and only a small part of the country had been affected. His own former Chief of Staff Lord (Pug) Ismay reacted in forthright terms when he wrote to his wife: "I was horrified at Dickie's (Mountbatten's) speech ... It seems to me immaterial whether one hundred thousand or a million have actually died: or whether only 3% of the country is in turmoil. The essential facts are that there is human misery on a colossal scale..."[10]

Mountbatten's considered thinking smacks of strange consolation that only a part of the country went through flames and that only a hundred thousand (one lakh) people lost their lives!

And he was not alone in this logic of mitigation. Even Attlee seemed to harbour such sentiments. Though he deplored the slaughter in India, he defended the policy of going "forward on the lines we did." "Any other course would have led to greater slaughter," he said in a Commons exchange with Churchill on 30 October 1947.

Almost 14 years later (1961) in a cold re-call he records in his memoirs — *A Prime Minister Remembers* :

"It took a lot of work and a lot of negotiation. But he (Mountbatten) won, and eventually the day came when we passed the Independence of India Act in the House of Commons.

"At the bitter end of course Winston (Churchill, the Leader of the Opposition), was very strongly opposed and several Indian authorities like Anderson (Sir John) and Butler (R.A. Butler), all thought we were being precipitate. The argument always is of course: 'Go slow and things will get better.' But there are occasions when if you hesitate and go slow things get not better but worse. I was quite sure this was one of the instances where the dictate 'go slow' could not be applied and we must go ahead and fix the date. And it came off.

"There followed, as you know, massacres, but they were not just the result of handing over, or any feebleness by the Government. They'd been brewing for a long time. They started with one lot killing the other in Bengal. Then they did the same in Bihar and on up to the UP (United Provinces) and so on eventually up to the Punjab, where there were a very sticky lot of people, not only a good many Moslems and Hindus but also the Sikhs, very undependable and rather a rough people: they were the biggest cause of the trouble. Whether we could have stopped it then if we'd still been in control I don't know — it's very doubtful. But there it was. I can only say that the death toll would have been far higher if we hadn't come out — if we'd tried to hold India...

"We would have preferred a United India. We couldn't get it, though we tried hard. But broadly speaking the thing went off well, I think. That was because we handed over power in India on a definite announced date and they knew they had to take it. That was absolutely essential... the experiment came off and that when we came out of India, we left behind so much goodwill."[11]

Really! Up to a million dead and 12 million uprooted from their hearths and homes, yet the thing went off well?

Notes

1. Attlee C.R., *As It Happened*, p. 182 (Heinemann, 1954).

2. *The Manchester Guardian*, 6 March, 1947.

3. *Ibid*, 7 March, 1947.

4. Ziegler Philip, *Mountbatten — the official biography*, p. 356 (Collins, London, 1985).

5. Wavell Lord, *The Viceroy's Journal*, 4 February 1947, p. 417 (OUP, 1973).

6. *Transfer of Power*, ed. N Mansergh, Vol X, p. 294 (HMSO).

7. *Ibid*, p. 301

8. The Viceroy's Verdict, *The Spectator*, London, 4 September 2004 (Letters page).

9. Ziegler Philip, *Mountbatten*, p. 388 (Collins, London, 1985).

10. *Ibid*, p. 437.

11. Attlee C.R., *A Prime Minister Remembers, Interviews by Francis Williams*, pp. 211–12 (Heinemann, London, 1961).

10

Mid-summer Blunder

The 3rd of June 1947. The die was cast. The day belonged to Lord Louis Mountbatten, the great grandson of Queen Victoria who had been crowned Empress of India nearly three quarters of a century earlier. The empire that began with the Battle of Plassey in Bengal near Calcutta in 1757 grew by putsh and thrust into the Crown Jewel until it became too hot to wear by the end of the 1939–45 world war.

A war weary Britain under its post-war Labour Government, with its conscience pricked by its democratic ideology and several promises of varying self-rule, had finally come to the realisation that enough was enough. Suffering under massive strokes of financial crises with its victorious population still groaning under food rationing and other shortages, the Labour Prime Minister, Mr Clement Attlee, declared on 20th February 1947, that come what may Britain would be pulling out of India by a date not later than June 1948. Years of hard talks with Indian leaders had finally crystallised into the agreement of 3rd June 1947, when in concert with London, it was announced in New Delhi by Britain's last Viceroy that power would be transferred to Indian hands on the basis of the country's partition and the creation of Pakistan.

For Mountbatten, who was basking in glory as the Supreme Commander of the Allied armed forces in South East Asia, a job for which he had been first sounded by Winston Churchill, the wartime Premier, on 15 August 1943, and whose victory over the Japanese forces led to the surrender of Japan in August 1945, the job of Viceroy of India offered a momentous opportunity for a unique achievement in the political field. He could pull off what no other Viceroy or political leader, including Sir Stafford Cripps in his two avatars in 1942 and 1945-46, had succeeded in doing.

For Mr Jinnah, the creator of the soon-to-be born Pakistan, it was a moment of quiet victory. His dream was coming true but he wasn't showing, at least not outwardly, any gratitude to the British who were offering him Pakistan virtually on a platter. But he allowed himself one shout, Pakistan Zindabad, as he concluded his broadcast on the All India Radio that historic night of 3rd June 1947 in New Delhi. With a heavy heart Mr Jawaharlal Nehru for the Congress and Sardar Baldev Singh for the Sikhs also broadcast their acceptance of the plan while Lord Mountbatten spoke first for Britain's decision to transfer power to Indian hands.[1]

The plan, copies of which had been given to the Congress and Muslim League leaders on 2nd June, was kept as a secret till its announcement in New Delhi and London on 3rd June. While most of the world came to know about it on the morning of the 4th of June, London's *Daily Express* scooped it and informed its readers of the broad details on 3rd June itself. The paper's resourceful correspondent, Sydney Smith, had managed to find some key informant, most probably in the Viceroy's camp and beat British competition with his scoop.

The next day, the 4th of June, 1947 too belonged to Lord Mountbatten who managed to spring a surprise devastating for its spontaneity and speed. He called a press conference, probably the first such self-sought encounter with the media by any Viceroy. It was a *tour de force*. True to his military mould, in reply to a question among the 200-odd correspondents from the sub-continent and a sprinkling from the foreign press corps, the Viceroy dropped the bombshell that Britain would pull out of India not in years or months but in ten short weeks, by the 15th of August 1947 itself. Both parties, the Indian National Congress led by Mr Nehru and the Muslim League led by Mr Jinnah, had no qualms or questions over this advancement of Britain's departure date from June 1948 to 15th August 1947. The June

1948 date was flexible to within one month — 30 days from 1st June to 30th June.[2] Mountbatten was quitting full ten months ahead.

Had Mountbatten consulted Prime Minister Attlee and the Cabinet back home or even the Congress and the Muslim League leaders before pulling this 15th August rabbit out of his hat? Most probably not.

Attlee, who had been mulling over the "Indian problem" since his first visit to India as a member of the all-white Simon Commission in 1928, must have felt like a totally satisfied backseat driver or punter on seeing that his gamble was working out even faster than his own target date. More than a year after the event in September 1948, Mountbatten claimed to have broached the topic of the transfer of power with Indian leaders who were said to have agreed unanimously on the choice of 15th August. "I (Mountbatten) was able to inform representatives of the Princes of this that day (3rd June 1947)."[3] However, there is no record of any such decision or discussion, either in Cabinet (British) papers, or in the Viceroy's staff papers. There was no mention of it even in VP Menon's account who was present all through the period. But once mentioned, "that date seems to have taken root at once and never thereafter to have been questioned."[4]

As Mountbatten's official biographer, Philip Ziegler, points out : The most startling piece of information (15th August as the date of transfer of power) provided at the 4th June press conference "was delivered casually, almost as a passing thought" that was "not even included in the excerpts telegraphed to London." Asked by a correspondent how long would he stay as His Excellency the Viceroy and thereafter as Governor–General, Mountbatten replied: "That is a most embarrassing question," adding "I think the transfer could be about the 15th of August."

"There is no evidence that this or any other precise date had been established beforehand with his advisers, with Whitehall (Prime Minister Attlee and his office), or with Indian leaders," says Ziegler.

Though Mountbatten had once told Jinnah on 17 May 1947 that

transfer of power should take place "as early as possible — preferably by 1st October (1947)," he gave no hint to London that he was thinking of an even earlier date. Ziegler refers to a letter dated 11 June 1947 in which Mountbatten tells his daughter Patricia that when he mentioned 15 August (1947) "even my own staff was horrified and kept saying 'It can't be done. It can't be done.'"[5]

In London the reaction of Attlee's private secretary, Sir Leslie Rowan, was pretty similar, but the Prime Minister simply told him: " Accept Viceroy's proposal."[6]

In fact, the summer of 1947 was one of the worst crisis-ridden periods of the Attlee government. The economy was in a shambles, to put it mildly. The Prime Minister and his government were neck deep in the post-war sterling-dollar crisis to give too much attention to India. The alacrity with which Attlee accepted whatever Mountbatten proposed would have been astonishing if it were not for the economic crisis in which Britain found herself in 1947. The USA, Britain's financial saviour and lender which gave a $3.5 billion loan at a rather steep interest rate of 2 per cent, forced Britain to make the sterling fully convertible into dollar by 15 July 1947 — just the period when India was hurtling into partition and its unknown consequences.

The last installment of repayment of that US war loan was cleared over 60 years later in December 2006![7]

Full convertibility proved a disaster. The rapid depletion of sterling that followed forced the government to suspend convertibility in less than 40 days — just when communal massacres and counter massacres were gathering uncontrollable speed in the Punjab in far off India. Foreign holidays were almost banned and meat rations were reduced for victorious Britons who had won the war but were struggling hard to cope with peace. Demobilisation was accelerated and government spending was severely slashed as India, the Empire's Crown jewel-turned-thorn, shook to its roots.

Britain's domestic crisis during 1947 pushed India almost out of mind and out of sight of most people and members of parliament except a very few who were directly concerned with pushing the Indian independence legislation through parliament or opposing it. Even former Prime Minister Winston Churchill, the defender of the empire who had once said that he had not "become His Majesty's first minister to preside over the dismemberment of the empire," seemed to have lost the initial zeal to oppose it soon after being charmed, at least outwardly, by Mountbatten and his chief of staff Lord Ismay. Rather too quickly he gave up opposition to what he only a few days earlier had castigated as Attlee government's policy of "scuttle". Both the Treasury and Opposition benches seemed to have become pretty tired of India and left it all to Mountbatten.

Few things seemed to be further away from their minds than events in India, Burma, Palestine or Egypt, even though they did make frequent headlines in newspapers.

Virtually left in sole charge of India, Mountbatten decided to work out the terms and conditions of the transfer of power and the impending divorce between Mr Jinnah's new land of Pakistan and the rest of old India as he went along. Goods, chattels, tables, chairs, typewriters, bank gold, notes, coins, horses, carriages, and even the last Viceroy's bodyguards were the easy ones to divide.

Not so the real issues of dividing power, authority, armed forces and the territory of an empire unified by rail, road and stratagem over the previous 200 years starting with the definitive first occupation of the territory of Bengal by the East India Company's Nabob, Robert Clive. Mountbatten's exit strategy now was to make a clean escape by putting the onus of responsibility for division on the Indians themselves.

While congratulating himself for reminding Indian leaders about the "Administrative Consequences" of their acceptance of his partition plan, Mountbatten himself failed to visualise the real administrative consequences that would severely constrict his own ability to carry out any decisions. He simply came a cropper on two major issues, one a wishful thinking about the celebration of the Raj legacy and the other of immensely greater importance for an orderly transfer of power.

Fondly and in true blue royal style, he had been busy designing flags of the two new Dominions with the British Union Jack in the upper canton of each flag as a memento and lasting legacy of the British Empire. The first to turn down this suggestion was Mr Jinnah who told point blank (in Mountbatten's words) that "it would be repugnant to the religious feelings of the Muslims to have a flag with a Christian cross alongside the crescent. He (Jinnah) also said that it would be difficult to make the extremists in the Muslim League accept such an idea at the present time." The response of Pandit Nehru for India, perhaps a wee bit more polite, was no better. Nehru said that "although Mahatma Gandhi, Sardar Patel, and others had originally expressed their willingness to accept it, they had now come to the conclusion the the general feeling among the Congress was that the leaders were pandering too much to the British, and that this had reached a point at which it was inadvisable to press the (Viceroy's) design on them."[8]

On the far greater issue of orderly transfer of power, Mountbatten had assumed that a common Governor-General for the two successor states during the interim period would be easily acceptable to both sides. He was proved blunderously wrong. After long delays Jinnah told Mountbatten on 2 July, 1947 that while deciding to have British officers as heads of all three Defence Services of Pakistan, he would himself be the Governor-General of the new country. Mountbatten did all he could to persuade Jinnah to have a Common Governor-General with British staff until 31 March, 1948 the date chosen for the completion of the partition operation. But Jinnah was adamant, even if it may "cost Pakistan crores of rupees in assets," which he feared new India may not hand over easily. It is ironic that later his perceived arch enemy, Mahatma Gandhi, championed the handover of Pakistan's share of assets, a gesture which earned him the opprobrium of many Hindus in India and became a horrendous contributor to his assassination by a fellow Hindu!

Mountbatten, who was fondly expecting to be requested by the two new Dominions to become their common Governor-General, was inconsolably shocked by Jinnah's rebuff. In his letter of 5 July to Attlee, he described this development as a "bombshell," owning it up as "my own fault," and saying: "I should have foreseen it, and (should) have cleared the position with both Jinnah and the Congress one way or the other three or four weeks ago."[9]

The same day in his letter to his daughter Patricia he poured out his heart: "Your poor old Daddy has finally and irretrievably 'boobed' and I have now landed myself in a position from which I cannot conceivably extricate myself with honour. Either I accept to stay with the Dominion of India and be forever accused of taking sides...or I let down the Congress leaders...Mummy feels I should preserve my reputation for impartiality and go on 15th August. The others feel I cannot let down Nehru and must stay. In both cases I'm in the wrong. In fact I've made a mess of things through overconfidence and overtiredness. I'm just whacked and worn out and would really like to go.

"I'm so depressed darling, because until this stupid handling of the Jinnah situation I'd have done so well. It has certainly taken me down many pegs."[10]

The "higher advice" which he had sought of Attlee by sending Lord Ismay to London boiled down to the instruction to stay on as the Governor-General of India, which he did. Churchill and the Conservatives, though unhappy with Jinnah's attitude, also agreed with Attlee's judgement.

Mountbatten had not just messed up things through overconfidence, he had lost control of steering the partition of India peacefully and avoiding the holocaust that followed.

Mountbatten further compounded the situation by advising the HMG (His Majesty's Government) to withdraw all British military personnel at the earliest against the advice of Field-Marshal Sir Claude Auchinleck, the Commander-in-Chief in India. The C-in-C wanted the British forces to be retained in India to cover the early stages of the reconstitution of the Indian armed forces. He also wanted the British forces to stay on until 1st January 1948 "to safeguard British lives."

Auchinleck, whose father had seen action at Cawnpore and other places during the 1857 Indian Mutiny when several British lives were lost, was perhaps afraid of a repeat of 1857 and a possible loss of British lives. He therefore wanted to keep British troops clean out of the Indian faction fighting. Mountbatten too wanted to divest British forces of any role in Indian affairs and to leave it to the Indians to sort out their affairs.

As a result of Mountbatten's extra cautionary policy the power to enforce law and order in the interim period became grossly weakened even though British officers nominally continued to retain their position till 15th August. (The first ship carrying British personnel to Blighty left Bombay on 17 August.) This policy declaration on the non-use of British forces to stop communal flare-ups and to restrict their deployment to protect only British lives and interests became an open invitation to violence by religious fanatics on both sides.

A further blow came with the decision to disband the Punjab Boundary Force, on the midnight of 1–2 September 1947, exactly one month after its creation on 1 August. The mixed Hindu–Muslim force under the British commander, Major-General TW Rees, was perhaps the only saving grace in a sea of anarchy in central Punjab. Carved out of the old 4th Indian Division, as yet kept out of division along communal lines, and commanded by Rees, it had two advisers each from the Indian and Pakistani sides who included Brigadier Ayub Khan (later C-in-C of Pakistan Army and President of Pakistan) and Brigadier Thimayya (later C-in-C of the Indian Army).[11]

Almost wholly made up of Gurkhas, Baluchis, Rajputs, Sikhs and Dogras, the PBF did yeoman's service in saving hundreds of lives in the central districts of Punjab despite total absence of help from civil or police machinery which had suffered a near complete breakdown. Yet it was decided, on the ill-considered judgement of all concerned, especially the Indian and Pakistani sides whose newspapers had started questioning its impartiality and effectiveness, to wind it up. Instead of augmenting or supporting the force, the view gained currency that the soldiers would become increasingly loath to act against their co-religionist trouble makers. The disbanding of the PBF left the field wide open for yet more massacres and counter-massacres.

Having declared abdication of power in advance of 15th August, Mountbatten could not control anything when things started going wrong. All those assurances given by Attlee and Mountbatten himself to use tanks and aircraft to suppress anybody creating trouble came to naught.[12]

In their quest for keeping its neutral image clear of any personal blame or responsibility, the outgoing British administration lost the intent and will to keep things under control. The riots and killings in Punjab which followed the resignation of Unionist Party (Hindu, Muslim, Sikh coalition) Prime Minister Sir Khizar Hayat Khan on the night of 2nd March 1947 and the assumption of direct civil rule by Sir Evan Jenkins, the Punjab Governor, under Section 93, were to a large extent the result of the unwillingness of the British civil and military authority to deal with the situation with a heavy hand in the run-up to 15th August 1947.

The expulsion or escape of Hindu and Sikh minorities from Hazara and other areas of the North West Frontier Province and neighbouring Punjab districts had started even before 3rd March, but after 3rd March it was mayhem let loose.

Feeding the flames of communalism, Master Tara Singh, the Sikh leader, brandishing his kirpan (short sword) and shouting from the steps of the Punjab Legislative Assembly chamber in Lahore on 3rd March raised the war cry: *"Pakistan Murdabad* (Death to Pakistan)! *Raj Karega Khalsa, Aaki Rahe Na Koi* (Sikhs, the pure, will rule; no resister shall remain). 'LIVE OR DIE APPEAL TO SIKHS' was the headline on the news items next morning in Punjab's main English daily, *The Tribune*. Quoting the Master (school teacher) the small but striking news story said: "Let the Khalsa Panth (Sikh

Community) now realize the gravity of the situation. I expect every Sikh to do his duty. We shall live or die but not submit to Muslim domination. Khalsa! Rise and gird up your loins. The most momentous hour has arrived. May God be our guide and guard us."

Tara Singh's inflammatory outburst sparked revenge and rioting in Lahore with Hindus and Sikhs paying dearly in Multan, Rawalpindi and other cities in quick succession and Muslims becoming targets in Amritsar and other eastern places in the province. His own birthplace, Harial village in Rawalpindi district was one of the first to go up in flames. The village school where he and his uncle, Gokal Singh, taught Hindu, Muslim and Sikh children was razed to the ground. Gokal Singh and a second uncle, Ram Chand, were killed while the granthi (Holy Text reader) of the local gurdwara was burnt alive.

The killings in the Multan and Rawalpindi areas which were later to lead to a chain reaction were not exactly simultaneous. The slaughter of about 130 Sikh and Hindu civilians (Governor Jenkins put the figure at only 20 in his note to the Viceroy, Lord Wavell) in Multan on 4th March in a few short hours could have served as a warning. The administration could have struck hard at the perpetrators of the atrocity and made an example of it. The killings that followed in Rawalpindi at the other end of the province took place a full two days and in some areas three or four days later between 7th and 9th March, though tension and odd stabbings had started earlier. Once again, as in Multan, the Rawalpindi slaughter of Sikhs and Hindus remained unpunished with any exemplary heavy hand. Military units were at hand but not deployed actively. Paltry fines on the offending groups in some of the areas were no deterrent for murder and arson.

In Lahore and Amritsar, the province's two big cities, sporadic violence continued but the loss of life was about equal among Muslims and non-Muslims. This deathly parity prevented the fanatics in the two cities from indulging in bigger orgies of destruction. Nevertheless, sporadic killings continued till the transfer of power in mid-August on the British watch, after which massacres and counter-massacres took hold of the Punjabis on both sides of the divide on a scale unprecedented in recent human history, not excluding the 1990s butchery witnessed in the aftermath of the break-up of Yugoslavia.

In his report on the riots in Punjab, Governor Jenkins divides the gruesome events from 4th March 1947 to 2nd August, 1947 in three phases. During phase-I from 4th March to 20th March, carnage was at its worst in rural Rawalpindi, though Multan urban and rural areas were the first to go up in flames. The cities of Lahore and Amritsar continued on slow boil. Phase-II up to 9th May saw escalation of rioting and arson in Lahore and Amritsar along with outbreaks of violence in the eastern district of Gurgaon on the borders of the central capital of New Delhi. Phase-III, covering the period mid-May to 2nd August 1947, saw wider areas engulfed in the carnage with Lahore and Amritsar bearing the brunt of the violence.

The death roll in all three phases up to 2nd August, according to the Governor's report, summarised in *The Great Divide* by H.V. Hodson, added up to 1,044 killed in urban areas, and 3,588 in rural areas with 2,023 seriously injured in urban areas and 550 in rural areas. Taking into account further casualties in the province's eastern district of Gurgaon, near New Delhi, the Governor's report tots up a consolidated toll of about 5,000 killed and 3,000 injured. The 5,000 death toll Included 1,200 Muslims and 3800 non-Muslims while the 3,000 injured comprised a roughly equal number of Muslims and non-Muslims.[13]

Appalled at this continuing carnage, Jinnah met Mountbatten on 23rd June 1947. Recalling the meeting, Mountbatten in his "Report on the Last Viceroyalty" records: "He (Jinnah) begged me to be absolutely ruthless in suppressing trouble in Lahore and Amritsar." He (Jinnah) said: "I don't care whether you shoot Muslims or not, it has got to be stopped". Next day on 24th June, "Pandit Nehru came to see me (Mountbatten) and spoke in a similar strain. He suggested turning over the cities of Lahore and Amritsar to the military, withdrawing the police, and declaring martial law."

The Viceroy consulted Governor Jenkins, who said he had already discussed similar proposals with Lahore Area (Military) Commander and Inspector General of Police, as also "political party leaders" of the province, and decided against martial law as the answer to the prevailing situation.

Accepting Governor Jenkins's analysis, the Viceroy had a tough time convincing Congress, Muslim League and Sikh leaders, that the martial law option was not a practical one: "I was violently attacked by the leaders of both parties for the complete failure of the 'British' to maintain law and order in the Punjab under Section 93 Government (Governor's direct rule). *Pandit Nehru demanded the sacking of every official in the province from the Governor downwards that same day.* (italics added). Sardar Patel said that the British had had little difficulty in keeping law and order when it was a question of putting down the Congress and freedom movements...

"Then the Muslim (League) members started attacking me and saying that there would be no Lahore left for them to inherit."[14]

In his candid assessment of the 1947 events in Amritsar, Penderel Moon, the British civil servant of the old ICS cadre who served India with great credit both before and after the transfer of power, records: "One of the worst failures of civil authority was in Amritsar." Recalling the 1919 Jallianwala Bagh (park) massacre, Moon contrasts the brutal success and ease with which Brigadier-General Reginald Dyer had suppressed the city's population with a mere 90 men of whom only half carried guns with the 1947 failure to take any action when the British District Magistrate had 144 troops at his command, besides the regular police.

Like the Grand Old Duke of York

> *"Who had ten thousand men,*
> *He marched them up the top of a hill*
> *And marched them down again"*

the District Magistrate marched his troops into the city and marched them out again, leaving the city in the hands of arsonists and murderers.[15]

(Moon, however, broadly agreed with the analysis of Jenkins.)

It was not just the Amritsar magistrate who failed but the entire administration of Governor Jenkins who was in charge of the place until 15th August. The responsibility to maintain law and order lay squarely with him. He was clearly not up to his job and deserved to be sacked as demanded by Pandit Nehru. But Mountbatten thought otherwise and his defence of Jenkins prevailed. Thanks to Jenkins, Punjab kept burning and sliding further into chaos.

Had limited martial law been clamped right at the start of the Multan and Rawalpindi riots in early March the situation would not have deteriorated as far as it did. A few exemplary arrests, bouts of curfew and strict censorship of riot news involving confiscation of pamphlets and weapons of communal warfare right from the beginning of March, especially immediately after the Multan and Rawalpindi flare-ups, would have gone a long way in controlling violence and promoting a peaceful transfer of power. The ground situation was war-like and called for war-time measures. During the 1939–45 war strict censorship was the order of the day in Britain. Sir Cyril Radcliffe, as the director general of the Ministry of Information in London, was the master controller of news censorship. Nothing less than a similar ban on riot news and activity was required in Punjab too. Sir Cyril, instead of doing a bad job of drawing the partition lines in utter haste, could have been the good chief censor at the start of the troubles in Punjab.

Inevitably questions are asked. Whatever happened to Mountbatten's 4th June 1947 press conference talk of not allowing any more violence or strife by sending out troops to "the known bad spots"?

What happened to Mountbatten's talk of securing the agreement of Prime Minister Attlee and his Cabinet on 23rd May 1947, on "using whatever force might be necessary to check the first signs of any widespread outbreak of communal violence"?[16]

What about Mountbatten's reported assurance to Maulana Abul Kalam

Azad: "I am a soldier, not a civilian. Once partition is accepted in principle, I shall issue orders to see that there is no bloodshed and riot"?

What about his further soldierly promises of sternest measures to nip the trouble in the bud? "I will order the Army and Air Force to act and I will use tanks and aeroplanes to suppress anybody who wants to create trouble"?[17]

What about Mountbatten's 11th July 1947 reprimand to the Maharaja of Patiala? "I saw the Maharaja of Patiala on 11th July and impressed upon him once again that the Sikhs, if they showed any sign of fighting, would have the armed forces of India against them and would be crushed".[18]

The prevailing British explanation was that communal frenzy among India and pro-Pakistan civil and military personnel had become so uncontrollable that it would have been impossible for the handful of British army and civil officers to effectively command their Indian staff to work impartially and stop rioting and revengeful killings.

That is an oversimplification. The ground reality was indeed different. The continued presence of British officers was pretty effective whenever it was exercised. The authority of British officers continued to be obeyed pretty well by the Indian subordinates in spite of communal infection and consequent doubts.

The confidence with which British officers could demonstrate, nay impose or enforce, their neutrality is instructive. Stationed at Peshawar, Brigadier GR Morris, who had opted to stay on and serve Pakistan, had to hurriedly finish his breakfast and morning coffee one day on being suddenly informed by Captain Edward Behr of the Brigade Intelligence that "our battalions are fighting each other." An accidental discharge of a round of fire from a Sikh soldier's rifle during cleaning had hit the canvas sheet of a lorry carrying Muslim soldiers. In the communally charged atmosphere of the times the accidental shot sparked firing between the two sides across the parade strip.

Brig Morris got into the open Army jeep and asked Capt Behr to drive right through the middle of the opposing battalions. After commanding his force to "Attention" Brig Morris bellowed: "Cease Fire". And all was quiet on that frontier with the erring battalions expressing their regrets.[19]

Not just the British officers. Even the Indian and soon-to-become Pakistani officers held on to their old bonds and stamped their authority. Colonel Muhammad Idris of the Second Cavalry set aside an order from (future) Pakistan Army Headquarters asking for all departing Indian troops to be stripped of their arms before leaving. Col Idris, however, told his departing men: "Wherever you go, we shall always remain brothers because we have spilled blood together," and declared: "These men are soldiers. They have come with their arms. They will leave with them."[20]

The biggest proof of the effectiveness of the British top brass came on 28th October, 1947 when the conflagration over Kashmir was practically on the point of getting out of hand and nearly exploding into a full scale open armed conflict or war between nascent Pakistan and new India. Whatever be the origins of that Kashmir eruption following the invasion of Kashmir by tribesmen and the Indian military response to it, the fact is that on hearing that the Indian Army units had been flown into Kashmir, Mr Jinnah's first reaction was to order sending the Pakistan Army into Kashmir to "protect Muslims" or save Kashmir from merging with India.

Reacting to the Indian army's airlift into Kashmir's capital Srinagar, Quaid-e-Azam Jinnah asked his acting army chief, General Sir Douglas Gracey, on 27 October to send two brigades of the Pakistan regular army into Kashmir. A reluctant Gracey instead phoned (after midnight) the British Supreme Commander in the sub-continent, Field-Marshal Sir Claude Auchinleck, who promptly flew into Lahore the very next morning from New Delhi to save the situation. The 'Great Auk' (as Auchinleck was reverently known in Indian military circles) reasoned with Mr Jinnah and explained that the presence of Indian troops in Kashmir was legally unquestionable, since the Kashmir ruler, Maharaja Hari Singh, had signed accession with India, and any action by the Pakistan Army would force him (Auchinleck) to withdraw all British officers, including Commanders-in-Chief of both India and Pakistan.

The desperate move was abandoned. Mr Jinnah cancelled his planned order to send the Pakistan Army into Kashmir.

Auchinleck, who as Supreme Commander was administering the division of the Indian Army and was also the Chief of the Joint Defence Council, thus saved the two countries from an immediate open war, underlining the effectiveness and importance of British presence in the transitional period.[21]

Had the British Army and civil machine stayed on to supervise not just the division of defence forces but also of civil authority till June 1948, the sub-continent would have been largely spared the terrible massacres which the two countries suffered.

Had all British personnel been assured of their pay, perks and rankings, many more would have stayed on a while longer to oversee a peaceful handover of power.

Post-haste sailings of British military and civilian personnel to Blighty caused an untimely exodus. Even then almost half of them chose to serve the new independent Dominions.

Most of all, the advancing of the transfer of power date by nearly 300 days from June 1948 to mid-August 1947 was sheer lunacy. In his 3rd April 1947 interview with Mountbatten, almost two months before the declaration of that lunatic date on 4th June, Mahatma Gandhi, while reluctantly considering the idea of partition, stressed that the British must retain firm charge of the Centre (united India) until their departure (June 1948). But alas, as Gandhi confessed later, he had been sidelined by everybody, even by his own Congress party.

Barring a handful of leading players, most leaders from New Delhi to London seemed to accept without question, some with great satisfaction, even joy, this declaration of British departure by 15th August.

Yet there was no logic in it, nor any urgency, except that of a British scuttle, which unthinkingly though unintentionally, led to massacres, taking a staggering toll of at least one million lives lost and 12 million men, women and children uprooted from their ancestral homes and hearths and sending them on forced walkathons of hundreds of miles while fleeing for their lives under the merciless August sun and the shadow of the gun.

Had the Attlee Government at the outset made it a condition of the transfer of power that the freedom package would come with a common Governor-General and common Commander-in-Chief of Armed Forces for India and Pakistan with army and civil administration under them until June 1948, the two sides, whatever their reservations, would have accepted it as *fait accompli*. That would have paved the way for a gradual handover of power, largely avoiding the bloody massacres that transpired. The mid-August 1947 handover of power was nowhere in the Indian or most British minds. It was solely Mountbatten's idea and a devastating brain wave at that!

Notes

1. Appendix, Pandit Nehru and Quaid-e-Azam Jinnah's, 3 June 1947 speeches on All India Radio, New Delhi.

2. Appendix, Prime Minister Attlee's letter of Instructions to Viceroy Lord Mountbatten, on flexibility of June 1948 date.

3. *Transfer of Power*, Vol X, p. 872 Mountbatten claims he discussed the choice of 15th August with Indian Princes (HMSO, London, 1981).

4. Hodson, H.V. *The Great Divide*, p. 370 (OUP 1969). No evidence to back Mountbatten's claim on 15 August date in any official documents.

5. Ziegler Philips, *Mountbatten — the official biography*, p. 388 (Collins, London, 1985).

6. *Ibid*, Attlee to P.S. Lerlie Rowan, p 387–88.

7. *The Guardian* report reprinted in *The Hindu* of 30 December 2006.

8. *Mountbatten's Report on the Last Viceroyalty*, p. 271 (Manohar print, New Delhi, 2003).

9. *Ibid*, p. 204-205.

10. Ziegler Philips, *Mountbatten*, p. 398.

11. Conell John, *Auchinleck,* p. 902–904 (Cassell, London, 1959).

12. Appendix, Attlee's 20 February 1947 Statement.

13. Hodson, H.V. *The Great Divide,* p. 343–45.

14. *Mountbatten's Report on the last Viceroyalty,* p. 179–80.

15. Moon Penderel, *Divide and Quit,* p. 280–81 (*The Partition Omnibus,* OUP, 2002).

16. *Mountbatten's Report on the last Viceroyalty,* p. 152.

17. Azad Moulana Abul Kalam, *India Wins Freedom—the complete version,* p. 207 (Orient Longman, New Delhi, 2005).

18. Mountbatten to Maharaja of Patiala, *Report on the last Viceroyalty,* p. 22 (Manohar).

19. Lapierre Dominique and Collins Larry, *Freedom at Midnight,* p. 413 (Vikas print, New Delhi 2003).

20. *Ibid,* p. 288.

21. Connell John, *Auchinleck,* p. 931.

The sole arbiter Cyril Radcliffe (centre) flanked by non-binding consultant High Court judges for the Punjab Boundary Commission (from right) Teja Singh and Mehar Chand Mahajan (for India) and Din Mohammed and Mohammed Munir (for Pakistan)

11

Cyril Radcliffe — The Boundary Man

Cyril John Radcliffe, the man almost universally reviled both in India and Pakistan — perhaps unjustly, made his mark in history by presiding over the boundary commissions in the Punjab and Bengal and drawing the lines of partition of India, the jewel in the crown of the British Empire. After the last Viceroy Lord Mountbatten, Radcliffe (as he is best known in the Indian sub-continent), is the most memorable British name in the sub-continental history. Perhaps less known, the credit or debit for this feat of demarcation belongs also to Lord Archibald Wavell, the Viceroy before Mountbatten. For the maps drawn according to Wavell's

The Hindustan Times

'Breakdown Plan' of 27 December 1945 and his delimitation of Pakistan, for the consideration of the then Secretary of State for India, Lord Pethick-Lawrence, and the Cabinet tell quite an intriguing story. Wavell's maps constituted a model and legacy for boundary demarcation by Sir Cyril (later Lord) Radcliffe.[1]

Radcliffe's labours in India were neatly summed by poet WH Auden in fluent lines:

> In seven weeks it was done, the frontiers decided
> A continent for better or worse divided
> The next day he sailed for England, where he quietly forgot
> The case as a good lawyer must. Return he would not
> Afraid, as he told his Clerk, that he might be shot.

Auden, of course, allowed himself the poetic licence of simplifying things, perhaps overlooking the fact that Radcliffe completed his job not in seven weeks but in 40 days, if you don't count the day of his departure at the end of his first and last visit to the Indian sub-continent. Nor did he sail back to England. In fact, he fled by air on the 17th of August 1947 from Palam airport in New Delhi where he had landed the previous month on the 8th of July.

His biographer, Edmund Heward, though, calculated Radcliffe's work lasting five weeks and one day. But Auden caught the mood of the man and the moment absolutely right by pointing that: "Return he would not/ Afraid, as he told his Clerk, that he might be shot."

Radcliffe himself said as much in a letter to his step-son Mark Tennant that after seeing Lord Mountbatten sworn-in as new India's first Governor-General: "I station myself firmly on the Delhi Airport until an aeroplane from England comes along. Nobody in India will love me for my (boundary) award about the Punjab and Bengal and there will be roughly 80 million people with a grievance who will begin looking for me. I do not want them to find me …:"[2]

Radcliffe, when he was first sounded out for the Indian job on 13th June 1947 by the Lord Chancellor, Lord Jowett, at the instance of Lord Listowell, the Secretary of State for India, had a flourishing practice at the bar, reportedly earning in those days a hefty sum of around £60,000 a year. The Indian job carried an offer of merely £5,000 a year plus living accommodation and other expenses related to work, including expenses paid for the contemplated visit to India by his wife and two step-sons. As it transpired none of his family visited India as his own stay proved too short, hot and hectic. Even the measly £5,000 salary or fee never materialized.

Within three days of that first sounding, Radcliffe had given his "yes" for the job and he conveyed his acceptance directly to Prime Minister Attlee. Obviously he was looking for neither money nor easy time in the last days of the Raj but most certainly for a name and a role in history. And succeed he did.

Radcliffe might not have got his job if the United Nations had been approached for nominating somebody to the post as was first tentatively mooted by the Indian leaders. The UN idea was quickly dropped as it could result in the appointment of a total stranger to the Indo–British situation. Pandit Nehru and Mr Jinnah instead suggested to the British government to look for some legal luminary to head the Arbitral Tribunal and the boundary demarcation machinery. The choice quickly fell on Radcliffe whose nomination was agreed upon by all sides.

Mr Jinnah had asked Mountbatten for some top member of the British bar, not one who may have served in India in some capacity which could strain his impartiality, and whose decision would be final. Pandit Nehru readily concurred. When informed of the possible choice of Radcliffe both leaders promptly accepted it.

Mr Jinnah somewhat knew of Radcliffe's high prestige at the bar while Mountbatten had known about him since his (Radcliffe's) days at the Ministry of Information in London during the Second World War. As Philip Ziegler, Mountbatten's official biographer, puts it : "I (Mountbatten) saw certain amount of him when he was the Director-General at the Ministry of Information during the War and formed a high opinion of him."[3]

Radcliffe who read at Hailebury College, the same school as that of Prime Minister Attlee much earlier, had a first class honours degree from New College, Oxford, and had a meteoric legal career. He took silk in 1935 and by 1938 had become a prominent personality at the Chancery bar. The outbreak of the Second World War saw him catapulted into the Information Ministry where he quickly rose by 1941 to the post of Director-General. He resumed his legal practice in 1945 and in 1949 was made a Lord of Appeal in Ordinary, the first man (other than former law officers) for over 60 years to be appointed to the House of Lords directly from the bar.

There is a widespread impression in India, Pakistan and Bangladesh that Radcliffe knew nothing about India before being chosen for the job of chief demarcator of its dismemberment. Not quite so. His eldest brother died in

India while serving in the Army. He was deeply soaked in the Kipling lore and his visits to Calcutta and its British cemeteries and life in Simla as seen by him during his brief stay in the country are quite touching and evocative of the Raj. As a legal luminary he had handled a few Indian cases before 1947, including one about a mosque in Lahore in which he had acted as arbitrator and won the praise of his clients.

The blood letting that followed his demarcation of boundaries didn't have all to do with Radcliffe alone. The blame also lies elsewhere. It was the woefully short period in which he was asked to deliver the job. He was asked to do what could not but be a hatchet job of dividing the sub-continent in less than 40 days. In fact, he felt utterly surprised when he was told by Mountbatten on his arrival in India that the job had to be finished by 15th August. Radcliffe even went on to ask Jinnah and Nehru if he could have more time to do the job a bit more properly. Both leaders refused and wanted the boundaries demarcated by 15th August, earlier if possible!

Radcliffe did his best and threw all of his energies into the task. As he said in a letter to his step-son, Mark Tennant, "I have worked and travelled and sweated — oh I have sweated the whole time." He had initially been given the impression (perhaps by Lord Jowett) that his task might take six months, if not 18 months. But he delivered it less than six weeks after his arrival in India and made his escape from the country on the very day his boundary award was published for public knowledge. It had been handed to Indian and Pakistani leaders a day earlier on 16th August 1947, though it had been lying in the safe custody of the last Viceroy since 13th August. Mountbatten had told the leaders of the two new Dominions that it would be better to announce the boundary award till after the independence celebrations which could otherwise be marred in the heat and eruption of public reaction to various details.

Radcliffe had accepted his brief but not without insisting on the all-important condition that his findings would constitute not the traditional recommendations with the chairman's casting vote but a firm unchallengeable umpire's final award by him alone. He set up his office (and residence) in an outhouse in the Viceroy's House with a small staff that included an officer from the Indian Political Service, Christopher Beaumont as his private secretary, one superintendent, five stenographers, five typists, one junior clerk, and eight peons, besides an assistant secretary, Rao Sahib VD Ayer, for purely secretarial duties.

The two boundary commissions, each comprising four High Court judges, two Muslims for Pakistan and two non-Muslims for India, were set up, one for the Punjab and the other for Bengal, with Radcliffe as the chairman of both commissions. At the outset he made the impossible request to the judges to be impartial and show willingness for compromise in their recommendations. One of the Punjab judges is said to have confessed to him that impartiality by him could only earn him the divorce from his wife. The times were so charged that the coolest of judges, though diplomatically proper and courteous, could not afford to be impartial. None of them was a Mahatma Gandhi though even Gandhi has never been considered impartial by the Pakistanis, nor indeed by a substantial section of his own Hindu countrymen, one of whom shot him dead on 30th January 1948 for being too partial to the Muslims of Pakistan by asking India to release funds for Pakistan.

During mid-year 1947 Radcliffe was running against time. It was no ordinary court case he was handling. Its complexity could have thrown biblical Daniel himself off course. He was ploughing a lone furrow, virtually all by himself, sharing the burden of his work with no one else. He seemed to have kept himself away from the general party scene of the Raj. He certainly kept himself at a distance from the Viceroy and his staff, which was also the Viceroy's wish who wanted to keep his own impartiality above suspicion. That, of course, does not mean that Radcliffe led a hermit's life during his Indian stay. He met and dined with a fair few members of the British hierarchy, including Sir Maurice Gwyer, the former Chief Justice of India, Sir Evan Jenkins, the Governor of Punjab, and others. He enjoyed his visits to Calcutta, Lahore and Simla, even entertaining member judges on the boundary commissions and others. But he studiously kept a good distance from Mountbatten's Viceregal entourage.

Expectedly enough there were quite a lot of calls upon the boundary commissions in both provinces by individuals and groups to allot certain tracts of land and areas to India or Pakistan. Some of the representations came from top leaders too. The Punjab's Sikh community wanted areas where its shrines like Nankana Sahib, the birthplace of Guru Nanak, the founder of Sikh religion, to be included in India. At the very least, the Sikhs wanted a Vatican like status for their chief shrine Nankana Sahib. They felt bitterly disappointed and betrayed by the British whom they had served so loyally over the years. But that was not to be.

Likewise the Buddhists of Chittagong Hill Tracts in the eastern region, the area with nearly 97 per cent Buddhist population, wanted their habitat to become part of secular India rather than that of an avowedly Muslim Pakistan. But the sole chairman of the two boundary commissions had his own ideas, guided by the nature of his brief and his own perception. His brief specifically held out the principle of contiguity of Muslim and non-Muslim population dominated areas to be awarded to Pakistan and India respectively. His brief also included the words 'other factors', presumably meaning something like an economic or geographic lifeline overriding the population and contiguity principle.

One of the most controversial parts of Radcliffe's Punjab boundary award, vociferously questioned by Pakistan, is the inclusion of Ferozepur and Zira tehsils or subdivisions in East (Indian) Punjab. It has been suggested time and again by Pakistani official and non-official circles that the two subdivisions had been first allotted to West (Pakistani) Punjab but later demarcated under (pro-India Mountbatten's) pressure for inclusion in East (Indian) Punjab. Mountbatten is also charged with putting similar pressure (on Radcliffe) for awarding a chunk of Gurdaspur district adjoining the Jammu and Kashmir state to India.

Pakistani objectors have claimed that on 8th August 1947, Mountbatten's secretary, Sir George Abell, sent a map given by Radcliffe for onward pass to undivided Punjab's Governor, Sir Evan Jenkins , showing the border areas of

Ferozepur, Zira and Gurdaspur as part of future West (Pakistan) Punjab. The map was said to have been sent to Punjab Governor as advance information to help him make necessary police and administrative arrangements to meet any contingency on the day of the announcement of the boundary award and actual allocation of territory.

Abell's accompanying letter is reported to have said: "I enclose a map showing roughly the boundary which Sir Cyril Radcliffe proposes to demarcate in his award and a note describing it. There will not be any great changes in the boundary, but it will have to be accurately defined by reference to village and rail boundaries in the Lahore district. The award itself is expected in the next 48 hours and I will let you know later about the probable date of announcement." (The enclosure is believed to have shown the Ferozepur and Zira tehsils or sub-divisions of Ferozepur district going to West Punjab in Pakistan.)

So, the Pakistanis have claimed, everything had been decided on 8th August 1947 and none but Mountbatten, under pressure from his friend, Nehru, could have made Radcliffe change his mind and include the two tehsils or sub-divisions in East Punjab, India, in the award which became ready by 13th August when it was handed over to Mountbatten for safe-keeping till its disclosure to the leaders of the two sides before public announcement.

Months later on 9th April 1948, the issue was raised by Sir Archibald Carter in the House of Commons. The Government spokesman's reply made by the Commonwealth Relations Office on the basis of Sir Cyril Radcliffe's own draft stated: "I understand from Sir Cyril that he found the treatment of the area (Ferozepur and Zira sub-divisions of the Ferozepur district) a question of considerable difficulty and on this point he (Sir Cyril) reached a final conclusion differing from that which he was disposed to adopt at the time when Sir George Abell asked him for advance information.

"Sir Cyril has informed me his award of August 13 was the result of his own unfettered judgment and that at no stage was any attempt made by the

Punjab boundary as demarcated by the Boundary Commission,
headed by Cyril Radcliffe

Transfer of Power, Ed. N Mansergh

*Bengal and Assam boundary demarcating East Pakistan (later Bangladesh)
by the Boundary Commission, headed by Cyril Radcliffe*

Transfer of Power, Ed. N Mansergh

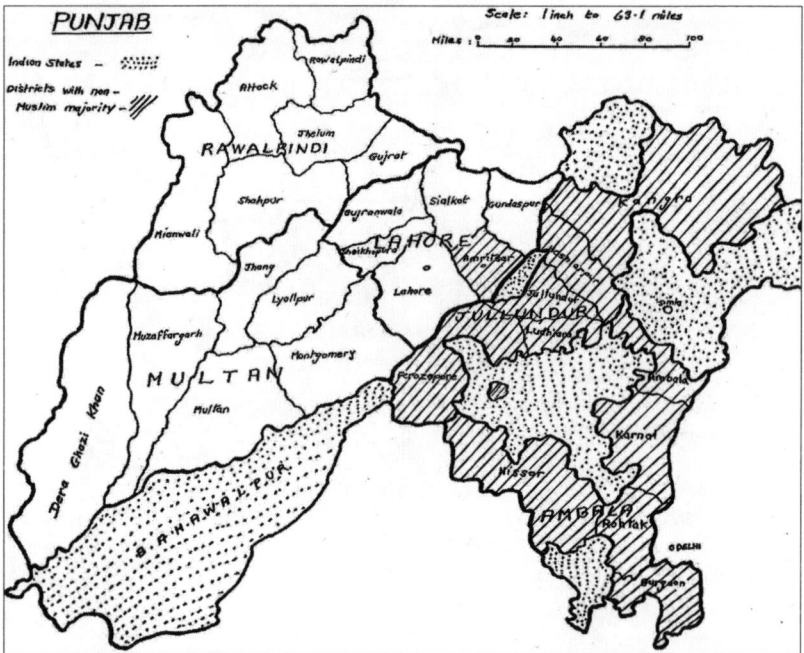

*Lord Wavell's Punjab Partition map suggested (1946) to HM Government,
London, showing non-Muslim majority areas (shaded with lines)
and princely states (shaded with dots) leaving Muslim majority
areas (white)*

Transfer of Power, 1942–47, Vol VI, Edited by Nicholas Mansergh

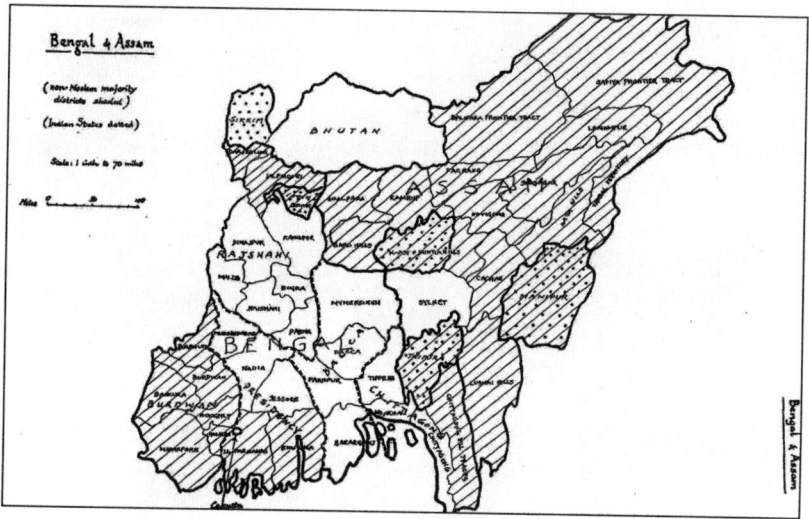

*Lord Wavell's Bengal and Assam Partition map suggested (1946) to HM
Government, London, showing non-Muslim majority areas
(shaded with lines), princely states (shaded with dots)
and Muslim majority areas (white)*

Transfer of Power, 1942–47, Vol VI, Edited by Nicholas Manserg

Partition forewarned as early as 1945: Punjab map from
India Divided by Dr Rajendra Prasad.
Book finished in December 1945
and Published January 1946

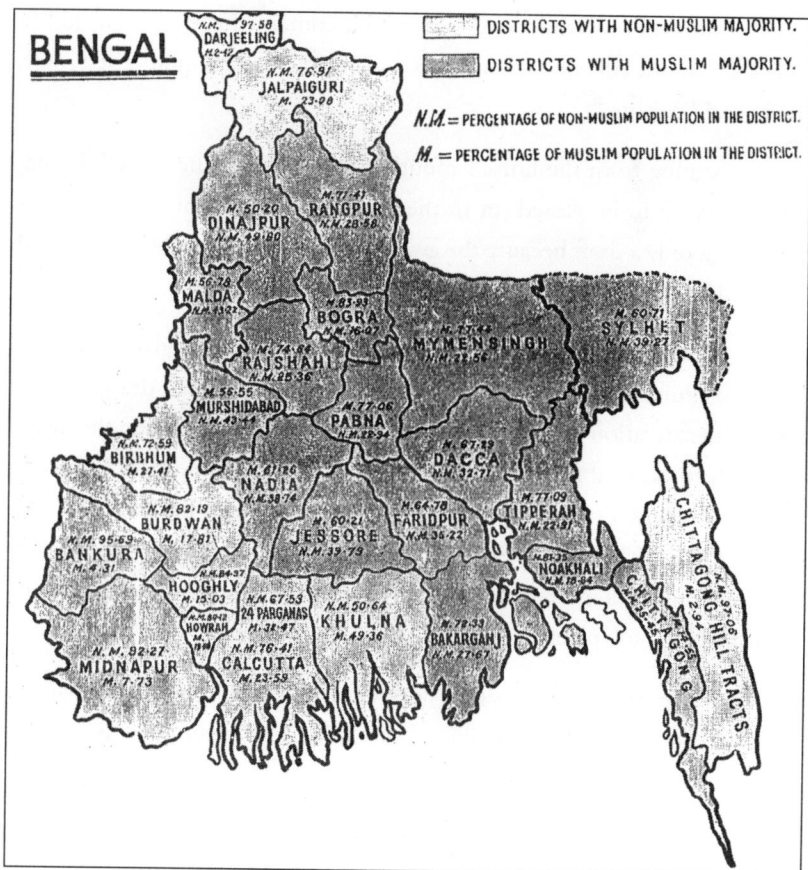

Bengal and Assam map from *India Divided* by Dr Rajendra Prasad.
Book finished in December 1945 and
Published January 1946

Governor-General (Mountbatten) to influence his decision. That this is so I have no doubt."

Four months later on 13th August 1948, Radcliffe wrote to Sir Archibald: "I do not think it quite correct to speak of provisional and final awards. There could be no awards until I had decided to make a report to the Viceroy and only this document which contained the report could be called an award. All the earlier drafts — and there were quite a few, were drafts and no more."

So coming from the horse's mouth, the map which he (Radcliffe) had given to Abell to be passed on to the Punjab Governor, Sir Evan Jenkins, was at best only a draft because the award itself was made ready only on 13th August 1947 when it was handed to Mountbatten.

Years later Radcliffe in an interview at his house in England to Kirpal Singh, of Punjabi University, Patiala, told him how he had drawn several lines of demarcation before reaching the final conclusion. While the award was in the process of finalisation, one such sketch map appears to have been sent to Governor Jenkins. But that could not have been the final one. The date of the letter accompanying the map or the date of the map when it was sketched remains a mystery, says Singh in his book, *The Partition of Punjab*, published by the University in 1971.

The suggestion that pressure from Mountbatten made Radcliffe alter his draft appears to have been attributed to Christopher Beaumont, Radcliffe's private secretary.

Beaumont is believed to have recalled an incident that took place on the midnight of 11th August 1947 when VP Menon, Mountbatten's trusted Reforms Commissioner and by inference an Indian, a Hindu and a follower of Nehru, sought to see Radcliffe who was working on his Report or Award, but Beaumont disallowed his request for a meeting. Menon is then said to have stated that he had been sent by Mountbatten to which Beaumont is said to have curtly replied that that (Mountbatten's reference) made no difference.

Next day, 12th August 1947, Radcliffe had lunch with Mountbatten and Lord Ismay, Mountbatten's Chief of Staff. What passed there nobody knows as no record was kept.

Forty-five years later after that cruel August, Beaumont is quoted to have said in an article, by a journalist, published in London's *Daily Telegraph* on 24th February 1992 that he (Beaumont) thought that the alteration (in Radcliffe's report) took place under pressure from Nehru and the Maharaja of Bikaner whose state would have been adversely affected if the canal headworks in Sulemanke in the Ferozepur district had gone to Pakistan. (In his Award, Radcliffe nonetheless included Sulemanke in Pakistan.)

The highly conjectural report in the *Daily Telegraph* was carried under the tendentious headline: "How Mountbatten bent the rules and the Indian border." The pre-conceived ideas of certain reporters and newspapers, favouring one side or another, are sadly quite often a reality. Beaumont's word could hardly be challenged by Radcliffe from beyond the grave.

Radcliffe's brief was to draw his boundary lines on the basis of "ascertaining the contiguous majority areas of Muslims and non-Muslims" while taking into account "other factors".

In his Award (para 10) Radcliffe says: "I have hesitated long over those not inconsiderable areas east of the Sutlej River and in the angle of the Beas and Sutlej Rivers in which Muslim majorities are found. But, on the whole, I have come to the conclusion that would be in the true interest of neither state to extend the West Punjab to a strip on the far side of the Sutlej and there are factors such as the disruption of railway communications and water systems that ought in this instance to displace the primary claim of contiguous majorities."

So Radcliffe did take into account "other factors" by awarding, to the eternal chagrin of Pakistan, part of the Muslim majority (51 per cent) district of Gurdaspur to India which he, like Wavell, considered essential for "geographical reasons". The award of most of Gurdaspur district and whole of Amritsar district had also the effect of leaving a majority of Sikh population within India rather than in Pakistan, if both or even Gurdaspur alone had been included in Pakistan.

Quite unaware or unconscious of its strategic importance at the time, Pathankot tehsil (sub-division) of Gurdaspur district was to provide the fateful road link between India and the Jammu and Kashmir state without which the whole of the state, including its Hindu majority region of Jammu and the Buddhist majority region of Ladakh, could have been an easy prize to be annexed by Pakistan. Even the Muslim majority region (Valley) of Kashmir at that time, led as it was by Nehru's ally Sheikh Abdullah of the secular National Conference, favoured India rather than Pakistan. From the Indian standpoint, it was the Pathankot (Gurdaspur district) road link that was to prove critically vital for the rescue of the Kashmir state ruled by Maharaja Hari Singh from being forcibly annexed by Pakistan in 1947. The invasion of the state by Pakistani army irregulars and tribesmen within a few days of the partition and the subsequent conflict between India and Pakistan over the following half-century has been the direct legacy of the partition of the country.

In fact Radcliffe tried to fine tune Wavell's model by awarding only part of Gurdaspur district, not the whole of it as Wavell outlined, to India.

Also from the Indian standpoint, Radcliffe's award in the eastern sector was nothing short of a monstrosity.[4] He awarded the Chittagong Hill Tracts (CHT) — with 97 Buddhist or non-Muslim majority population — to East Pakistan (later Bangladesh). The CHT, which could have developed an existing dirt track into a road link to India, was also denied even the smallest sea outlet. The subsequent squeezing out of the Buddhist population and the organized influx of Muslim population into the Hill Tracts area remains an unending tragedy for the tribal (Buddhist) people of the region. By 1991 the Muslim population in the Chittagong Hill Tracts had risen to 48.2 per cent from just 2.8 per cent in 1947[5]. The ensuing uneasy, often bitter, relations between East Pakistan and successor Bangladesh with India over the following half-century remain the direct consequence of Radcliffe's ill-informed and hastily drawn boundary.

Even worse, Radcliffe's lack of knowledge of the topography of eastern India left the entire north-eastern India without any sea outlet and condemned the region to interminable problems of critical transport links and lifelines. As a consequence the seven states of Assam, Meghalaya, Arunachal Pradesh, Nagaland, Manipur, Mizoram and Tripura are surrounded by international land borders and virtually cut off from the rest of India except via the 20-kilometre 'chicken neck' opening around Siliguri in northern West Bengal. The huge bottleneck that it created has in turn dealt a devastating blow to the economy of the region and millions of its people, often straining the unity of India and encouraging secessionist splinter groups with overt and covert help from non-friendly regimes fishing in troubled waters.

Besides there was the issue of over 200 enclaves waiting to explode. They were pockets of habitation called Chit mahals or enclaves or adverse possessions of princely states like Cooch Behar with a Hindu ruler, parts of whose territory were located in Muslim majority areas.

The objections and counter-objections to Radcliffe's boundary award by both Indian and Pakistani sides are strong, even ferocious, and beyond any mutual agreement. The harsh and unpalatable fact is that, warts and all, Radcliffe's award was final and could not be questioned as had been agreed by the two sides at the time of his appointment.

Had he more time at his disposal, as he begged of Mountbatten, Jinnah and Nehru, Radcliffe perhaps could have done a better job, though it is doubtful if even that would have satisfied either party. As it turned out it was the best of a bad job done in 40 days, thanks again to Mountbatten who authored the advance of the British pullout from June 1948 to August 1947. Asked by Indian journalist Kuldip Nayar in October 1971 in London, if he was satisfied with the way he drew the border lines between India and Pakistan, Radcliffe replied: "I had no alternative; the time at my disposal was so short that I could not do a better job. Given the same period I would do the same thing. However, if I had two to three years, I might have improved on what I did."[6]

The mere fact that Radcliffe completed his job in record time is quite a feat. However, the credit or debit for it does not belong wholly to him. Besides Mountbatten, it also belongs at least in good measure to a third person — Wavell, the Viceroy (1943–1947) before Mountbatten. In fact the idea of a notional division of India on a religious basis had been there for a long time in British minds, though its timing acquired clarity and finality only with post-war Labour Prime Minister Attlee's announcement of the 3rd June 1947 plan. Indications of the shape of things to come had become visible even during Lord Linlithgow's Viceroyalty from 1936 to 1943 and certainly during Wavell's term. The two missions involving Sir Stafford Cripps, first alone in 1942 and later in 1945–46 as member of the Cabinet delegation, brought out the division issue for public debate in India and Britain.

It was Wavell who not only prodded the British government in London to devise contingency plans for the departure from India, thereby earning himself the ingratitude and displeasure of the leaders in power in London, but also provided the basis of the maps for such a division for the consideration of the Secretary of State, Pethick-Lawrence, and the Cabinet in London.[7]

In his communication, accompanied with maps, Wavell clarifies: "If compelled to indicate demarcation of genuinely Moslem areas I recommend that we should include:

(a) Sind, North-West Frontier Province, British Baluchistan, and Rawalpindi, Multan and Lahore divisions of Punjab, less Amritsar and Gurdaspur districts.

(b) In Bengal, the Chittagong and Daccca divisions, the Rajshahi division(less Jalpaiguri and Darjeeling), the Nadia, Murshidabad and Jessore districts of the Presidency division; and in Assam the Sylhet district.

"In the Punjab the only Moslem majority district that would not go into Pakistan under the demarcation is Gurdaspur (51 per cent Moslem). Gurdaspur must go with Amritsar for geographical reasons and Amritsar being the sacred city of Sikhs must stay out of Pakistan…"

In fact, Wavell's maps suggesting the partition of Punjab and Bengal had become an open secret by 1945 itself. Dr Rajendra Prasad, the future first president of India, had published maps indicating Muslim and Hindu majority districts of Punjab and Bengal in his book *India Divided,* completed in December 1945 and published in January 1946, as a warning against the planned vivisection of India by the British rulers.[8]

By and large Radcliffe's maps bear a close similarity, except for Chittagong Hill Tracts and Khulna in the eastern sector and Gurdaspur and Ferozepur in the western sector, to Wavell's maps demarcating the boundaries.

In the face of such historical evidence and pressure of time schedule, it is difficult not to believe that Radcliffe pretty substantially reproduced Wavell's boundary maps. His 40-day wonder or blunder was certainly not entirely his own. All bouquets and brickbats must be shared by Radcliffe, Wavell and Mountbatten, the man who advanced the British pullout from India by a full 10 months — from June 1948 to 15 August 1947 — and left no time for Radcliffe to do a proper job.

Notes

1.   *Transfer of Power* (TOP), Vol. VI, pp. 964–65, 700–701 and maps, eds. N Mansergh and Pendrel Moon, HMSO, London.

2.   Heward Edmund, *A Life of Lord (Cyril) Radcliffe,* p. 42, Barry Rose, Chichester.

3.   Ziegler Philip, *Mountbatten—The Official Biography,* p. 402, Collins, 1985.

4.   Roy Tathagata, *My People Uprooted,* p. 133, Ratna, Kolkata, 2001.

5.   Verghese B.G., *India's Northeast Resurgent,* p. 375, Koark, Delhi, 1996.

6.   Nayar Kuldip, *Distant Neighbours,* p. 34, Vikas, Delhi, 1972.

7.   Nayar Kuldip, *Scoop!,* p. 34 Harper Collins, Delhi, 2006.

8.   Prasad Dr Rajendra, *India Divided,* Hind Kitabs, Bombay,1946.

RACE AND RELIGION

Punch, 1947

12

Massacres and Population Exchange

Mountbatten's 3rd June 1947 Plan, the basis of the Indian Independence Bill, was a settlement, more a compromise than an agreement, among three parties — the Indian National Congress led by Pandit Nehru, the Muslim League led by Mr Jinnah and the British government led by Labour Prime Minister Clement Attlee.

It was a settlement that spelled a substantial compromise on the starting objective of all three parties. The Congress had to accept the unacceptable partition of the country; the Muslim League had to accept a 'moth-eaten' Pakistan — losing half of Punjab and half of Bengal — and without the corridor linking West Pakistan and East Pakistan, thus separating the two parts by a thousand miles of foreign territory; and the British Empire having to leave India as a dismembered, broken up country which it had so assiduously and proudly shaped into a united edifice buttressed with a world class united Army.

The British establishment and the Indian Congress, though reconciled to partition as a last resort, in their own ways kept hoping, for quite some time, that the separating units would sooner or later come together again. The Muslim League under Mr Jinnah, though, never talked of rolling back into a united or federal arrangement, yet Mr Jinnah never tired of reminding the critics and doubters that minorities in Pakistan need never have any apprehension or fear for their life, property or religious faith. He promised equal citizenship to all in Pakistan — the next best to a re-united or federal combination.

Prime Minister Attlee while moving the Second Reading of the Indian Independence Bill in the House of Commons on July 10, 1947, expressed his "earnest hope" that this severance (partition) "may not endure". He regretfully accepted the coming reality of partition and said: "We have all wished to maintain the unity of India — But it has not been found to be practicable...We and the Indian statesmen have had to accept the only alternative — partition...

"For myself, I certainly hope this severance may not endure: that the two Dominions...in course of time, come together again to form one great member State of the British Commonwealth of Nations (cheers). But this is entirely a matter for the Indians..."[1]

Some other members of the British establishment from time to time, had even expressed (privately) the opinion that Pakistan was an unviable idea, economically and militarily.

Several Indian Congress leaders had openly expressed the hope that Pakistan and India would re-unite sooner than later.

Congress President Acharya JB Kripalani on a visit to Karachi, soon to be capital of the new state of Pakistan, told the Sindh Assembly and Provincial Congress Party members that the Congress would continue to strive for the achievement of its ideal of a United India in a peaceful manner and advised against any migration by the minority Hindus and Sikhs.

"Congress has not given up the ideal of a United India. In fact, I hold that there can be no peace or prosperity in the two parts of India unless they come close together. There is no question of oneness. We have a federal constitution. The provinces, whether in Pakistan or in India, will have the maximum provincial sovereignty consistent with the defence of the country and its prosperity."[2]

About a week later on 10 August, Congress leader Mrs Sarojini Naidu, the Governor-designate of the United Provinces and an old admirer of

Mr Jinnah whom she once called 'Ambassador' of Hindu–Muslim unity, said in New Delhi that the division of the country could only be temporary and that constitutional lawyers could not separate the people. This separation had been brought about either by anger or fear or sorrow. Those separated would come back again, she fervently believed.[3]

The fond hopes proved to be shatteringly wrong.

Mr Jinnah, who never looked back at a united or federal India, nevertheless looked for friendly relations with India and said so before and after the creation of Pakistan. His famous address at the inaugural session of the Pakistan Constituent Assembly in Karachi asking citizens of Pakistan to go about freely to their temples, mosques and churches[4] and a BBC radio interview in London over a year earlier[5] are testimony to his secular thinking and assurances to minorities.

The question answer session at a press conference he held at his residence in New Delhi barely a month before the birth of Pakistan throws interesting light on the clear vision he had for Pakistan. Some excerpts:

Q: Could you as Governor-General (of Pakistan) make a brief statement on the minorities problem?

Mr Jinnah: "At present I am only Governor-General-designate...let me tell you that I shall not depart from what I have said repeatedly with regard to the minorities. Everytime I spoke about the minorities, I meant what I said, and what I said I meant.

"Minorities, to whichever community they may belong, will be safeguarded, their religion or their faith or belief will be protected in everyway possible. Their life and property will be secure. There will be no interference of any kind with their freedom of worship. They will have protection with regard to their religious faith, their life, their property, their culture. They will be in all respects citizens of Pakistan without any distinction of caste, colour, religion or creed.

"They will have all their rights and privileges and, no doubt, along with it goes the obligation of citizenship…and as long as the minorities are loyal to the state and owe true allegiance to it and as long as I have any power, they need have no apprehension of any kind."

Q: "Would you like the minorities to stay in Pakistan, or would you like an exchange of population?"

Mr Jinnah: "As far as I can speak for Pakistan, I say that there is no reason for any apprehension on the part of the minorities in Pakistan. It is for them to decide what they should do. All I can say is that there is no reason for any apprehension as far as Pakistan is concerned. It is for them to decide. I cannot order them?

Q: "Will Pakistan be a secular or theocratic state?"

Mr Jinnah: "You are asking me a question that is absurd. I do not know what a theocratic state means."

A correspondent suggested that a theocratic state meant where only people of a particular religion, for example, Muslims, would be full citizens and non-Muslims would not be full citizens.

Mr Jinnah: "Then it seems to me that what I have already stated is like throwing water on a duck's back. For goodness' sake, get out of your head the nonsense that is being talked about. What this theocratic state means I do not understand."

Another correspondent suggested that the questioner meant a state run by Maulanas (Mullahs).

Mr Jinnah: "What about a government run by Pandits in Hindustan? When you talk of democracy, I am afraid you have not studied Islam. We learnt democracy 13 centuries ago."

Asked what would be the relations between Pakistan and India, Mr Jinnah said: "I have already answered that long ago and I repeat it here.

I sincerely hope that they will be friendly and cordial. We have a great deal to do, both States, and I think we can be of use to each other, not to say the world. Being neighbours, from our side I do not think you will find goodwill wanting and I hope and appeal to the Press and news agencies to impress this more upon Hindustan."[6]

Mr Jinnah's dream of a modern, secular Pakistan looked unshakeable. He even commissioned a Hindu poet, jagan Nath Azad son of well known Urdu poet Tilok Chand Mehroom of Lahore, to write the first national anthem of Pakistan. The anthem, which continued to be sung as the new nation's primary song till six months after Mr Jinnah's death in September 1948, had the following opening lyrics:

Ay Sarzameené Pak

Zarrey teray hain aaj sitaaron sé taabnak

Roshan hai kehkashaan sé kaheen aaj teri khaak

Ay Sarzameené Pak

(O Land of Pak / The stars have lit up every bit and particle of yours / The rainbow shines on every speck of your dust/O Land of Pak

The Quaid-e-Azam (The Great Leader) was not to know that Pakistan was to be ruled by none other than Maulana (sorry General) Zia-ul-Haq who, with generous help from the USA and Saudi Arabia reduced the country to a theocratic State, anathema to the Quaid himself. The imposition of extreme Sharia and Islamisation of Pakistan under Gen Zia (1977–88) was to put Pakistan in the frontline of Jihadist militancy that not only threatened the benefactors, America and Saudi Arabia, but also beneficiary Pakistan. The Taliban ideology in Pakistan, initially to defeat the Soviet forces in Afghanistan at the behest of America and Saudi Arabia, was to make Pakistan and Afghanistan the launch pad of al-Qaeda under the awesome leadership of Osama bin-Laden. al-Qaeda's 9/11 attack on New York's World Trade Twin Towers in the commercial, intellectual and cultural heart of America was to set Pakistan on yet another American journey, this time against the Islamic, theocratic, tigers which it had been riding earlier. The same tigers, however, did not spare Pakistan itself, culminating in the assassination of Benazir Bhutto and two earlier attempts on the life of General Pervez Musharraf, nearly 20 years after General Zia's regime.

Much as Mr Jinnah decried theocracy and hoped for normalisation of relations between Muslims and Hindus after the establishment of Pakistan, the events surrounding the birth of Pakistan belied all his and everybody else's expectations. Hatred and violence were writ large on the northern expanse of the sub-continent. Population exchange, at worst thought to be voluntary, became an ugly and permanent reality.

Promises of equal citizenship, friendship and good neighbourliness were plentiful yet the speed of daily occurrences became uncontrollable. Promises and assurances couldn't stop the massacres. Innocents were on the move — abandoned by the gods — on forced marches to the unknown. Nearly 12 million luckless souls — men, women and children — were marching across Cyril Radcliffe's boundary line in two-way processions from the newly named East Punjab to West Punjab and from West Punjab and the rest of western Pakistan to East Punjab and other areas over the Indian border. Or were they the mourners in countless funeral processions? Or worse, for anything up to one million of them never completed their last journey. Nobody knows, for sure, exactly how many crossed the Hades or the Radcliffe rekha, lakeer or line. God alone knows how many failed to make that crossing. Or as some believers, in helpless rebellion, asked: "Does He care?"

And there were at least another half million making the one-way journey in those early days from the eastern part of Sonar Bangla or Golden Bengal (newly christened East Pakistan) to West Bengal in India. While the western sector (of the sub-continent) rushout was a two-way affair, the eastern migration was practically a slow trickle out from East Pakistan

(Bangladesh after 1971) to India's West Bengal. A few, very few, did make the reverse journey in this sector. Luckily, thanks to Mahatma Gandhi and united Bengal Premier Husain Shaheed Suhrawardy, the eastern sector was spared any largescale bloodshed or migration in the immediate days around the division of the province.

But first to the blood-soaked land of the five rivers (Punjab) in the western sector of the sub-continent. Who killed more people? Who looted most or lobbed more fire bombs? 'You did it, you did it' has been the historic refrain from both sides. Never mind who plunged the most knives, the incontrovertible fact is that up to one million innocents got killed in the most horrific way and another 12 million got uprooted from their hearths and homes in the western sector alone.

Lahore, Amritsar, Multan and Rawalpindi cities had become the flashpoints soon after the resignation of the United Punjab Prime Minister Sir Khizar Hayat Khan Tiwana on 2nd March, 1947 and the inflammatory speech of the Sikh leader Master Tara Singh the next day outside the Punjab Legislative Assembly when he shouted *Pakistan Murdabad* (Death to Pakistan) and called upon Sikhs to be ready for a do-or-die battle.

Such fiery harangues by Master Tara Singh and Giani Kartar Singh sparked demonstrations by Hindus and Sikhs in Lahore and retaliatory attacks on them by Muslim National Guards and their supporters on 4th March. Amritsar and Multan cities witnessed almost simultaneous rioting which soon spread to rural areas. Rawalpindi was not far behind. Within three days 140 deaths had been recorded at the Amritsar mortuary and 275 casualties treated at the city's two main hospitals. The actual toll was most certainly much higher than the official figures.

Multan witnessed its first riots on March 5 where a procession of Hindu and Sikh students protesting against police firing at Lahore students the previous day was attacked by a mob led by Muslim National Guards shouting *'Leyke rahenge Pakistan'* and *'Pakistan Zindabad'* (We will not rest till we get Pakistan and Long Live Pakistan). Besides widespread arson and looting of minority Hindu and Sikh shops and houses, the local tuberculosis hospital run by a Hindu charity was attacked and patients butchered in their beds and the building set on fire.[7] The trouble soon spread to villages in the outlying district which saw a repeat of atrocities enacted in the city.

Rawalpindi, the home district of Master Tara Singh attracted the particular attention of Muslim National Guards forces. By 6th March, Muslim gangs were roaming the rural areas surrounding Rawalpindi city and spreading the rumour that the city's Jumma Masjid (mosque) had been razed to the ground by Sikh and Hindu mobs who had also killed scores of Muslims. The rumour spread like wildfire provoking a Muslim mob to burn down several shops in the Masjid area. "The Muslim mob was divided into different groups by the (Muslim) League leaders. Each group was directed to a different locality. The mob proceeded to their allotted targets with instructions to kill. A part of the mob consisting of about one thousand people attacked the Amarpura Abadi (population cluster)…The mob (armed with assorted weapons) entered the mohalla (locality) raising slogans like *Allah Hu Akbar, Pakistan Leyke rahenge* and *Inn Hindu aur Sikh moozion ko maro* (God is Great, We shall get Pakistan and kill these wretched Hindus and Sikhs)." The upshot was 13 non-Muslims were burnt alive and scores of houses set on fire. Another seven people were killed in the cantonment area where they had been lured to join a peace committee, according to witnesses assisting a fact finding Indian team of the Ministry of Relief and Rehabilitation. The killing spree continued for three more days till 10th March. Many more were killed in the surrounding areas leading to hundreds of people fleeing their homes and seeking refuge in Sikh states of eastern Punjab.

One of the most desperate happenings occurred in a small hamlet called Thoha Khalsa in Rawalpindi district where 90 women decided to commit suicide by drowning rather than fall into the hands of molesters and rapists. *The Statesman* recorded the story in a double column in its northern India edition on an inside page (No 3) in a dead pan narrative in its 14th April issue thus:

WOMEN JUMP INTO WELL TO AVOID CAPTURE

FROM OUR STAFF CORRESPONDENT

"The story of 90 women of the little village of Thoha Khalsa, Rawalpindi District, who drowned themselves by jumping into a well during the recent disturbances, has stirred the imagination of the people of the Punjab.

They revived the Rajput tradition of self-immolation when their men-folk were no longer able to defend them. They also followed Mr Gandhi's advice to Indian women that in certain circumstances even suicide was morally preferable to submission.

Thoha Khalsa, situated at the foot of a hill, until recently belonged to members of a minority. It was small, prosperous and pretty.

About a month ago, a communal army of around 3,000 strong, armed with sticks, tommy guns and hand grenades surrounded it. The villagers defended themselves as best as they could. They had two guns which they put to good use. But in the end they had to raise the white flag.

Negotiations followed. A sum of Rs. 10,000 was demanded by the besiegers. It was promptly paid. The intruders gave a solemn assurance that they would not come back. The promise was broken the next day.

They returned to demand more money and in the process hacked to death 40 of the defenders. Heavily outnumbered, they were unable to resist the onslaught. Their women held a hurried meeting and came to the conclusion that all was lost except their honour. Following the example of Indian women of by-gone days, they decided to evade inglorious capture. Ninety women jumped into a small well. Only three were saved. There was not enough water in the well to drown them all."

By April as many as 10,000 Sikhs were housed in refugee camps in Patiala and Kapurthala States which were to turn into a kind of recruiting centres of avenging jathas (bands) of Sikhs around 15th August (independence day).

With the collapse of civil authority on both sides of the dividing line, the field was clear for mobs led by Muslim National Guards in West Punjab and Sikh–Hindu jathas in East Punjab.

Come 17th August when Cyril Radcliffe's Boundary Award was made public, the gloves were off completely.

The Punjab Boundary Force, said to be 50,000-strong but with an effective strength of less than a third, was designed as a bulwark against this mayhem. It was carved out of the Indian Army's undivided 4th Division with a mix of Rajput, Sikhs, Baluch, Frontier (Muslim) Rifles, Dogra and Gurkha soldiers under non-partisan British command. Created on 1st August 1947 under the command of Major-General TW Rees, the hero of Mandalay in the Burma campaign of the Second World War, the PBF was disbanded on midnight 1–2 September.

Rees had two senior advisers each from India (Brigadiers Brar and Thimayya) and Pakistan (Brigadier Ayub Khan, who later became C-in-C and President of Pakistan and Brigadier Nasir Ahmed). The operational area under PBF, Rees wrote in the introduction to his report, consisted of 12 central districts of united Punjab and covered about 37,500 square miles, larger than Ireland, with a population of around fourteen and a half million — Muslims, Hindus and Sikhs in the approximate proportion of 55:25:20.

The "Synopsis" of his report records: "The political upheavals in India had resulted in a cleavage and bitter enmity between Muslims and non-Muslims in the Punjab, exacerbated by the March (1947) massacres of Sikhs by Muslims in Rawalpindi and the north-west Punjab.

"The cities of Lahore and Amritsar, which set the pace for the rest of the Punjab, were ablaze in the early days of August; and presently the Sikhs, who had recently been preaching violent resistance to any unfavourable boundary award, started their revenge for the Rawalpindi massacres. Their plans were put into execution and the mass-slaying of Muslims began in

Amritsar district, and spread west and east; the Muslims started retaliation; and rapidly the whole of the central Punjab was ablaze; loot, rapine, the destruction of villages and mass slaughter of men, women and children in indescribable savagery, by both communities, became widespread."

Sketching the "political and historical background" of the events, the Rees report points out: "All police became totally partizan, even before partition. So, on 15th August, in the East Punjab, in the Jullundur civil division alone, government was minus 7,000 policemen due to loss of their Muslim police. And already Lahore and Amritsar were burning...and migration of refugees both ways had started."

Detailing the "course of events" Rees recounts how "mass violence by Sikh jathas on Muslims (in the rural areas of Amritsar) started retaliation by Muslims on non-Muslims in Gujranwala and in Lahore."

Similarly Lt-Gen Sir Francis Tuker, GOC, Eastern Command, India, recounts from the note, in fact a long report, of a British officer of the PBF posted in East Punjab. The force suddenly stopped receiving any civilian cooperation by about 4th August when all British civilian officers had left their jobs and were replaced by Indian (and Pakistani) police and other (designate) staff. Tuker reproduces the officer's report which says: "Up to this date (4th August) the DIG of police, the Commissioner, the SP (Superintendent of Police) and the DC (Deputy Commissioner) had all been British, and further to this the police force was mainly Muslim. This ensured the protection of minorities (Muslims)." The British officers having gone, the Muslim police was disarmed in advance of being sent to Pakistan as they had opted for service there. The minority community in the Hoshiarpur and Jullundur districts of East Punjab was thus left high and dry.[8]

Nearly five days earlier on 31 July some 14 men from village Jhand were killed and their houses set on fire. Similarly in Talwandy Arayan village 15 people were killed. The massacres in Hoshiarpur city and rural district took a toll of over 500 lives with Muslim houses in several villages being put on fire. Jullundur district too went up in a "big way", said the Boundary Force Officer's report to General Tuker.

"By about 25th August it was painfully obvious that the officials (Hindu and Sikh) of the Eastern Punjab were quite prepared to accept a large-scale massacre and exodus of Muslims from that area," Tuker quoted. Convoys of Muslim refugees harried by Sikh jathas were swelling and marching towards Pakistan. On the opposite side in West Punjab the Muslim National Guards were busy scoring their own victories. Parts of Lahore were in flames. "The massacre of non-Muslims who had taken shelter in Hargobind Gurdwara (Sikh temple) on Temple Road, Lahore, was another incident of extreme barbarity. About 350 non-Muslims were confined in this Gurdwara which was being guarded by a unit of Hindu military. On August 14, the Hindu guard was replaced by a Muslim guard. The same evening a number of fireballs were thrown inside the Gurdwara and when the non-Muslims, driven by the flames, came out they were shot dead by the Muslim guards or stabbed. Every one of the three hundred and fifty was killed..."[9]

The ethnic cleansing of Lahore is well recorded. "Of the three lakh (300,000) non-Muslims living in Lahore before the trouble began only 10,000 were left on August 19, and, by the end of August, there were not more than a few Hindus and Sikhs in houses and these, too, were waiting for an opportunity to go away."[10]

Perhaps the worst of massacres occurred in Sheikhupura town, barely 23 miles from the provincial capital Lahore, and the countryside surrounding it. The Muslim majority district had a population of about 7 lakh (700,000) out of which two lakhs (200,000) were Hindu and about one lakh (100,000) Sikhs. The Sikhs were prosperous farmers and lived in the countryside and suburban towns. The Hindus lived in market towns or mandis and controlled business and trade. There was no trouble till the end of July, 1947 and only minor incidents till 18th August, four days after independence or establishment of Pakistan when Baluch troops took charge of the town and district. Joining hands with the civil administration and Muslim National Guards the troops formed what the minorities viewed as a troika of military, civil administration and Muslim League (political) axis. Stabbing of non-Muslims started at the railway station on 20th August and widespread arson in Sheikhupura town and surrounding district went unchecked. The town's Hindu and Sikh residents were told to come out of their burning houses for shelter at two rice ginning factories and the local Namdhari Gurdwara. About 9,000 people came for shelter there. On arrival there men, women and children were asked to stand up in long lines. The young girls and women were snatched and "distributed as booty" among goondas or badmashes and sex-crazed hoodlums. The rest of the 9,000 faced firing by the military and police till their ammunition was exhausted when other methods were employed to deal with the remnants. Mini-massacres were conducted in smaller market towns and villages.

Six days later on 29th August Pakistan Prime Minister Liaquat Ali Khan and Indian Prime Minister Pandit Nehru visited the place but it was too late.[11]

Sheikhupura became a byword in the aftermath of this massacre. Muslim hoodlums would intimidate minorities into submitting to their demands for handing over valuables, property, and girls for conversion to Islam. "If you don't do what you are told, we will do another Sheikhupura here" became their standard warning.[12]

What for some was truly August — the month of independence — was for others the month of murderous destiny. Two nations were born in the middle of that burning August and literally had a baptism of fire. Free India and free new Pakistan. New flags flew all over the landmass of the two countries. And lots of flags were carried on blood-soaked poles by blood-thirsty killers and looters masquerading as defenders of Islam, Hindu or Sikh faith as they shouted *Allah Hu Akbar, Sat Sri Akal, Jai*

Bajrang Bali (God is Great, and Victory of Hindu god Bajrang Bali). And who did these faith bands target? The unarmed, the weak — men, especially women, and even children. They roamed the land as Muslim National Guards, Sikh jathas and Hindu nationalist RSS volunteers. They drove people out of their homes and hovels, waylaying them in cornfields, on highways and byways, in buses, streets, on rail station platforms and trains. There was no place to hide from these faith gangs. Where were the new political masters of the two countries? They were exhorting people to stay calm, respect and defend minorities. They were making speeches and issuing press statements, reiterating pledges to do all in their power to quell riots and restore law and order. An exasperated Prime Minister Liaquat Ali Khan of Pakistan, sitting beside India's Prime Minister Pandit Nehru, burst out: "Our people have gone mad." Had the people gone mad? No. Only the faith gangs and those who let these gangs free to roam. Wittingly or unwittingly, the administration on both sides became paralysed and largely non-functional.

Stabbing, shooting and violence by religions gangs which burst sporadically before the Division Day — 17th August when Cyril Radcliffe's Boundary Award was published — acquired a new spurt after the D-Day. The gangs of looters and murderers — Sikhs and Hindus in East Punjab and Muslims in West Punjab who belonged to areas unaffected by the boundary announcement — became bolder in the absence of law and order. Their raids on fleeing minorities and abandoned houses and shops became ever so brazen by the hour. The civil administration which was a mix of Muslim and Non-Muslim staff before the D-Day suddenly became one-sided in strength — exclusively Muslim in Muslim-majority West Punjab and exclusively Hindu-Sikh in East Punjab. Civil servants and police staff had been given the option to work in Pakistan or India and an overwhelming majority of Muslims chose to go to Pakistan while Hindus and Sikhs chose to go to India, leaving thousands of posts unmanned for several days and weeks. In fact, Muslim police officers were disarmed forthwith in East Punjab while

Hindu-Sikh police officers were disarmed in West Punjab. Absence of minority community officers made the minority community on each side virtually defenceless. The gangs of looters and killers saw the opportunity and made a killing, forcing the minority communities to abandon their homes and flee for their lives.

It was to control this chaos that the Punjab Boundary Force was created. As Major-General Rees records in the 'Conclusion' to his report: "The Punjab Boundary Force had a life of one month. It had come into being when internecine strife had already been going on for four or five months. After the violence of the March–April massacres, the trouble had simmered down to a state of widespread tension all over the province with occasional bursts of varying severity…As 15th August and partition approached, the tempo increased, especially in Lahore and Amritsar. There for the first fortnight of August, while the remaining British officials were handing over control… massacres had started in rural areas. About this time occurred the split in the Punjab police and for the rest of August there was little effective government administration for the PBF to cooperate with…But as the slaughter and persecution went on day after day, there gradually came both to the leaders and the masses, the realization not only of the folly but also the realization of the immediate danger of retaliation…Meanwhile both communities were maddened. There were a few notable cases of humanity and kindness shown to the other side but these were very exceptional; and throughout the Punjab there were many millions of embittered men and women fanatically involved in communal fighting…use of troops alone was not the right answer to the problem. Clearly, the psychological approach had to be achieved, and the people brought to reason by their own leaders.

"But the psychological moment had not been reached during August 1947. It was not to be reached for many weeks, until there had been a further long orgy of killing and retaliation by both sides culminating during the last ten days of September in several savage train attacks (in one alone over a thousand men, women and children were butchered.) And "it was not till well into November…that there was any real cessation of terror."[13]

"During the first furious impact of the struggle, the PBF stood firm, rock-like, in a welter of confusion and anarchy. Indeed during the second half of August 1947, the civil administration having broken down, the only effective organisation in the Punjab was the Army…"

After doing a valiant job for one month, the PBF was disbanded on the midnight of September 1-2, 1947, just when it was needed the most. Instead of strengthening the Force and persuading General Rees to carry on, political and military authorities on both sides, unable to put their heads together, took the matters under their own separate (incompetent) commands. Sure enough, violence spiralled out of control.

Meanwhile, the long caravans and convoys of thousands of people of minority communities were inexorably moving towards the other side of the boundary line.

Nobody is sure which caravan of uprooted people crossed the border first. But there was a sudden spate of border crossings in both directions within the very first week of independence (15–22 August). Then there was no stopping them for at least another eight weeks. The governments on both sides kept the doors open for the victims from the opposite side and provided whatever succour they could with pathetically inadequate arrangements. The two governments simply did not have the wherewithal to handle modern history's biggest migration of millions of people. Men, women and children, old and infirm, babes just born and those waiting in their mothers' wombs to be born were on the move, even as politicians on each side kept repeating assurances of protection, equal rights, even home return to uprooted minorities. Promises, promises. Hollow promises all. Hollow, not for want of concern or affection but for lack of foresight, preparation and physical competence.

Minority communities in villages and towns across the entire land mass of the province were subjected to selective looting, rape, abduction, forced religious conversions and evictions. The unprecedented ferocity of violence in both parts of the province finally established a balance of terror which in turn brought the realisation in both camps that there could be no victor in this war of attrition. But it took nearly three months for this realisation to sink in — at a cost of a million lives with another 12 million subjected to cross-migration in foot-marching convoys the like of which has never been seen in man's brutish, nasty and short history.

Several such caravans were seen from the air by Alan Campbell-Johnson, Mountbatten's Press Secretary, who was flying in a Dakota along with Pandit Nehru, Liaquat Ali Khan, Mountbatten and others.

"We flew first in a north-westerly direction towards Ferozepur and Kusur, upon which columns of Moslems from Jullundur and Ludhiana in the East, and of non-Moslems from the bottle-neck of the Balloki Head bridge across the River Ravi, were converging. We passed first over Kallanur, which was supposed to be surrounded by non-Moslems, but there was no sign of any such activity, only a few people on the outskirts waving at us, and then on to Hissar, junction of road and rail, where again nothing seemed to be disturbing the peace of this quiet Sunday morning.

"Only when we reached Bhatinda, an important railway junction, did we come across the first signs of major upheaval. Two trains, crammed with their human cargoes, were in the station. We could see the refugees clambering on to the tops of the carriages, bursting out of the sides, in occupation of the engine and tender itself. On arrival at Ferozepur we saw another such refugee train and more rolling-stock. As we approached the Ravi we had our first aerial vision of the scale of this desperate exodus. We were looking down on one of the greatest movements of population in recorded history, and then only on a small segment of it...

"As we flew back into India we came down low over the northern-most of the Moslem refugee convoys making its slow and painful way along the main Lyallpur–Lahore road. Their exodus brought them across the Beas

River, and involved an elaborate detour to save them from passing through Amritsar. We estimated that it took us just over a quarter of an hour to fly from one end to the other of this particular column at a flying speed of about a hundred and eighty miles per hour. *This column therefore must have been at least forty-five miles long.* (Italics added)

"At the conference on Sunday, Nehru and Liaquat had told us how, to begin with, they had set their faces against any wholesale transfer of populations, but how events had rapidly become too large for them and had dictated the course of their policy.

"Today we saw for ourselves something of the stupendous scale of the Punjab upheaval. Even our brief bird's-eye-view must have revealed nearly half a million refugees on the roads. At one point during our flight Sikh and Moslem refugees were moving almost side by side in opposite directions. There was no sign of clash. As though impelled by some deeper instinct, they pushed forward obsessed only with the objective beyond the boundary."[14]

Reporters on the ground saw it more graphically: The Staff Correspondent of the (more neutral) British-owned daily, *The Statesman*, from New Delhi, had this to report.

STREAM OF REFUGEES ON
FEROZEPORE–LAHORE
ROAD : HARROWING TALES

"Lahore, August 20.—A 50-mile car journey from Ferozepore to Lahore today brought home to me the extent of the tragedy now being enacted in the two Punjabs.

"I alighted from the Frontier Mail at Ferozepore, now running via Bhatinda to find that troops had occupied the station. The platform, I was told, was the scene of a clash yesterday. Starting from the station, trouble spread to the cantonment. Similar happenings are reported from the nearby town of Moga and many villages in that tehsil. The area between Ferzepore and Faridkot is equally disturbed.

"I had hardly made my way out of the cantonment into the countryside beyond when another aspect of the problem revealed itself. Villagers, men, women and children from the green fields around were converging on the road to Pakistan. Its boundaries lay four miles away. One end of the heavily guarded Sutlej bridge is in India and the other in the Muslim Dominion.

"They were refugees. They had just turned their backs on the country in which they had lived and worked for generations.

"Some women had babes in arms, I saw others with trunks on their heads—unbelievably heavy trunks. Men were carrying ploughs and driving their cattle. They were all following the caravan of bullock-carts heavily laden with beds and beddings. Their expressions were as sad as their future was uncertain. I did not see a single smile in the two-mile-long procession of refugees."[15]

Another report in the same newspaper carried the headline:

150,000 REFUGEES CROSS
INDIAN BORDER IN
FOUR DAYS

The report's opening paragraph said:

"Five foot-columns of non-Muslim-refugees totalling more than 150,000, have crossed the Indian border from West Punjab in the last four days, said a military spokesman in Delhi on Tuesday. Details of the strength of these convoys are as follows: Column 10 — 20,000; Columns 11, 12 and 13 — 30,000 each; and Column 14 — 40,000. Column 15 — 30,000 — which has passed Balloki headworks, is also on its way to Khem Karan."[16]

Such was the staggering scale of transfer of population which bedevilled the people of the two countries.

Two years on, it was the turn of the inmates of the Lahore Pagal Khana (mental asylum) to be put through Operation Population Exchange.

In his masterly critique of this exchange in his short story titled *Toba Tek Singh*, Urdu novelist Sadat Hasan Manto delivers his verdict on this operation of monumental lunacy through the utterances of the principal pagal (asylum inmate), also named Toba Tek Singh. Like Shakespeare's Fool in *King Lear* and Mercutio in *Romeo and Juliet*, Manto's pagal pronounces his judgement on this population exchange business with the ringing refrain in Punjabi: Dhur Phite Moonh (Shame on everybody or Plague on both your sides).[16] Toba ends his life with an almighty scream and a crashing fall on the "No Man's Land" between the two countries.[17]

Notes

1. Reuter report in *The Statesman*, New Delhi.

2. *Ibid*, 4 August 1947.

3. *Ibid*, 11 August 1947.

4. Appendix VI.

5. Appendix VII.

6. *The Statesman*, New Delhi, 14 July 1947.

7. Khosla G.D., *Stern Reckoning*, p. 104 (OUP).

8. Tuker Lt. Gen., *While Memory Serves*, p. 442.

9. Khosla G.D. *Stern Reckoning*, p. 124 (OUP).

10. *Ibid*, p. 125.

11. Singh Kirpal, *Partition of Punjab*, pp. 692–93 (Punjabi University, Patiala).

12. Khosla G.D. *Stern Reckoning*, p. 126.

13. Rees Major General T.W., Chief of the Punjab Boundary Force, Rees Report.

14. Campbell-Johnson Alan, *Mission with Mountbatten*, p. 200-201.

15. *The Statesman*, 12 August 1947.

16. *Ibid*, 15 October, 1947.

17. Manto Sadat Hassan, *Toba Tek Singh*, Appendix IX.

Faqir Chand Vohra

13

From Attock to Wah Camp
A family's Journey

Attock city, christened Campbellpore during the British Raj and back to its original name after the Raj, is where the story begins. Centuries earlier Attock and its surrounding region had been the stomping ground of adventurers like Alexander the Great (circa 327 BC) and Indian Emperors before and after him. It was here that a centre of learning or university like Taxila grew and flourished for nearly 1,500 years, along with Nalanda and Patliputra in eastern India, before fading away around 12th to 13th centuries AD just when Oxford and Cambridge were starting on their glorious journey. Attock Fort, which looks over the mighty Indus River was built much later by the Mughal Emperor Akbar (completed about 1583 AD) when Queen Elizabeth the First reigned over the British Isles.

Onwards to the British Raj and its finale. It's mid-August 1947, nearly 10 days on either side of the 15th August time-line, the partition or independence day of India as also the birth of Pakistan. The journey is short, just about 30 miles, but perilous. The witness, aged 13, is stumbling through the traumatic daze enveloping his family. They are, among countless others, on the move, more accurately on a politically forced march. Here is what the 13-year-old Sat Paul has to tell of that fateful run from pillar to unknown post.

Attock Fort and city on the border of the North West Frontier Province and the Punjab province of undivided India, is where the family's journey starts. High on the raised ground is Attock Fort, while Attock Railway Station is the strategic tri-junction from where branch lines spread out slightly south eastwards to Rawalpindi and the rest of the sub-continent, westward to the Frontier province on the road to Peshawar, Khyber Pass and Afghanistan, and slightly southwest to the Punjab districts of Mianwali and Dera Ismail Khan.

Dotted along the stretch between Attock and Rawalpindi were some of the historic towns and villages with minority community concentrations. Panja Sahib, the Sikh holy shrine with railway station at Hasan Abdal, was and is only a short few miles from Rawalpindi, the divisional headquarters and military hub on whose outskirts lies Islamabad, the modern new capital of Pakistan. Attock has flowered into a tourist spot after the British Raj while old Wah camp has been turned into a formidable military cantonment and a nuclear weapons base.

Much before the frenetic August 1947 days, the Sikh community had come under attack by the Muslim (League) National Guards, the militia raised over the previous few months. The Sikhs and Hindus who formed a minority of about 10 per cent in a predominantly Muslim region, had to leave their homesteads in villages and small towns and take shelter in bigger cities like Rawalpindi for safety. The immediate neighbourhood of Rawalpindi itself was one of the first conurbations after Multan to witness the killing of Sikhs and Hindus in the first fortnight of March 1947 within days of the resignation of the anti-Muslim League Unionist Prime Minister of Punjab, Sir Khizar Hayat Khan Tiwana, on 2nd March. By about 8th March some of the Hindus and Sikhs were being evacuated from rural areas of Attock, Mianwali and Gujarat districts of the province to somewhat safer areas. It's a matter of history that top British officers of the district — Commissioner, Deputy Commissioner and Director-General of Police — failed to prevent the massacre of Sikhs in Rawalpindi area.

The Attock–Rawalpindi stretch was also the region where lay the home village (Haryal) of Sikh leader Master Tara Singh. He had brandished his naked Kirpan, the traditional short sword kept on a strap by the Sikh faithful, and shouted slogans like "Pakistan Murdabad (Death to Pakistan)" outside the Punjab Legislative Assembly in Lahore on 3rd March which contributed in no small measure to the killings of Sikhs and Hindus by the Muslim League militants.

It was on the same Attock–Rawalpindi rail stretch that teenager Sat Paul had seen turban wearing, bearded Sikh passengers being picked off by Muslim fanatics, while Hindu passengers like himself who wore no turbans escaped because they looked no different from Muslims.

By mid-August, Sikhs and Hindus were beginning to be evacuated from Attock town's outlying areas. From Attock heights, overlooking the mighty river Sindh and across the bridge could be seen the civilian town of Khairabad (Blessed Town). Sikhs and Hindus were timely evacuated from there to safety by Frontier Gandhi Khan Abdul Ghaffar Khan's Khudai Khidmatgars (Servants of God) also known as Surkhposh or Red Shirts. Empty houses were soon set on fire by the bands of the Muslim (League) National Guards and Khairabad presented an eerie sight from Attock Fort across the river bridge.

Mobs led by Muslim National Guards, who torched Khairabad, also heralded the birth of the new country with slogans like Pakistan Zindabad (Long live Pakistan). They were soon to surround the railway colony of Attock where Sat Paul's father, Faqir Chand Vohra, was the Station Master.

Station Master Faqir Chand was a fine cricketer, a strong swimmer and a popular personality of the little town. Confident of his place in the town, he was smoking his hookah (hubble bubble) in the courtyard of his bungalow one August evening when he heard the din of a slogan shouting mob in the neighbourhood.

Unnerved by all that noise he thought that the mob would go away after shouting a few slogans and even firing the odd shot in the air. He was confident that they won't touch the house of a popular man like him. After all he had spent the best part of his life among them and in the Attock region. He had no fear. He belonged there as much as any Muslim citizen. He had no thought of quitting the land of his birth or going over to Hindustan or new India. He didn't even speak Hindustani, the Urdu-Hindi language of far-off Delhi and the United Provinces, though he could understand it.

Faqir Chand had officially opted for service in the newly christened country of Pakistan, confident that life would continue as earlier under the new Muslim majority rulers. Hadn't Quaid-e-Azam Mohammad Ali Jinnah, the founder of Pakistan, himself just promised safety and equality for all citizens of the new nation? Hadn't he in his famous address to the Constituent Assembly in Karachi on 11th August declared: "You are free; you are free to go to your temples, you are free to go to your mosques or to any other place of worship in the State of Pakistan. You may belong to any religion or caste or creed, that has nothing to do with the fundamental principle that we are all citizens and equal citizens of one State. Now I think we should keep that in front of us our ideal, and you will find that in course of time Hindus will cease to be Hindus and Muslims will cease to be Muslims, not in the religious sense, because that is the personal faith of each individual, but in the political sense, as citizens of the State"?

But Faqir Chand hadn't reckoned with the wind of change that had swept the landmass of Punjab from the borders of NWFP in the west to Gurgaon in the east on the outskirts of New Delhi, the capital of united India. His old Muslim friends and colleagues hadn't turned enemies but long time colleagues and acquaintances had become powerless before the surging Muslim National Guards (the counterparts of the firebrand Hindu RSS militia).

A mob of non-locals from outlying areas (no badges or banners) shouting slogans and beating a drum had actually gathered outside his house. The adjoining quarters occupied by three Assistant Station Masters had just been looted. Some inmates who offered some resistance had been injured, as he was to find later. But Faqir Chand and his wife Budh Wati, who had five young boys including Sat Paul and two little girls with them, kept their cool and offered no resistance and let the looters take away what they wanted.

The family had almost escaped unscathed physically when a shot fired by one of the departing mob hit Faqir Chand in his left thigh which left him bleeding profusely. A home spun bandage by wife Budh Wati stopped the bleeding until the next morning when Muslim staff colleagues who came to know of the incident took him to the local hospital.

Younger son Tilak Raj, barely 11 years old, accompanied his Baooji, as Faqir Chand was called by his children, to the hospital. He kept bedside vigil night and day looking after his father and calling nurses or meeting doctors on their rounds.

As long days and longer nights fraught with fear rolled by, the time arrived when the Attock garrison's new Muslim Commanding Officer felt that he could no longer ensure the safety of the minority community because Muslim refugees from new India's East Punjab were beginning to arrive in Pakistan with their own harrowing tales, sharply raising the communal temperature.

A fine officer and a truly noble specimen of humanity, the Commanding Officer did not let his own personal loss come in the way of helping others. His own family members had been butchered by Hindu and Sikh fanatics on the other side of the border at Jullunder in East Punjab. Almost apologetically he suggested that Station Master Faqir Chand's family along with other Hindu and Sikh railway staff and their families in Attock be moved to Wah refugee camp, bursting at the seams with about 10,000 young and old bodies and souls.

The injured Station Master was also moved from Campbellpore to Wah Camp make-shift hospital where his condition started deteriorating rather fast as the bullet lodged in his thigh had not been removed at Campbellpore. The poison had spread, leading to "jaw locking" also known as the "tetanus" condition. Baooji's life was ebbing away. His dying words to his son Sat Paul were: "I am going now. Your brothers (three of the older sons who were already on the other side of the border in India) will take care of you."

At Wah Camp hospital Faqir Chand had several visitors from Attock station, old Muslim colleagues who had come to know of his injury. One of them was the chief of the telephones wing of the station. He had brought with him two of the Station Master's loved possessions. One was his beloved hookah or hubble bubble, complete with its smoking pipe, the tobacco container or chillum, the small earthen vase with a hole at the bottom linked to the water bowl at the base from which the smoke comes filtered. The hookah was the community pipe for Faqir Chand and his inner circle of friends and colleagues, Hindus as well as Muslims who would gather for the odd puff and social banter or daily gossip.

The other pride possession which the old Muslim colleague brought was the Station Master's white turban, the lightly starched headgear with its toora (crest) rising at an angle into the air. The turban called Pug or Pugree in Punjabi is symbolic of a man's pride and social status. It's something which money can't buy, though the yards of cloth can be bought at any shop. It signifies the social esteem in which one is held and the respect which one commands among one's community.

It was a touching presentation to the bullet-ridden Station Master Faqir Chand Vohra delivered at the hospital in Wah Camp from where Sikh and Hindu refugees were to make their fateful journey to new India. Thousands of them, including Faqir Chand's wife, five younger sons and two little daughters, somehow made that journey through bloodied trains and stations across the plains of Punjab. But Faqir Chand, the head of the family, never made it.

Instead of making the journey to India, Faqir Chand breathed his last at Wah Camp in his beloved old India or new Pakistan. A funeral pyre had to be arranged and wood had to be gathered for his cremation in the scarcity ridden and tension charged atmosphere at Wah Camp where survival of the living was as difficult than cremation of the dead. But with dogged courage and wounded hearts Sat Paul, his mother Budh Wati and his six younger siblings watched Baooji's body cremated according to the Hindu rites with flames rising high unto the heavens.

APPENDIX I

Statement made by Prime Minister Attlee in the House of Commons, 20 February, 1947

INDIAN POLICY

1. It has long been the policy of successive British Governments to work towards the realisation of self-government in India. In pursuance of this policy, an increasing measure of responsibility has been devolved on Indians, and today the civil administration and the Indian Armed Forces rely to a very large extent on Indian civilians and officers. In the constitutional field, the Acts of 1919 and 1935 passed by the British Parliament each represented a substantial transfer of political power. In 1940 the Coalition Government recognised the principle that Indians should themselves frame a new constitution for a fully autonomous India, and in the Offer of 1942 they invited them to set up a Constituent Assembly for this purpose as soon as the war was over.

2. His Majesty's Government believe this policy to have been right and in accordance with sound democratic principles. Since they came into office, they have done their utmost to carry it forward to its fulfilment. The declaration of the Prime Minister of 15 March last, which met with general approval in Parliament and the country, made it clear that it was for the Indian people themselves to choose their future status and constitution and that in the opinion of His Majesty's Government the time had come for responsibility for the government of India to pass into Indian hands.

3. The Cabinet Mission which was sent to India last year spent over three months in consultation with Indian leaders in order to help them to agree upon a method for determining the future constitution of India, so that the transfer of power might be smoothly and rapidly effected. It was only when it seemed clear, that without some initiative from the Cabinet Mission, agreement was unlikely to be reached that they put forward proposals themselves.

4. These proposals, made public in May last, envisaged that the future constitution of India should be settled by Constituent Assembly composed in the manner suggested therein, of representatives of all communities and interests in British India and of the Indian States.

5. Since the return of the Mission, and interim Government has been set up at the Centre composed of the political leaders of the major communities, exercising wide powers within the existing constitution. In all the provinces Indian governments responsible to legislatures are in office.

6. It is with great regret that His Majesty's Government find that there are still differences among Indian parties which are preventing the Constitution Assembly from functioning as it was intended that it should. It is of the essence of the plan that the Assembly should be fully representative.

7. His Majesty's Government desire to hand over their responsibility to authorities established by the constitution approved by all parties in India in accordance with the Cabinet Mission plan. But unfortunately there is at present no clear prospect that such authorities will emerge. The present state of uncertainty is fraught with danger and cannot be indefinitely prolonged. His Majesty's Government wish to make it clear that it is their definite intention to take the necessary steps to effect the transference of power to responsible Indian hands by a date not later than June 1948.

8. This great sub-continent now containing over four hundred million people has for the last century enjoyed peace and security as a part of the British Commonwealth and Empire. Continued peace and security are more than ever necessary today if the full responsibilities of economic

development are to be realised and a higher standard of life attained by the Indian people.

9. His Majesty's Government are anxious to hand over their responsibilities to a Government which, resting on the sure foundation of the support of the people, is capable of maintaining peace and administering India with justice and efficiency. It is therefore essential that all parties should sink their differences in order that they may be ready to shoulder the great responsibilities which will come upon them next year.

10. After months of hard work by the Cabinet Mission a great measure of agreement was obtained as to the method by which a constitution should be worked out. This was embodied in their statements of May last. His Majesty's Government there agreed to recommend to Parliament a constitution worked out in accordance with the proposals made therein by a fully representative Constituent Assembly. But if it should appear that such a constitution will not have been worked out by a fully representative Assembly before the time mentioned in paragraph 7, His Majesty's Government will have to consider to whom the powers of the central Government in British India should be handed over, on the due date, whether as a whole to some form of central Government for British India, or in some areas to the existing provincial Governments, or in such other way as may seem most reasonable and in the best interests of the Indian people.

11. Although the final transfer of authority may not take place until June 1948, preparatory measures must be put in hand in advance. It is important that the efficiency of the civil administration should be maintained and that the defence of India should be fully provided for. But inevitably, as the process of transfer proceeds, it will become progressively more difficult to carry out to the letter all the provisions of the Government of India Act, 1935. Legislation will be introduced in due course to give effect to the final transfer of power.

12. In regard to the Indian States, as was explicitly stated by the Cabinet Mission, His Majesty's Government do not intend to hand over their powers

and obligations under paramountcy to any Government of British India. It is not intended to bring paramountcy, as a system, to a conclusion earlier than the date of the final transfer of power, but it is contemplated that for the intervening period the relations of the Crown with individual States may be adjusted by agreement.

13. His Majesty's Government will negotiate agreements in regard to matters arising out of the transfer of power with representatives of those to whom they propose to transfer power.

14. His Majesty's Government believe that British commercial and industrial interests in India can look forward to a fair field for their enterprise under the new conditions. The commercial connection between India and the United Kingdom has been long and friendly and will continue to be to their mutual advantage.

15. His Majesty's Government cannot conclude this Statement without expressing on behalf of the people of this country their goodwill and good wishes towards the people of India as they go forward to this final stage in their achievement of self-government. It will be the wish of everyone in these islands that notwithstanding constitutional changes, the association of the British and Indian peoples should not be brought to an end; and they will wish to continue to do all that is in their power to further the well-being of India.

CHANGE OF VICEROY

The House will wish to know of an announcement which is being made public today. Field Marshal the Right Honorable Viscount Wavell was appointed Viceroy in 1943, after having held high military command in the Middle East, South-East Asia and India with notable distinction since the beginning of the war. It was agreed that this should be a wartime appointment. Lord Wavell has discharged this high office during this very difficult period with devotion and high sense of duty. It has, however, seemed that the opening of a new and final phase in India is an appropriate time to terminate this war appointment. His Majesty has been pleased to approve, as successor to Lord Wavell, the appointment of Admiral the Viscount Mountbatten, who will be entrusted with the task of transferring to Indian hands responsibility for the government of British India in a manner that will best ensure the future happiness and prosperity of India. The change of office will take place during March. The House will be glad to hear that His Majesty has been pleased to approve the conferment of an earldom on Viscount Wavell.

Appendix II

The Prime Minister's letter of instructions to Lord Mountabatten

10 Downing Street, Whitehall.

March 1947

My dear Mountbatten,

The statement which was issued at the time of the announcement of your appointment sets out the policy of the Government and the principles in accordance with which the transfer of power to Indian hands should be effected.

My colleagues of the Cabinet Mission and I have discussed with you the general lines of your approach to the problems which will confront you in India. It will, I think, be useful to you to have on record the salient points which you should have in mind in dealing with the situation. I have, therefore, set them down here.

It is the definite objective of His Majesty's Government to obtain a unitary Government for British India and the Indian States, if possible within the British Commonwealth, through the medium of a Constituent Assembly, set up and run in accordance with the Cabinet Mission's plan, and you should do the utmost in your power to persuade all Parties to work together to this end, and advise His Majesty's Government, in the light of developments, as to the steps that will have to be taken.

Since, however, this plan can only become operative in respect of British India by agreement between the major Parties, there can be no question of compelling either major Party to accept it.

If by 1st October you consider that there is no prospect of reaching a settlement on the basis of a unitary Government for British India, either with or without the co-operation of the Indian States, you should report to His Majesty's Government on the steps which you consider should be taken for the handing over of power on the due date.

It is, of course, important that the Indian States should adjust their relations with the authorities to whom it is intended to hand over power in British India; but as was explicitly stated by the Cabinet Mission, His Majesty's Government do not intend to hand over their powers and obligations under paramountcy to any successor Government. It is not intended to bring paramountcy as a system to a conclusion, earlier than the date of the final transfer of power, but you are authorised, at such times as you think appropriate, to enter into negotiations with individual States for adjusting their relations with the Crown.

You will do your best to persuade the rulers of any Indian States in which political progress has been slow to progress rapidly towards some form of more democratic government in their States. You will also aid and assist the States in coming to fair and just arrangements with the leaders of British India as to their future relationships.

The date fixed for the transfer of power is a flexible one to within one month; but you should aim at 1st June, 1948, as the effective date for the transfer of power.

In your relations with the Interim Government you will be guided by the general terms of the Viceroy's letter of 30th May, 1946, to the President of the Congress Party, and of the statement made by the Secretary of State for India in the House of Lords on 13th March 1947. These statements made it clear that, while the Interim Government would not have the same powers as a Dominion Government, His Majesty's Government would treat the Interim Government with the same consultation and consideration as a Dominion Government, and give it the greatest possible freedom in the day to day exercise of the administration of the country.

It is essential that there should be the fullest co-operation with the Indian leaders in all steps that are taken as to the withdrawal of British power so that the process may go forward as smoothly as possible.

The keynote of your administration should therefore be the closest co-operation with the Indians and you should make it clear to the whole of the Secretary of State's Services that this is so, and that it is their duty to their countries to work to this end.

You should take every opportunity of stressing the importance of ensuring that the transfer of power is effected with full regard to the defence requirements of India. In the first place you will impress upon the Indian leaders the great importance of avoiding any breach in the continuity of the Indian Army and of maintaining the organisation of defence on an all Indian basis. Secondly, you will point out the need for continued collaboration in the security of the Indian Ocean area for which provision might be made in an agreement between the two countries. At a suitable date His Majesty's Government would be ready to send military and other experts to India to assist in discussing the terms of such an agreement.

You will no doubt inform Provincial Governors of the substance of this letter.

Yours sincerely,
(signed) CR ATTLEE

Admiral the Right Hon
the Viscount Mountbatten of Burma,
KG, GCSI, GCIE, GCVO, KCB, DSO

APPENDIX III

Statement made by His Majesty's Government, 3 June 1947

INTRODUCTION

1. On 20 February 1947, His Majesty's Government announced their intention of transferring power in British India to Indian hands by June 1948. His Majesty's Government had hoped that it would be possible for the major parties to co-operate in the working-out of the Cabinet Mission Plan of 16 May 1946, and evolve for India a constitution acceptable to all concerned. This hope has not been fulfilled.

2. The Majority of the representatives of the provinces of Madras, Bombay, the United Provinces, Bihar, Central Provinces and Berar, Assam, Orissa and the North-West Frontier Province, and the representatives of Delhi, Ajmer–Merwara and Coorg have already made progress in the task of evolving a new constitution. On the other hand, the Muslim League Party, including in it a majority of the representatives of British Baluchistan, has decided not to participate in the Constituent Assembly.

3. It has always been the desire of His Majesty's Government that power should be transferred in accordance with the wishes of the Indian people themselves. This tasks would have been greatly facilitated if there had been agreement among the Indian political parties. In the absence of such agreement, the task of devising a method by which the wishes of the Indian people can be ascertained has devolved upon His Majesty's Government.

After full consultation with political leaders in India, His Majesty's Government have decided to adopt for this purpose the plan set out below. His Majesty's government wish to make it clear that they have no intention of attempting to frame any ultimate constitution for India; this is a matter for the Indians themselves. Nor is there anything in this plan to preclude negotiations between communities for a united India.

THE ISSUES TO BE DECIDED

4. It is not the intention of His Majesty's government to interrupt the work of the existing Constituent Assembly. Now that provision is made for certain provinces specified below, His Majesty's Government trust that, as a consequence of this announcement, the Muslim League representatives of those provinces, a majority of whose representatives are already participating in it, will now take their due share in its labours. At the same time, it is clear that any constitution framed by this Assembly cannot apply to those parts of the country which are unwilling to accept it. His Majesty's Government are satisfied that the procedure outlined below embodies the best practical method of ascertaining the wishes of the people of such areas on the issue whether their constitution is to be framed : –

(a) in the existing Constituent Assembly ; or

(b) in a new and separate Constituent Assembly consisting of the representatives of those areas which decide not to participate in the existing Constituent Assembly.

When this has been done, it will be possible to determine the authority or authorities to whom power should be transferred.

BENGAL AND THE PUNJAB

5. The provincial Legislative Assemblies of Bengal and the Punjab (excluding the European members) will, therefore, each be asked to meet in two parts, one representing the Muslim-majority districts and the other rest of the Province. For the purpose of determining the population of districts, the 1941 census figures will be taken as authoritative. The Muslim-majority districts in

these two provinces are set out in the Appendix to Announcement.

6. The members of the two parts of each Legislative Assembly sitting separately will be empowered to vote whether or not the Province should be partitioned. If a simple majority of either part decides in favour of partition, division will take place and arrangements will be made accordingly.

7. Before the question as to the partition is decided, it is desirable that the representatives of each part should know in advance which Constituent Assembly the Province as a whole would join in the event of the two parts subsequently deciding to remain united. Therefore, if any member of either Legislative Assembly so demands, there shall be held a meeting of all members of the Legislative Assembly (other than Europeans) at which a decision will be taken on the issue as to which Constituent Assembly the Province as a whole would join if it were decided by the two parts to remain united.

8. In the event of partition being decided upon, each part of the Legislative Assembly will, on behalf of the areas they represent, decide which of the alternatives in paragraph 4 above to adopt.

9. For the immediate purpose of deciding on the issue of partition, the members of the Legislative Assemblies of Bengal and the Punjab will sit in two parts according to Muslim-majority districts (as laid down in the Appendix) and non-Muslim majority districts. This is only a preliminary step of a purely temporary nature, as it is evident that for the purposes of a final partition of these provinces a detailed investigation of boundary questions will be needed; and, as soon as a decision involving partition has been taken for either province, a Boundary Commission will be set up by the Governor-General, the membership and terms of reference of which will be settled in consultation with those concerned. It will be instructed to demarcate the boundaries of the two part of the Punjab on the basis of ascertaining the contiguous majority areas of Muslims and non-Muslims. It will also be instructed to take into account other factors. Similar instructions will be given to the Bengal Boundary Commission. Until the report of a

Boundary Commission has been put into effect, the provisional boundaries indicated in the Appendix will be used.

SIND

10. The Legislative Assembly of Sind (excluding the European members) will at a special meeting also take its own decision on the alternatives in paragraph 4 above.

NORTH-WEST FRONTIER PROVINCE

11. The position of the North-West Frontier Province is exceptional. Two of the three representatives of this Province are already participating in the existing Constituent Assembly. But it is clear, in view of its geographical situation, and other considerations, that if the whole or any part of the Punjab decides not to join the existing Constituent Assembly, it will be necessary to give the Non-West Frontier Province an opportunity to reconsider its position. Accordingly, in such an event, a referendum will be made to the electors of the present Legislative Assembly in the North-West Frontier Province to choose which of the alternatives mentioned in paragraph 4 above they wish to adopt. The referendum will be held under the aegis of the Governor-General and in consultation with the provincial Government.

BRITISH BALUCHISTAN

12. British Baluchistan has elected a member, but he has not taken his seat in the existing Constituent Assembly. In view of its geographical situation, this Province will also be given an opportunity to reconsider its position and to choose which of the alternatives in paragraph 4 above to adopt. His Excellency the Governor–General is examining how this can most appropriately be done.

ASSAM

13. Though Assam is predominantly a non-Muslim province, the district of Sylhet which is contiguous to Bengal is predominantly Muslim. There has been a demand that, in the event of the partition of Bengal, Sylhet should be amalgamated with the Muslim part of Bengal. Accordingly, if it

is decided that Bengal should be partitioned, a referendum will be held in Sylhet district under the aegis of the Governor-General and in consultation with the Assam Provincial Government to decide whether the district of Sylhet should continue to form part of the Assam Province or should be amalgamated with the new Province of Eastern Bengal, if that Province agrees. If the referendum results in favour of amalgamation with Eastern Bengal, a Boundary Commission with terms of reference similar to those for the Punjab and Bengal will be set up to demarcate the Muslim majority areas of Sylhet district and contiguous Muslim-majority areas of adjoining districts, which will then be transferred to Eastern Bengal. The rest of the Assam Province will in any case continue to participate in the proceedings of the existing Constituent Assembly.

REPRESENTATION IN CONSTITUENT ASSEMBLIES

14. If it is decided that Bengal and the Punjab should be partitioned, it will be necessary to hold fresh elections to choose their representatives on the scale of one for every million of population according to the principle contained in the Cabinet Mission Plan of 16 May 1946. Similar elections will also have to be held for Sylhet in the event of it being decided that this district should form part of East Bengal. The number of representatives of which each area would be entitled is as follows :—

Province	General	Muslims	Sikhs	Total
Sylhet District	1	2	Nil	3
West Bengal	15	4	Nil	19
East Bengal	12	29	Nil	41
West Punjab	3	12	2	17
East Punjab	6	4	2	12

15. In accordance with the mandates given to them, the representatives of the various areas will either join the existing Constituent Assembly or form the new Constituent Assembly.

ADMINISTRATIVE MATTERS

16. Negotiations will have to be initiated as soon as possible on the administrative consequences of any partition that may have been decided upon :

(a) Between the representatives of the respective successor authorities or about all subjects now dealt with by the central Government, including defence, finance and communications.

(b) Between different successor authorities and His Majesty's Government for treaties in regard to matters arising out of the transfer of power.

(c) In the case of provinces that may be partitioned, as to the administration of all provincial subjects such as the division of assets and liabilities, the police and other services, the High Courts, provincial institutions, etc.

THE TRIBES OF THE NORTH-WEST FRONTIER

17. Agreements with tribes of the North-West Frontier of India will have to be negotiated by the appropriate successor authority.

THE STATES

18. His Majesty's Government wish to make it clear that the decisions announced above relate only to British India and that their policy towards Indian States contained in the Cabinet Mission Memorandum of 12 May 1946 remains unchanged.

NECESSITY FOR SPEED

19. In order that successor authorities may have time to prepare themselves to take over power, it is important that all the above processes should be completed as quickly as possible. To avoid delay, the different provinces or parts of provinces will proceed independently as far as practicable within the conditions of this Plan. The existing Constituent Assembly and the new Constituent Assembly (if formed) will proceed to frame constitutions for their respective territories: they will of course be free to frame their own rules.

IMMEIDATE TRANSFER OF POWER

20. The major political parties have repeatedly emphasized their desire that there should be the earliest possible transfer of power in India. With this desire His Majesty's Government are in full sympathy, and they are willing to anticipate the date of June 1948, for the handing over of power by the setting up of an independent Indian Government or Governments at an even earlier date. Accordingly, as the most expeditious, and indeed the only practicable way of meeting this desire, His Majesty's Government propose to introduce legislation during the current session for the transfer of power this year on a Dominion Status basis to one or two successor authorities according to the decision taken as a result of this announcement. This will be without prejudice to the right of the Indian Constituent Assemblies to decide in due course whether or not the part of India in respect of which they have authority will remain within the British Commonwealth.

FURTHER ANNOUNCEMENTS BY GOVERNOR-GENERAL

21. His Excellency the Governor-General will from time to time make such further announcements as may be necessary in regard to procedure or any other matters for carrying out the above arrangements.

APPENDIX

THE MUSLIM-MAJORITY DISTRICTS OF THE PUNJAB AND BENGAL ACCORDING TO THE 1941 CENSUS

1. THE PUNJAB

Lahore Division — Gujranwal, Gurdaspur, Lahore, Sheikhupura, Sialkot, Rawalpindi *Division* — Attock, Gujrat, Jhelum, Mianwali, Rawalpindi, Shahapur. *Multan Division* — Dera Ghazi Khan, Jhang, Lyallpur, Montgomery, Multan, Muzaffargarh.

2. BENGAL

Chittagong Division — Chittagong, Noakhali, Tippera.

Dacca Division — Bakerganj, Dacca, Faridpur, Mymensingh.

Presidency Division — Jessore, Murshidabad, Nadia.

Rajshahi Division — Bogra, Dinajpur, Malda, Pabna, Rajshahi, Rangpur.

Appendix IV

Pandit Nehru's 3 June 1947 speech on All India Radio, New Delhi

Nearly nine months ago, soon after my assumption of office, I spoke to you from this place. I told you then that we were on the march and the goal had still to be reached. There were many difficulties and obstacles on the way and our journey's end may not be near, for that end was not the assumption of office in the Government of India but the achievement of full independence for India and the establishment of a cooperative commonwealth in which all would have equal shares in opportunity and in all things that give meaning and value to life.

Nine months have passed, months of sore trial and difficulty, of anxiety and sometimes even of heartbreak. Yet looking back at this period with its suffering and sorrow for our people there is much which has been achieved— India has advanced nationally and internationally, and is respected today in the councils of the world. In the domestic sphere something substantial has been achieved, though the burden on the common man still continues to be terribly heavy and millions lack food and cloth and other necessities of life. Several development schemes are nearly ready and yet it is true that most of our dreams about the brave things we are going to accomplish have still to be realised. You know well difficulties which the country had to face, economic, political and communal. These months have been full of tragedy for millions and the burden on those who have the governance of the country in their hands has been great indeed.

My mind is heavy with the thought of the sufferings of our people in the areas of disturbance — the thousands who are dead and those, especially our womenfolk, who have suffered agony worse than death. To their families and to the innumerable people who have been uprooted from their homes and rendered destitute, I offer my deepest sympathy and assurance that we shall do all in our power to bring relief. We must ensure that such tragedies do not recur.

Today, I am speaking to you on another historic occasion when a vital change affecting the future of India is proposed. You have just heard an announcement on behalf of the British government. This announcement lays down a procedure for self-determination in certain areas of India. It envisages, on the one hand, the possibility of these areas seceding from India. On the other, it promises a big advance towards complete independence. Such a big change must have the full concurrence of the people, for it must always be remembered that the future of India can only be decided by the people of India, and not by any outside authority, however friendly. These proposals will be placed soon before the representative assemblies of the people for consideration. But meanwhile, the sands of time run out and decisions cannot await the normal course of events. So while we must necessarily abide by what the people finally decide, we had to come to certain decisions ourselves and to recommend them to the people for acceptance. We have, therefore, decided to accept these proposals and to recommend to our larger committees that they do likewise.

It is with no joy in my heart that I commend these proposals to you, though I have no doubt in my mind that this is the right course. For generations we have dreamt and struggled for a free, independent and united India. The proposal to allow certain parts to secede if they so wish is painful for any of us to contemplate. Nevertheless, I am convinced that our present decision is the right one even from the larger viewpoint. The united India that we have laboured for was not one of compulsion and of coercion but a free and willing association of a free people. In this way we shall reach that united India sooner than otherwise, and then she will have a stronger and more secure foundation.

We are little men serving a great cause, but because the cause is great, something of that greatness falls upon us also. Mighty forces are at work in the world today and I have no doubt that we are ushering in a period of greatness for India. The India of yesteryears, its history and tradition, the India in our minds and hearts, cannot change.

With a firm faith in our future I appeal to you to cooperate in the great task ahead and to march together to the haven of freedom for all in India. Jai Hind !

Appendix V

Mr Jinnah's 3 June 1947 speech on All India Radio, New Delhi.

I am glad that I am afforded the opportunity to speak to you directly via radio from Delhi. This is the first time, I believe, that a non-official has been given an opportunity to address the peoples through the medium of this powerful instrument, on political matters. It augurs well. I hope I shall have greater facilities in future to enable me to voice my views and opinion which would reach you directly rather than in the cold print of newspapers.

The statement of His Majesty's government embodying the plan for the transfer of power to the people of India has already been broadcast and will be released to the press to be published in India and abroad tomorrow morning. With these outlines of the plan, it is for us to give to our most earnest consideration. We have to examine it coolly, calmly and dispassionately. We must remember that we have to take momentous decisions and handle grave issues facing us in the solution of the complex political problem of this great subcontinent inhabited by four hundred millions of people. The world has no parallel for the most onerous and difficult task which we have to perform. Great responsibilities lie particularly on the shoulders of Indian leaders. Therefore, we must galvanise and concentrate all our energies, to see that the transfer of power is effected in a peaceful and orderly manner.

I must earnestly appeal to every community and particularly to Muslim India to maintain peace and order.

We must examine the plan, its letter and spirit, and come to our conclusions and take our decisions. I pray to God that at this critical moment He may guide us and enable us to discharge our responsibilities in a wise and statesmanlike manner in regard to the plan as a whole. It is clear that the plan does not meet, in some important respects, our point of view; and we cannot say or feel that we are satisfied or agree with some of the matters dealt with by the plan.

It is for us now to consider whether the plan as presented to us by His Majesty's government should be accepted by us as a compromise or a settlement. On this point I do not wish to prejudge the decisions of the council of the All-India Muslim League which has been summoned to meet on Monday, 9 June. The final decision can only be taken by that council according to our constitution, precedents and practice. But so far as I have been able to gather, on the whole I find the reaction in the Muslim League circles in Delhi quite hopeful. The plan, has got to be very carefully examined in its pros and cons in great detail before a final decision can be taken. But I must say that I feel that the viceroy has battled against various forces very bravely. The impression that he has left on my mind is that he was actuated by a high sense of fairness and impartiality. It is up to us now to make his task less difficult and help him as far as possible in order that he may fulfil his mission of transferring power to the people of India in a peaceful and orderly manner.

The plan that has been broadcast makes it quite clear in paragraph eleven that a referendum will be made to the electorates of the present Legislative Assembly in the North-West Frontier Province who will choose which of the two alternatives in paragraph four they wish to adopt. The referendum will be held under the aegis of the governor general in consultation with the provincial government. Hence, it is clear that the verdict and the mandate of the people of the Frontier Province will be obtained as to whether they want to join the Pakistan Constituent Assembly or the Hindustan Constituent Assembly.

In these circumstances, I request the Provincial Muslim League of the Frontier to withdraw the movement of peaceful civil disobedience which they had been forced to resort to. I call upon all the leaders of the Muslim League and the Musalmans in general to organise our people to face this referendum with hope and courage. I feel confident that the people of the Frontier will give their verdict by a solid vote to join the Pakistan Constituent Assembly.

I cannot but express my appreciation of the sufferings and sacrifices made by all classes of Musalmans and particularly the great part the women of the Frontier played in the fight for our civil liberties. Without apportioning blame, and this is hardly the moment to do so, I deeply sympathise with all those who have suffered, those who died and those whose properties were subjected to destruction. I fervently hope that the Frontier will go through this referendum in a peaceful manner and it should be the anxiety of everyone to obtain a fair, free and true verdict of the people. Once again, I most earnestly appeal to all to maintain peace and order. Pakistan Zindabad!

Appendix VI

Mr Jinnah's Presidential Address to the Constituent Assembly of Pakistan, 11 August 1947

Mr. President,
Ladies and Gentlemen,

I cordially thank you, with the utmost sincerity, for the honour you have conferred upon me — the greatest honour that is possible for this Sovereign Assembly to confer — by electing me as your first President. I also thank those leaders who have spoken in appreciation of my services and their personal references to me. I sincerely hope that with your support and your co-operation we shall make this Constituent Assembly an example to the world. The Constituent Assembly has got two main functions to perform. The first is the very onerous and responsible task of framing our future Constitution of Pakistan and the second of functioning as a full and complete Sovereign body as the Federal Legislature of Pakistan. We have to do the best we can in adopting a provisional constitution for the Federal Legislature of Pakistan. You know really that not only we ourselves are wondering but, I think, the whole world is wondering at this unprecedented cyclonic revolution which has brought about the plan of creating and establishing two independent Sovereign Dominions in this sub-continent. As it is, it has been unprecedented; there is no parallel in the history of the world. This mighty sub-continent with all kinds of inhabitants has been brought under a plan which is titanic, unknown, unparalleled. And what is very important with regard to it is that we have achieved it peacefully and by means of an evolution of the greatest possible character.

Dealing with our first function in this Assembly, I cannot make any well considered pronouncement at this moment, but I shall say a few things as they occur to me. The first and the foremost thing that I would like to emphasise is this — remember that you are now a Sovereign Legislature body and you have got all the powers. It, therefore, places on you the gravest responsibility as to how you should take your decisions. The first observation that I would like to make is this: You will no doubt agree with me that the first duty of a Government is to maintain law and order, so that the life, property and religious beliefs of its subjects are full protected by the State.

The second thing that occurs to me is this: One of the biggest curses from which India is suffering — I do not say that other countries are free from it, but, I think, our condition is much worse — is bribery and corruption. That really is a poison. We must put that down with an iron hand and I hope that you will take adequate measures as soon as it is possible for this Assembly to do so.

Black-marketing is another curse. Well, I know that black-marketeers are frequently caught and punished. Judicial sentences are passed or sometimes fines only are imposed. Now you have to tackle this monster which today is a colossal crime against society, in our distressed conditions, when we constantly face shortage of food and other essential commodities of life. A citizen who does black-marketing commits, I think, a greater crime than the biggest and most grievous of crimes. These black-marketeers are really knowing, intelligent and ordinarily responsible people, and when they indulge in black-marketing, I think they ought to be very severely punished, because they undermine the entire system of control and regulation of food-stuffs and essential commodities, and cause wholesale starvation and want and even death.

The next thing that strikes me is this: Here again it is a legacy which has been passed on to us. Along with many other things, good and bad, has arrived this great evil — the evil of nepotism and jobbery. This evil must be crushed relentlessly. I want to make it quite clear that I shall never tolerate any kind of jobbery, nepotism or any influence directly or indirectly brought to bear upon me. Wherever I will find that such a practice is in vogue, or is continuing anywhere, low or high, I shall certainly not countenance it.

I know there are people who do not quite agree with the division of India and the partition of the Punjab and Bengal. Much has been said against it, but now that it has been accepted, it is the duty of everyone of us to loyally abide by it and honourably act according to the agreement which is now final and binding on all. But you must remember, as I have said, that this mighty revolution that has taken place is unprecedented. One can quite understand the feeling that exists between the two communities wherever one community is in majority and the other is in minority. But the question is, whether, it was possible or practicable to act otherwise than what has been done. A division had to take place. On both sides, in Hindustan and Pakistan, there are sections of people who may not agree with it, who may not like it, but in my judgment there was no other solution and I am sure future history will record its verdict in favour of it. And what is more it will be proved by actual experience as we go on that that was the only solution of India's constitutional problem. Any idea of a United India could never have worked and in my judgment it would have led us to terrific disaster. May be that view is correct; may be it is not; that remains to be seen. All the same, in this division it was impossible to avoid the question of minorities being in one Dominion or the other. Now that was unavoidable. There is no other solution. Now what shall we do? Now, if we want to make this great State of Pakistan happy and prosperous we should wholly and solely concentrate on the well-being of the people, and especially of the masses and the poor. If you will work in co-operation, forgetting the past, burying the hatchet, you are bound to succeed. If you change your past and work together in a spirit that every one of you, no matter to what community he belongs, no matter what relations he had with you in the past, no matter what is his colour, caste or creed, is first, second and last a citizen of this State with equal rights, privileges and obligations, there will be no end to the progress you will make.

I cannot emphasise it too much. We should begin to work in that spirit and in course of time all these angularities of the majority and minority communities, the Hindu community and the Muslim community — because even as regards Muslims you have Pathans, Punjabis, Shias, Sunnis and so on and among the Hindus you have Brahmans, Vashnavas, Khatris, also Bengalees, Madrasis, and so on — will vanish. Indeed if you ask me this has been the biggest hindrance in the way of India to attain freedom and independence and but for this we would have been free peoples long long ago. No power can hold another nation; and specially a nation of 400 million souls in subjection; nobody could have conquered you, and even if it had happened, nobody could have continued its hold on you for any length of time but for this. Therefore, we must learn a lesson from this. You are free; you are free to go to your temples, you are free to go to your mosques or to any other places of worship in this State of Pakistan. You may belong to any religion or caste or creed — that has nothing to do with the business of the State. As you know, history shows that in England conditions, some time ago, were much worse than those prevailing in India today. The Roman Catholics and the Protestants persecuted each other. Even now there are some States in existence where there are discriminations made and bars imposed against a particular class. Thank God, we are not starting in those days. We are starting in the days when there is no discrimination, no distinction between one community and another, no discrimination between one caste or creed and another. We are starting with this fundamental principle that we are all citizens and equal citizens of one State. The people of England in course of time had to face the realities of the situation and had to discharge the responsibilities and burdens placed upon them by the government of their country and they went through that fire step by step. Today, you might say with justice that Roman Catholics and Protestants do not exist; what exists now is that every man is a citizen, and equal citizen of Great Britain and they are all members of the Nation.

Now, I think we should keep that in front of us as our ideal and you will find that in course of time Hindus would cease to be Hindus and Muslims would cease to be Muslims, not in the religious sense, because that is the personal faith of each individual, but in the political sense as citizens of the State.

Well, gentlemen, I do not wish to take up any more of your time and thank you again for the honour you have done to me. I shall always be guided by the principles of justice and fair-play without any, as is put in the political language, prejudice or ill-will, in other words, partiality or favouritism. My guiding principle will be justice and complete impartiality and I am sure that with your support and co-operation, I can look forward to Pakistan becoming one of the greatest nations of the world.

I have received a message for the United States of America addressed to me. It reads:

'I have the honour to communicate to you, in Your Excellency's capacity as President of the Constituent Assembly of Pakistan, the following message which I have just received from the Secretary of State of the United States:

'On the occasion of the first meeting of the Constituent Assembly of Pakistan, I extend to you and to members of the Assembly, the best wishes of the government and the people of the United States for the successful conclusion of the great work you are about to undertake.'

Appendix VII

Mr Jinnah's Interview to BBC London, 13 December 1946

I know, the people of Britain are deeply interested in India. I thank you ... and I feel we have your good wishes. As you know of the many races, creeds and religions that inhabit the vast subcontinent of India, there are two major nations, the Hindus and Muslims. Hundred million of Muslims cannot be characterised as a minority. We are 70 millions in the north-western and northeastern zones of India. We constitute a majority of 70 per cent against the caste Hindus in these homelands of ours. We want the division of India into Hindustan and Pakistan because that is the only practical solution which will secure freedom of both Hindus and Muslims and the achievement of stable and enduring Government for Hindustan and Pakistan which, I am confident, will settle down as friends and neighbours like Canada and United States and other sovereign states both in North and South America.

Hindu India and Muslim India must be separated because the two nations are entirely distinct and different and, in some matters, antagonistic to each other. Let me tell you some of the differences: We differ in our history, culture, language, architecture, music, laws, jurisprudence, calendar and our entire social fabric and code of life. One India is impossible to realise which will inequitably mean that the Muslims would be transferred from the domination of the British to the caste Hindu rule, a position that Muslims will never accept. As an All India minority, which will be under the rule of permanent Hindu majority of about three to one, which will virtually mean one nation ruling another by means of ballot boxes. The writ and fiat of such a government will neither command respect nor acceptance in religion and such a government will therefore be impossible. It can only function by force, but will never secure a willing approval and sanction of the hundred million of the Muslims.

Unless the gravity of this aspect of the problem is realised and tackled frankly and boldly by the British Government, chaos is inevitable which must have serious repercussions and endanger the world peace. Our scheme of division of India gives Hindus three-fourths of the country and the Muslims secure a dominant voice in the remaining one quarter of India, thereby giving the two nations scope and opportunity to develop in accordance with their own culture and ideology so as to contribute with at least (voice not clear) advancement of the world as a whole.

Muslims desire freedom more than anyone else because love for freedom, fraternity and liberty is the life-blood of their existence. But freedom must mean freedom both from the British exploitation and Hindu domination. Hundred millions of Muslims will never agree merely to a change of masters.

Mr Muller, BBC Interviewer: — Thank you, Mr Jinnah. You have just heard Mr Mohammad Ali Jinnah, President of the Muslim League and leader of one hundred million Muslims who has reviewed the Muslim case at this critical time in India's history.

Appendix VIII

Governor Francis Mudie's letter to Mr Jinnah on Sikhs

No. 2
GOVERNMENT HOUSE, LAHORE,
5th September, 1947.

DEAR MR JINNAH,

Many thanks for your letter of 26th August, which arrived just after you left on Monday. I will certainly write to you more often than once a fortnight to keep you in touch with the situation here. I will also, as you asked me to, write quite frankly.

The law and order position here has improved very definitely, but there are still great dangers. I got a telephone message from the Commissioner Multan last night that Muzaffargarh was giving trouble, and Dera Ghazi Khan is still disturbed. I think that the raiders took a pretty severe knock. There was serious trouble in Jhang, due, partly at least I think, to the incapacity and low morale of the Deputy Commissioner, but it seems to be quiet now. I am apprehensive about Lyallpur. In the next two days I am visiting Multan, Layallpur and Jhang. I had hoped to go to Dera Ghazi Khan, but cannot get a light aeroplane, which is the only way of getting there quickly. So I asked the Deputy Commissioner to meet me in Multan and bring the Nawab Leghari with him, if he can. I expect trouble in all the Western districts. The refugee problem is assuming gigantic proportions.

The only limit that I can see to it is that set by the Census reports. According
to reports, the movement across the border runs into a lakh or so a day. At
Chuharkana in the Sheikhupura District I saw between a lakh and a lakh and
a half of Sikhs collected in the town and round it, in the houses, on the roofs
and everywhere. It was exactly like the Magh Mela in Allahabad. It will take
45 trains to move them, even at 4,000 people per train; or, if they are to stay
there, they will have to be given 50 tons of ata a day. At Govindgarh in the
same district there was a collection of 30,000 or 40,000 Mazhbi Sikhs with
arms. They refused even to talk to the Deputy Commissioner, an Anglo-
Indian, who advanced with a flag of truce. They shot at him and missed.
Finally arrangements were made to evacuate the lot. I am telling every one
that I don't care how the Sikhs get across the border; the great thing is to
get rid of them as soon as possible. There is still little sign of 3 lakh Sikhs in
Lyallpur moving, but in the end they too will have to go.

The most serious recent development is the very rapid deterioration
in the reliability of the Army. Yesterday Pathans in a Frontier Force Rifle
battalion in Gujranwalla seized their arms and established a road block on
the main road, and their officers could do nothing with them. Brigadier
McDonald, who belongs to the regiment and can talk Pushto, was sent out
this morning and the situation is now under control. I do not know quite
what the mutiny was about. I imagine that the real trouble was that the
Commanding Officer is a bania and the Second in Command a Sikh! All the
Hindus and Sikhs of the Battalion are being sent today across the border.
The Muslims, will as soon as possible, be sent to Jhelum. Anyhow, this and
other incidents — I understand that things are worse in this respect in NWF
Province — have convinced the Military that their own non-Muslim troops
are number one priority for evacuees. And yet a proposal was seriously put
forward that the Military should take over our police.

I am getting very doubtful — and so is the General — whether the plan
of protecting evacuee camps by troops of their own nationality will work in
practice. But we will have to try it and keep the two armies absolutely apart.
I think that we could secure the safety of non-Muslim camps on our side,

but I doubt very much whether any Muslim camps in the East would be safe with a Sikh guard. So we will have to do our best to work the scheme on our side in order to keep it going on the other.

From various sources I hear that the political situation is deteriorating. Yesterday there was a minor refugee demonstration with shouts of "Pakistan Murdabad" — I am told that Shaukat is afraid to show his face in the Muslim Refugee Camp here. I warned my Ministry about a week ago that this sort of thing was inevitable, that when things go wrong on a large scale it is always the Government that gets the blame. At first they were inclined to attribute any unpopularity they may have sensed to the machinations of Firoz, Khaksars, etc. This was mere self-delusion and very dangerous. This feeling of resentment against things in general and against the Government in particular is bound to grow. The ways in which, as far as I can see, it can be countered are (a) propaganda reiterating what the Government is doing for the refugees and (b) an efficient administration.

Efficiency with my present staff is out of the question. We have one Financial Commissioner, instead of a normal two or three, and our present one, Akhtar Hussian, though loyal and a good technical revenue officer, is certainly not capable of doing two men's work. Out of three Commissioners of Divisions we have only one, and he is from all accounts, hardly up to the job. Out of five DIGs Police we have only three and two are recently joined outsiders, one from UP and one from CP Finally to crown all, we have no Chief Secretary — the Finance Secretary, a mediocre officer, is supposed to be doing both jobs. In all these matters the Ministry had to adopt the attitude of the ostrich.

They have got a "new scheme" by which no Chief Secretary is required: a senior departmental Secretary to Government apparently is called Chief Secretary and draws the pay. The shortage of Commissioners is to be met partially by abolishing the post of Commissioner of Lahore.

I have not yet troubled them on the subject of the Chief Secretaryship but on the general question of staff and, incidentally, that of the Commissionership of the Lahore Division. I called in Liaquat and Mohammad Ali and had a joint meeting with them and my Ministers. Largely by Liaquat's help I got the Ministers to agree to our trying to get back a number of ex-Punjab and ex-UP British ICS officers and to the retention of the Lahore Division. Shaukat was a bit difficult, I don't quite know why.

We had, from our point of view, a successful meeting with Nehru, Patel and company on Wednesday. Your Ministers and we had the day before drawn up a paper on refugee policy, which went through after about four hours rather desultory talk with one only drafting amendments. The main fight was over certain proposals of East Punjab by which their troops or officers would be allowed to enter West Punjab on various pretexts. Finally, I had it conveyed to Nehru that the conference would break down unless they gave way, which they did. I enclose a copy to the final paper for your Excellency's information.

Patel maintained silence for the first three hours and then said that we were all wasting our time, and delivered a lecture on how things should have been done months ago. According to Liaquat the mistakes which he claimed had been made were largely due to his own attitude in the Partition Council. He was really getting at Nehru, who sat with closed eyes, half asleep. After the meeting when my ADC was waiting to show Trivedi and Patel into their car he heard the following conversation:

"*Trivedi:* Panditji looks quite done up.

Patel: So he deserves to be, flying all over the country and making fools of us all."

I hope that we have now seen an end of the visits to this province of Nehru and his fellow politicians. By his hectoring manner he did considerable damage to the morale of the District Administration of Sheikhupura. Besides, he brings newspaper-men like Durga Das with him. I hope that it will be possible to prevent further visits to Lahore.

This all sounds very gloomy, but we are all in quite good heart. Moss and Amin-ud-Din are pillars of strength. If we can get some of our old officers back, the whole situation will change.

I do not know whether I have addressed you in this letter as you wish to be addressed. If not, will you please let me know?

Yours sincerely,
(Sd.) FRANCIS MUDIE.

His Excellency Quaid-i-Azam Mohammad Ali Jinnah,
Governor-General of Pakistan, Karachi.

Appendix IX

Toba Tek Singh

by Sadat Hasan Manto

(Translated from Urdu by Subhash Chopra)

Two or three years after the partition (of India), it occurred to the governments of Pakistan and Hindustan that like the normal felons/convicts in prisons, the inmates of the lunatic asylums should also be exchanged (as part of the exchange/transfer of population agreement between the two Punjabs of Pakistan and Hindustan). In other words, Muslim pagals (lunatics) from Indian asylums should be sent to Pakistan while Hindu and Sikh inmates of Pakistani asylums should be handed over to Hindustan (India).

Nobody knows whether it was right or wrong, nonetheless after high level talks between the wisemen of both sides a day was fixed for the transfer/ exchange of pagals. After thorough inquiries and investigations Muslims whose guardians/relatives were in Hindustan were allowed to remain there; the rest were despatched to the border (to be handed over to Pakistan). Since almost all Hindus and Sikhs had already migrated from Pakistan there was no question of retaining any one of them in Pakistan. All Hindu and Sikh pagals therefore were sent over to the border under police escort.

It is not known what transpired over there but here in the Lahore asylum the news of this exchange/transfer set of lot of talk/sparked lot of interest. A Muslim pagal who had been a regular reader of *Zamindar* (Urdu newspaper) for the past 12 years was asked by one of his friends: "Maulvi Sahib (Reverend Sir), What is this thing called Pakistan?" After grave consideration came the reply: "It is a place in Hindustan where cut throat razors are made."

The friend felt satisfied with the reply (and left it at that).

In a similar vein, a Sikh pagal asked another Sikh pagal; "Sardarji , Why are we being sent to Hindustan? We don't even know the language of that place."

The other one smiled : "I know the language of Hindustan. The Hindustanis are devils who strut about haughtily."

A Muslim pagal, while taking a bath one day shouted "Pakistan Zindabad" (long live Pakistan) so loudly that he slipped on the floor and passed out.

Some of the pagals were not really pagal or unhinged. Most of them were murderers whose relatives got them declared pagals by bribing officials so as to get them locked up in asylums to save them from the gallows.

They understood somewhat why India had been partitioned and what Pakistan was but they too did not know the whole story. They couldn't make any sense out of the newspapers and the sepoys or guards at the asylum were not of much help either because they were illiterate and ignorant; One couldn't make anything of their conversations tro. They just knew that a man called Jinnah, also known as Quaid-e-Azam (Great Leader), had created a separate country called Pakistan for the Muslims. But they knew nothing of this country's location or whereabouts. That's exactly why the pagals who were not completely unhinged were thoroughly confused as to whether they were in Pakistan or Hindustan.

And if they were in Hindustan, then where was Pakistan?

One pagal got so confused in this Pakistan–Hindustan and Hindustan-Pakistan rigmarole that his condition worsened, making him even more unhinged. While sweeping the floor one day he put aside the broom and climbed straight up a tree. Perched on a branch, he went into a two-hour long harangue on the delicate issue of Pakistan and Hindustan. When the sepoys asked him to come down, he climbed even higher up the tree. And when they threatened him, he shot back: "I want to live neither in Hindustan nor in Pakistan. I will live here in this tree only."

After a lot of trouble when his fits cooled off, he climbed down and started embracing his Hindu and Sikh friends, full of sobs and tears and utterly saddened at the thought that they would be leaving him and going to Hindustan.

A Muslim radio engineer with a Master's degree in Science who never mixed with other pagals and used to walk silently up and down a chosen path in the garden, suddenly took off all his clothes, deposited them with an chaprasi (orderly), and started strutting around stark naked in the garden.

A fat Muslim pagal, hailing from Chiniot who had been a Muslim League activist and who used to have 15 to 16 showers every day, suddenly gave up his habit. His name was Muhammad Ali. From his perch behind the fence one day he declared that he was Muhammad Ali Jinnah (the head of Muslim League and founder of Pakistan). Seeing him a Sikh pagal made a counter declaration that he was Master Tara Singh (the firebrand Sikh leader who shouted Pakistan Murdabad or Death to Pakistan outside the Punjab Assembly in Lahore just weeks before the partition of India). It looked almost certain that a blood spilling clash would take place behind the asylum fence. Sensing the danger and declaring the two dangerous, the authorities took them away and locked them up separately.

There was a young Hindu lawyer from Lahore who had become unhinged after a failed love affair. When he heard that Amritsar had been declared part of Hindustan he felt very distraught as it was the city of the girl he loved. Even though she had already ditched him yet in his love crazed state he could never forget her. So he would abuse all those Hindu and Muslim leaders who together had divided the country into two parts, making his beloved a Hindustani and him a Pakistani.

When the partition talk was in its early stages the love-lorn lawyer was counselled and consoled by several other pagal inmates of the asylum that he shouldn't take it to his heart as he too would be sent over to Hindustan where his beloved lived. But he wasn't the one who would leave Lahore city because he thought his legal practice won't flourish in Amritsar.

The European ward (of the asylum) had two Anglo-Indian pagals. They felt very distraught at finding that the Angrez (British) had quit after making India independent. Away from the gaze or hearing of other inmates, the two would often debate for hours the serious issue how their superior status in the asylum would be affected, wondering whether the European ward would be retained or abolished. Would they be served (European) breakfast any more or instead of the double roti (English sliced bread) would they have to stomach the bloody Indian chapati?

There was a Sikh who had been in the asylum for the past 15 or 16 years. He was often heard muttering strange, unintelligible gibberish like: "Ooper di gar gar di annexe di beydhiana di moong di daal of di laltain (Gurgling sounds from the upper part of the annexe of the unmindful lot and their lentil soup and the lantern). He slept neither during the day nor at night. The warders maintained that during his 15-year long internment he hadn't slept one wink. He wouldn't ever lie down to rest, though sometimes he would tek (lean) against some wall.

Constant standing led to swelling of his feet and calves of his legs but in spite of such physical torture he would not lie down to rest. He always listened attentively to any discussion among the asylum inmates about Hindustan, Pakistan and exchange of population. If anyone asked him about his thoughts (on the issue), he would answer in all seriousness: "Ooper di gar gar di annexe di beydhiana di moong di daal of di Government of Pakistan."

Later, however, the reference to the Pakistan government gave way to Toba Tek Singh government. And he started asking other pagals where was Toba Tek Singh, the place he came from. But nobody knew if it was in Pakistan or Hindustan.

Those who tried to explain would themselves become entangled in questions like how was it that Sialkot which used to be in Hindustan earlier was now said to be in Pakistan. Who knows, Lahore which is now in Pakistan could be in Hindustan tomorrow? Or entire Hindustan may become Pakistan! And who could put his hand on his chest and say for sure that one day both Hindustan and Pakistan might not vanish altogether from the face of the earth?

This pagal Sikh's kesh (hair) had become straggly and reduced to a few strands.

As he rarely had a bath, his hair had become enmeshed with his beard which gave his face a pretty ferocious look. But he was a harmless soul. In his long stint of 15 years he had never picked a quarrel with anybody. Older staff at the asylum knew this much about him that he had lot of farmland in Toba Tek Singh. He was a well to do landlord (farm owner) who happened to have become suddenly unhinged, whereupon his relatives tied him in thick iron chains and got him admitted in the asylum. His relatives used to visit him about once a month to see him and to enquire about his welfare. The visits continued over a long period but when Pakistan–Hindustan troubles started, their visits stopped.

His name was Bishen Singh but everybody at the asylum used to call him Toba Tek Singh. He couldn't tell what day of the month it was today or how many years had rolled by. But every month he knew intuitively when his relatives or near and dear ones were visiting. He would inform the guards when his relatives were about to come. He would have a good bath that day with soap and scrub. He would rub oil into his hair and comb it properly. He would take out his clothes, which ordinarily he rarely wore, and put them on. Thus well attired and appointed he would go to meet his visitors but would remain silent, if asked any questions though once in a while he would blurt out his refrain: "Ooper the gurr gurr di annexe di beydhiana di moong di daal of di laltain."

Bishen Singh had a daughter who had grown up inch by inch into a fine young woman in 15 years. But he couldn't even recognise her. When she was a child she used to burst into tears on seeing her poor father. As a young woman too she couldn't hold her tears on seeing him.

When the Pakistan–Hindustan troubles began, Bishen Singh started asking other pagals where was Toba Tek Singh (in Pakistan or Hindustan?). In the absence of any satisfactory answer, his anxiety grew by the day. Now his visitors had also stopped coming. Earlier he used to know intuitively about the forthcoming visits but now it seemed his inner voice too had stopped informing him of any visit.

He looked forward to see his visitors who used to express sympathy for him and bring fruits, sweets and clothes for him. Had he asked them where was Toba Tek Singh, they would have certainly told him whether it was in Hindustan or Pakistan because, he thought, they themselves came from Toba Tek Singh where his farmlands were.

The asylum also had an inmate who used to call himself Khuda (God). One day when Bishen Singh asked him where exactly was Toba Tek Singh, the Khuda as was his wont burst into a guffaw, saying: "It is neither in Pakistan nor in Hindustan because We haven't yet passed any orders."

Bishen Singh entreated several times with this Khuda that he should pass the orders to end this confusion. But he (Khuda) was too busy as he had too many other orders to pass. Fed up with this Khuda , Bishen Singh burst out: " Ooper di gurr gurr di annexe di beydhiana di moong di daal of Wahé Guru Ji da Khalsa tey Wahé Guru Ji ki Fateh — Jo Bolé, So Nihal , Sat Sri Akal!" (The Sikh invocation and chant).

This outburst was perhaps his way of telling this Khuda: "You are the God of Muslims only, because if you were the God of Sikhs also, then you would have surely listened to my prayer."

A few days before the exchange, a Muslim friend of his from Toba Tek Singh came to visit him. On seeing him , Bishen Singh turned suddenly and started walking back. But the guard stopped him and told him: "He has come to see you. He is your friend Fazal Deen."

Bishen Singh fixed Fazal Deen with one glance and started muttering something. Fazal Deen stepped forward and putting his hand on Bishen

Singh's shoulders said: "I have been thinking of coming to see you for a long time but couldn't — so busy. All of your relatives have gone safely to Hindustan. I helped as much as I could. Your daughter Roop Kaur..."

He stopped mid-sentence. Bishen Singh remembered something and uttered: "Daughter Roop Kaur..."

Fazal Deen haltingly said: "Yes she ... she too is quite well and fine ... has gone with them (to Hindustan)."

Bishen Singh remained silent. Fazal deen resumed: " They had said that I should keep enquiring about your health and well being. Now I have heard that you are going to Hindustan. Give my salaam to brother Balbir Sing and sister-in-law Wadhawa Singh. And also sister Amrit Kaur. Tell brother Balbir Singh that Fazal Deen is fine and well. One of the two brown buffaloes they had left (in Pakistan) has given birth to a male calf while the other had a female calf but that one died within six days ... and ... let me know if I can be of any service. I am always ready ... And here are some marundey (rice cakes) for you."

Bishen Singh handed the rice cakes packet to the guard standing nearby and asked Fazal Deen, "Where is Toba Tek Singh?"

Taken aback, Fazal Deen said: "Where? It is where it always was."

Bishen Singh again asked: "In Pakistan or Hindustan?"

"In Hindustan ... No, no, in Pakistan," said a baffled Fazal Deen.

Bishen Singh turned, muttering away: "Ooper di gurr gurr di annexe di beydhiana di moong di daal of di Pakistan and Hindustan of di Dhur Phité Moonh (Plague on both your sides)."

Preparations for this exchange (of pagals) were complete. Lists of pagals to be sent from this side to that side or from the other side to this side were ready and in hand. Even the date of exchange had been fixed.

It was bitter cold when lorry loads of Hindu and Sikh pagals from the Lahore asylum set off for the border under police escort. Officers overseeing the operation were also accompanying them. The Superintendents from both sides met at Wagah border and after the completion of preliminaries, Operation Exchange (of pagals) kicked off and continued through the night.

Getting the pagals out of the lorries and handing them over to officers from the other side was a tricky job. Some of them would not even come out. Those who agreed to come out were difficult to control as they would run away hither and thither. Those who kept themselves naked were dressed but they would instantly tear off the clothes Some were firing expletives, others singing or quarrelling among themselves. Yet others were weeping or sobbing. You couldn't hear a thing. Female pagals were yelling in their own way. Bitter cold made one's teeth chatter.

Majority of pagals were against this exchange. They couldn't understand why they were being uprooted from their place and thrown somewhere else. The few who could understand something were shouting slogans: "Pakistan Zindabad (Hail Pakistan). Pakistan Murdabad (Death to Pakistan)." As some of the Muslims and Sikhs felt outraged at hearing such slogans, rioting was narrowly averted on two or three occasions.

Now it was Bishen Singh's turn for exchange, and when the officer on the other side of Wagah border started entering his name in the register, Bishen Singh asked: "Where is Toba Tek Singh? In Pakistan or Hindustan?" The officer laughed: "In Pakistan."

On hearing this Bishen Singh jumped aside and ran towards other co-pagals still standing there. Pakistani guards caught hold of him and began taking him to the other side but he refused to budge, uttering: "Toba Tek Singh is here," and in high pitched voice shouted: "Ooper di gurr gurr di annexe di beydhiana di moong di daal of Toba Tek Singh and Pakistan."

They tried to persuade him that Toba Tek Sing had gone to Hindustan and even if it had not, it would be immediately transferred to Hindustan. But he wouldn't accept such talk. When an attempt was made to take him forcibly to the other side, he dug himself in the middle ground , standing on his swollen legs so firmly as if no power on earth could move him.

Since he was a non-violent person, it was decided not to use any more force against him. He was left standing there while other exchange work carried on.

Just before sunrise a sky rending cry rang out of the gullet of Bishen Singh who had been standing alone by himself. Officers from all sides rushed to the spot and found how the man who had stood on his legs for the last 15 years was lying slumped face down on the ground. On this side of the barbed wire lay Hindustan, on the other side behind identical barbed wires lay Pakistan. On the piece of ground in the middle called NO Man's Land lay Toba Tek Singh!

Bibliography

Ahmed Salahuddin, *Bangladesh Past and Present,* APH Publishing Corp, Delhi, 2004.

Ali Riyaz, *God Willing—Politics of Islamism in Bangladesh,* Rowman & Littlefield Inc., Lanham, MD, 2004.

Attlee C.R., *As It Happened,* Heinemann, 1957.

Attlee C.R., *A Prime Minister Remembers,* Heinemann, 1961.

Azad Maulana Abul Kalam, *India Wins Freedom,* (The Complete Version),

Orient Longman, 1988.

Bandopadhaya S.K., *Quaid-i-Azam Muhammad Ali Jinnah And the Creation of Pakistan,* Sterling, New Delhi.

Bagchi J. & Dasgupta S. (Ed), *The Trauma and the Triumph, Stree,* Kolkatta, 2003.

Bhattacharjea Ajit, *Countdown to Partition,* Harper Collins, 1997.

Bhalla Alok, *Partition Dialogues,* Oxford, 2006.

Bence-Jones Mark, The Viceroys of India, Constable, London, 1982.

Blitho Hector, *Jinnah—Creator of Pakistan,* John Murray, 1954.

Bose Sumantra, *Kashmir—Roots of Conflicts, Pathas to Peace,* Harvard University Press, 2003.

Brecher Michael, *Nehru – A Political Biography,* Oxford, 1959.

Bhasin Avtar Singh, *Some Called it Partition,* SIBA Exim, Delhi, 1998.

Bhutto Benazir, *Daughter of the East,* London, Hamish Hamilton, 1988.

Bhutto Benazir, *The Peace Dividend* (Keynote Address), Roli Books, India, 2004.

Burke S.M. and Salim Quraishi, *The British Raj in India-An Historical Review,* OUP, Karachi, 1995.

Burki Shahed Javed, *Pakistan — Fifty years of Nationhood,* Westview Press (Colorado), 1999.

Chakrabarty Bidyut, *The Partition of Bengal and Assam,* Routledge Curzon, 2004.

Chatterji Joya, *Bengal Divided,* Cambridge University Press, 1995.

Campbell-Johnson Alan, *Mission with Mountbatten, Dutton,* New York, 1953.

Connell John, *Auchinleck,* Cassell, 1959.

Clarke Peter, *The Cripps Version – The Life of Sir Stafford Cripps,* Allen Lane (Penguin), 2000.

Das Durga, *India from Curzon to Nehru,* Collins, 1969.

Das Manmath, *Partition and Independence of India,* Vision Books, New Delhi, 1982.

Dobbin Christine E., *Basic Documents in the Development of India and Pakistan,* Van Nortrand Reinhold, London, 1970.

Edwardes Michael, *Raj,* Pan Books, 1967.

French Patrick, *Liberty or Death,* HarperCollins, 1997.

Godbole Manohar, *The Holocaust of Indian Partition,* Rupa, New Delhi, 2006.

Gopal S, Nehru, *A Biography* (3 vols), Jonathan Cape, London, 1975-84.

Gopal S (Ed), *Nehru, Selected Works,* Nehru Memorial Fund, New Delhi, 1999.

Harrison Kenneth, *ATTLEE ,* Weidenfield and Nicolson, 1982.

Hodson H.V., *The Great Divide,* Oxford, 1969.

Ismay, *The Memoirs of Lord Ismay,* Heinemenn 1960.

Jacques Kathryn, Bangladesh, India and Pakistan, Macmillan, 2000.

Jahan Rounaq, *Bangladesh — Promise and Performance,* Books, London, 2000.

Jalal Ayesha, *The Sole Spokesman,* Cambridge University Press, 1983.

Joshi Shashi, *The Last Durbar,* 2006.

Kalla. K.L., *Cultural Heritage of Kashmir,* Anmol Publications, New Delhi, 1996.

Kasturi Bhashyam, *Walking Alone – Gandhi and India's Partition,* Vision Books, 2001.

Katyal K.K., *Journey to Amity,* Har Anand, 2006.

Khan Wali, *Facts are Facts—The Untold Story of India's Partition,* Vikas, 1987.

Khan Yasmin, *The Great Partition*, Penguin Viking, 2007.

Kher. R.S., *SAARC*, Dominant Publication, New Delhi, 2004.

Khosla G.D., *Stern Reckoning*, Oxford , 1989.

Lapierre Dominique & Collins Larry, *Freedom at Midnight*, Vikas, New Delhi.

Lapierre Dominique, *Mountbatten and the Partition of India*, Vikas, New Delhi, 1982.

Madhok Balraj, *Kashmir, Kargil Indo-Pak Relations*, D.A.V. Publication, New Delhi, 2000.

Menon V.P., *Transfer of Power in India*, Princeton University Press, 1957.

Mansergh Nicholas (Ed), *Transfer of Power* (12 vols), HMSO, London, 1970-83.

Mirza Muzaffar, *The Great Quaid*, Ferozesons, Lahore, 1995.

Mountbatten Lord Louis, *Report on the Last Viceroyalty*, Manohar.

Mountbatten Pamela, *India Remembered*, Pavilion, 2007.

Moore R.J., *Escape from Empire — Attlee and the Indian Problem*, Oxford: Clarendon,1979.

Moon Pendrel, *Divide and Quit*, Chatto and Windus, London, 1964.

Nanda B.R, *Witness to Partition—A Memoir*, Rupa, New Delhi, 2003.

Nayar Kuldip, *Distant Neighbours — A Tale of the sub-continent*, Vikas, 1972.

Nayar Kuldip, *Scoop!*, HarperCollins, Delhi, 2006.

Philips C.H., Singh H.L. and Padey B.N., *The Evolution of India and Pakistan: Select Documents*, Oxford, 1962.

Prasad Rajendra, *India Divided*, Hind Kitabs, Bombay, 1946.

Rafique M. Afzal, *Speeches and Statements of Liaquat Ali and Jinnah*, Lahore.

Reynolds Reginald, *White Sahibs in India*, Socialist Book Centre, London, 1946.

Rees, Major-General T.W., *Rees Report, Document* , British Library, London.

Roy Tathagata, *My People Uprooted*, Ratna Prakashan, Kolkata, 2001.

Sarila Narendra Singh, *The Shadow of the Great Game*, HarperCollins 2005.

Sarila Narendra Singh, *The Untold Story of India's Partition*, HarperCollins 2005.

Sengupta Nitish, *Bangal Divided—1905-1971*, Penguin/Viking, 2007.

Siddiqa Ayesha, *Military Inc.— Inside Pakistan's Military Economy*, Pluto, 2007.

Singh Kirpal, *Partition of the Punjab*, Punjabi University, Patiala, 1972.

Tai Yong Tan and Gyanesh Kudaisya (ed), *The Aftermath of Partition in South Asia*, Routledge, 2000.

Talib Gurbachan Singh, *Muslim Attacks on Hindus and Sikhs in 1947*, S.G. P.C, Amritsar, 1950.

Wavell Lord, *The Viceroy's Journal—edited by Pendrel Moon*, Oxford, 1973.

Wolpert Stanley, *Jinnah of Pakistan*, Oxford, 1989.

Wolpert Stanley, *Shameful Flight*, Oxford, 2006.

Ziegler Philip, *Mountbatten – the Official Biography*, Collins, 1971.

Zakaria Rafiq, *The Man Who Divided India*, Popular Prakashan, Bombay, 2001.

NEWSPAPERS AND PERIODICALS

Dawn, Delhi and Karachi, 1947.

The Civil and Military Gazette, Lahore, 1947.

The Tribune, Lahore, 1947.

The Hindustan Times, New Delhi, 1947.

The Statesman, New Delhi and Calcutta, 1947.

The Manchester Guardian, 1947.

The Times, London, 1947.

The Daily Express, London, 1947.

PERIODICALS

Punch, London, 1947.

The Spectator, London, 2006.

South Asian Journal, SAFMA, Lahore, 2004-2009.

Index